THE
CHINA VOYAGE

ALSO BY TIM SEVERIN

Tracking Marco Polo

Explorers of the Mississippi

The Golden Antilles

The African Adventure

Vanishing Primitive Man

The Oriental Adventure

The Brendan Voyage

The Sindbad Voyage

The Jason Voyage:
The Quest for the Golden Fleece

The Ulysses Voyage:
Sea Search for the Odyssey

Crusader:
By Horse to Jerusalem

In Search of Genghis Khan

THE
CHINA VOYAGE
Across the Pacific by Bamboo Raft

TIM SEVERIN

ADDISON-WESLEY PUBLISHING COMPANY

Reading, Massachusetts   Menlo Park, California   New York

Don Mills, Ontario   Wokingham, England   Amsterdam   Bonn

Sydney   Singapore   Tokyo   Madrid   San Juan   Paris

Seoul   Milan   Mexico City   Taipei

First published in Great Britain by Little, Brown and Company

Library of Congress Cataloging-in-Publication Data

Severin, Timothy.
  The China voyage : across the Pacific by bamboo raft / Tim Severin :
photographs by Joe Beynon and Rex Warner.
    p.   cm.
  Originally published: London: Little, Brown, 1994.
  ISBN 0-201-48394-7
  1. Severin, Timothy—Journeys.   2. Pacific Ocean—Discovery and
exploration.   3. Rafts.   I. Beynon, Joe.   II. Warner, Rex.
III. Title.
G480.S48   1995
910'.964—dc20   95-17915
                                                                    CIP

Photographs by Joe Beynon
and Rex Warner
Drawings by Nina Kojima and Trondur Patursson
Jacket design by Suzanne Heiser
Map by Alec Herzer
Raft illustration by Arthur Saluz

1 2 3 4 5 6 7 8 9-MA-98 97 96 95
First printing, July 1995

C ONTENTS

Part One: Asia

Part Two: Ocean

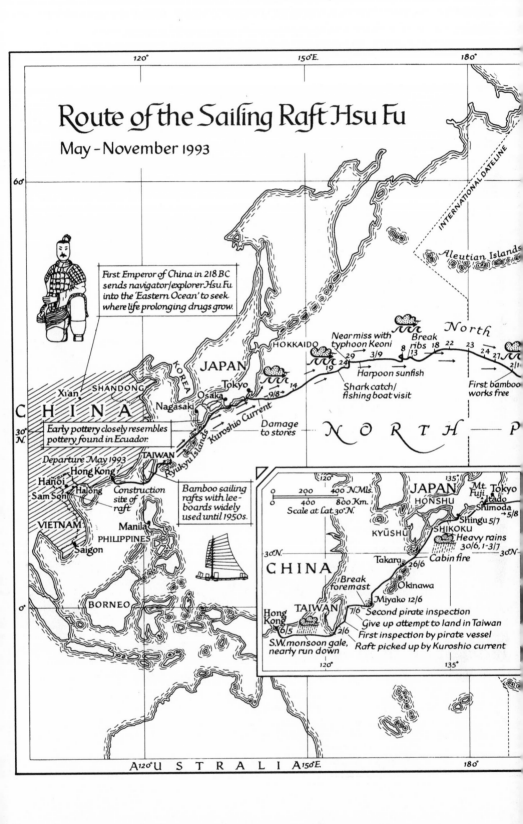

Route of the Sailing Raft Hsu Fu

May – November 1993

First Emperor of China in 218 BC sends navigator/explorer Hsu Fu into the 'Eastern Ocean' to seek where life prolonging drugs grow.

INTERNATIONAL DATELINE

Aleutian Islands

North

Near miss with typhoon Keoni 29 3/9

Break ribs 18 22 23 24

8 13 27

19 24

Harpoon sunfish

First bamboo works free

Shark catch/ fishing boat visit

HOKKAIDO

JAPAN

Tokyo

Osaka

~9/8 14

Nagasaki

Xi'an SHANDONG

C H I N A

KOREA

Kuroshio Current

Ryukyu Islands

Damage to stores

N O R T H   P

Early pottery closely resembles pottery found in Ecuador.

Departure May 1993

Hong Kong

Hanoi

Sam Son

Halong

VIETNAM

Saigon

Construction site of raft

Manila

PHILIPPINES

TAIWAN

Bamboo sailing rafts with lee-boards widely used until 1950s.

BORNEO

Inset map:

200 400 N.Mls.

400 800 Km.

Scale at Lat. 30°N.

JAPAN Mt. Fuji Tokyo

HONSHU Itado

Shimoda 5/8

Shingu 5/7

KYŪSHŪ SHIKOKU

Heavy rains 30/6, 1–3/7

CHINA

Takara 26/6 Cabin fire

30°N. 30°N

Break foremast Okinawa

Miyako 12/6

Hong Kong 7/6 Second pirate inspection

6/5 2/6 Give up attempt to land in Taiwan

First inspection by pirate vessel

S.W. monsoon gale, nearly run down Raft picked up by Kuroshio current

TAIWAN

Bottom margin: A₁₂₀° U S T R A L I A ₁₅₀°E. 180°

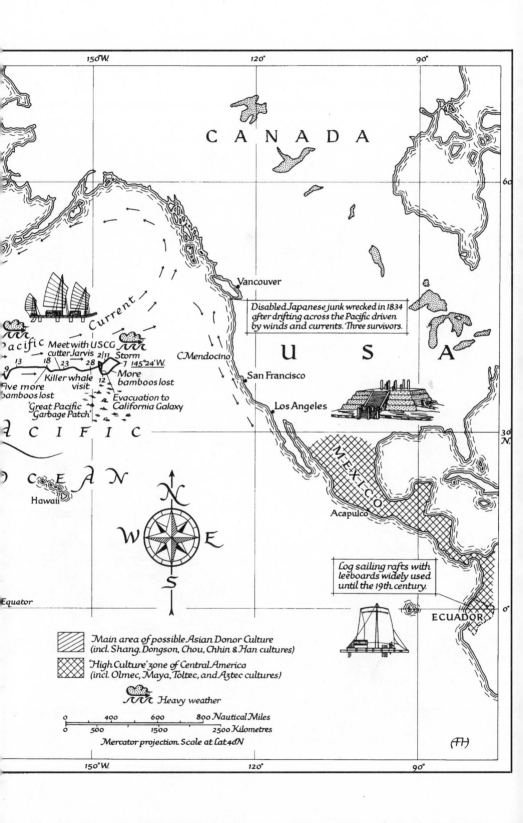

150°W.   120°   90°

C A N A D A

Vancouver

Disabled Japanese junk wrecked in 1834
after drifting across the Pacific driven
by winds and currents. Three survivors.

U   S   A

60

Current

C.Mendocino

San Francisco

Los Angeles

Pacific   Meet with USCG
       cutter Jarvis 2/11   Storm
9   13   18   23   28 → 7 145°24'W.
       Killer whale   12   More
        visit   bamboos lost
Five more   Evacuation to
bamboos lost   California Galaxy
    'Great Pacific
     Garbage Patch'

P A C I F I C

MEXICO

30
N.

O C E A N

Hawaii

Acapulco

Log sailing rafts with
leeboards widely used
until the 19th century.

N

W   E

S

Equator

ECUADOR

0°

Main area of possible Asian Donor Culture
(incl. Shang, Dongson, Chou, Chhin & Han cultures)

'High Culture' zone of Central America
(incl. Olmec, Maya, Toltec, and Aztec cultures)

Heavy weather

0   400   600   800 Nautical Miles
0   500   1500   2500 Kilometres
Mercator projection. Scale at Lat. 40N

(FH)

150°W.   120°   90°

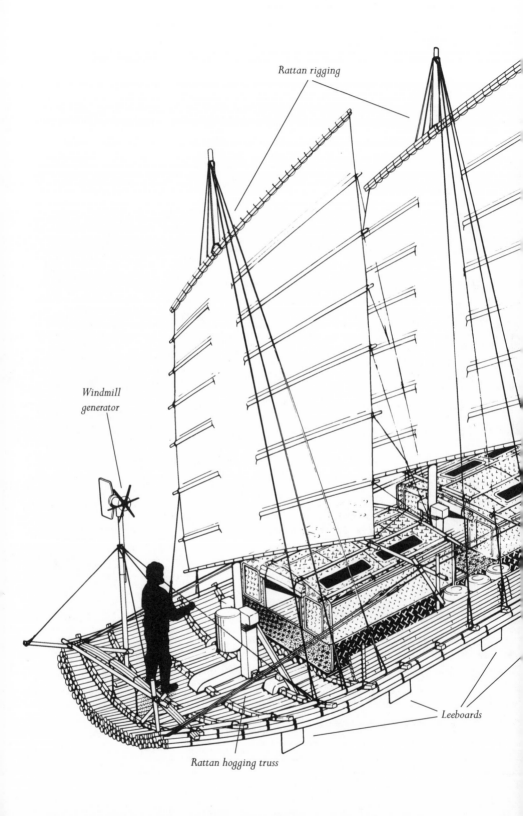

Rattan rigging

Windmill
generator

Leeboards

Rattan hogging truss

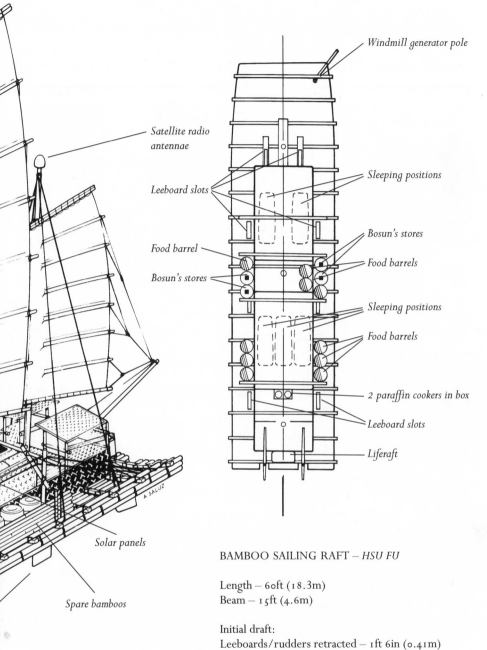

Windmill generator pole

Satellite radio antennae

Leeboard slots

Sleeping positions

Bosun's stores

Food barrel

Food barrels

Bosun's stores

Sleeping positions

Food barrels

2 paraffin cookers in box

Leeboard slots

Liferaft

A SALUZ

Solar panels

Spare bamboos

BAMBOO SAILING RAFT – *HSU FU*

Length – 60ft (18.3m)
Beam – 15ft (4.6m)

Initial draft:
Leeboards/rudders retracted – 1ft 6in (0.41m)
Leeboards/rudders extended – 4ft 11in (1.3m)

Sail area, approx – 800 sq ft

PART ONE

ASIA

Drawings by
Nina Kojima

1

ANCIENT RAFTS
ACROSS THE PACIFIC

The pirate ship came at us out of the darkness. All we could see were the lights, green, red and white, of a small vessel steering straight at us from astern. The lights approached very quickly until we could hear the rumble of the engine over the sound of the waves, and see a white bow-wave ahead of the darker shape of what looked like a small fishing vessel. It was a black night with no moon, just a few stars and a gentle sea. Only Nina, the Japanese artist, and I were on watch. The rest of the crew – Mark, Joe, and Loi were in their sleeping bags in the cabins. The strange ship must have spotted us on radar, because it was clearly interested in us. It drew level, then cut back its engine, and came wallowing close alongside. The bright beam of a floodlight sprang out and flickered up and down the length of our vessel, examining us. What they saw was very odd – a slightly curved bamboo platform barely emerging above the water and carrying two thatched cabins, like huts deep in some tropical jungle. Above, like great fans, were the distinctive shapes of three Chinese junk sails. We were barely moving through the water, an easy prey. For a few moments the light continued to search us, then abruptly the engine note increased and the boat moved off.

'I wonder what they wanted?' I asked Nina in my ignorance. 'Look! They've stopped, and are turning back.' Sure enough, the half-seen vessel had swung round and was heading back towards us, this time on the opposite side. Now it passed even closer and made a circle, so tight that the wash slopped on to our deck. I shone a torch at our inquisitive visitor, and saw a green hull with a broad white band painted around it. A cluster of men, dimly seen as black shapes, was gathered in the waist of the vessel. 'Perhaps they are thinking of giving us a tow,' I muttered to Nina. 'That would be very useful. We're in Japanese waters now. Try giving them a shout.' But before Nina could call out an enquiry, the strange vessel again decided to leave us. With the water churning in its wake, it accelerated into the darkness, swung across our bows and headed off into the darkness. Three days later, when we had reached the nearby Japanese island of Miyako, we learned the truth. An officer of the Japanese Coastguard was interviewing Nina about our voyage from Hong Kong, when she mentioned the visit of the strange fishing boat. Immediately the officer came alert.

'Can you describe the boat? What colour was it ?' he asked. Nina told him. 'That boat,' said the Coastguard officer bluntly, 'is a known pirate vessel. We've been trying to intercept it for some weeks. Usually pirates stay out of Japanese waters, but that particular vessel is so bold that it even came to one of the islands and gave trouble. You were very lucky. They probably decided your raft was not worth attacking.' And, I thought to myself, we had nearly asked the pirates to give us a tow.

Pirates had not been very high on my list of concerns when I began to prepare the China Voyage expedition nearly three years before. Then my thoughts had been about more obvious matters such as the risk of typhoons, how to raise enough money to finance the project, or whether a raft of bamboos would stay afloat long enough to carry five or six people across the vastness of the Pacific Ocean from China to America. Above all, I had to be sure that such a dangerous journey was justified. Ever since studying the history of exploration at Oxford University, I had been aware of the theory that long before Columbus reached the New World, mariners from Asia had visited America and influenced the early High Cultures there, notably those of Central America like the Mayans. But I had set aside the idea as impractical. The Pacific is twice the width of the Atlantic, and can breed storm systems which are 3,000 miles in diameter. I was sceptical that early sailors could have crossed that gale-swept expanse except on very rare occasions, if at all.

Also the evidence for cultural contact between early America and ancient Asia was inconclusive. For more than two centuries some unorthodox scholars had claimed to see similarities between early Asian and American architecture, art forms, calendars, language, and so forth.

4

The evidence they quoted ranged from the highly scientific – for example that there were similarities between the DNA structure of native Americans and Asian peoples – to the highly subjective and slightly bizarre. In a sensational case in the 1920s an eminent anthropologist-traveller Sir Grafton Elliot Smith asserted that an eighth-century Mayan stone carving, found in Honduras in Central America, depicted the heads and trunks of two elephants ridden by mahouts. Elephants had been extinct in the New World for thousands of years, so it was claimed that the stone carvers could only have known about elephants if they had been in contact with Asia. A blazing row broke out between those who claimed to see long-nosed elephants in the carving, and their opponents, who scoffed that these were representations of long-beaked macaws, a perfectly normal American bird. The arguments kept flaring up and fading again over decades, and in the meantime the carving itself was so badly eroded by the weather that today it would be difficult to see either macaws, elephants or anything else cut in the original stone, and the debate depends on early sketches made of the mysterious sculpture.

So the long-running argument about whether there had been trans-Pacific contact rumbled on and on. Nothing was definitive, and there was such a mass of evidence that the detail was bewildering. Then I read the opinion of one scholar whose reputation towered among Orientalists. Professor Joseph Needham of Cambridge University was acknowledged as the greatest living authority on the history of Chinese civilisation and science. His seven-volume book on the subject, published in no less than twenty-five parts, had been described as the single most comprehensive work of scholarship of modern times. In it Professor Needham announced firmly that he believed there had been cultural exchange by sea between America and Asia in ancient times. What is more, he proposed – and this is what really caught my attention – that the most likely vessel the Chinese would have used for any trans-oceanic trips was the bamboo sailing raft. Needham believed that rafts were so ancient in Chinese culture that they were the true ancestors of the Chinese junk, whose design still copied the raft's distinctive curve and blunt ends. Thus, a tiny drawing of what looked like a raft was one of the earliest Chinese pictograms for a boat.

I was intrigued, not just about the bamboo rafts, but about Needham himself. Thirty years earlier I had been a university student preparing my very first expedition, which was to follow Marco Polo's overland route to China on a motorcycle. Already Joseph Needham was one of the most eminent Oriental scholars of the day, and I had written to him asking for advice. To my surprise he had replied to my letter and invited me to call on him at his Cambridge college. There, as a very junior student, I met a tall, imposing man, who was courteous and helpful, finding time to encourage a novice historian to go travelling and do field work. His kindness had made a profound impression on me, and after my Marco Polo expedition had turned out well, I had been happy to send him a book as thanks.

Now, thirty years later, it seemed almost unbelievable that the same Joseph Needham should still be alive. But he was: ninety-two years old, white-haired and frail, his big frame now bowed over with arthritis and confined to a wheelchair, but as courteous and shrewd as ever. This time I explained to him that I was proposing to test the idea that a bamboo raft could cross the Pacific, and my method would be to build a replica using traditional materials, and set out from Hong Kong to sail by way of Taiwan and Japan to see if the vessel would reach the coast of California. Did he consider that my idea was worthwhile, and that it could add usefully to the debate about possible trans-Pacific contacts? Once again Joseph Needham offered encouragement. He still held his view that mariners from Asia had reached the New World long before Columbus, and indeed he had published a large monograph volume on the subject. 'The voyage,' he stated, 'is extremely important, not only in the study of exploration but also in the study of civilisation in general.'

Obviously my next step was to find out whether bamboo sailing rafts were still to be found in Asia and, if so, to try to learn how they were built and handled. When Needham had done his research for his magisterial study on Chinese nautical technology published in 1971 thousands of bamboo rafts were to be found on the west coast of Taiwan, facing the Chinese mainland. There they were used for fishing and coastal transport, and they seem formerly to have been sailed across the ninety-mile-wide Taiwan Strait to the mainland, because Needham cited Chinese historical records which spoke of sea raiders from Taiwan landing on the coast of mainland China from boats made of bundles, which they could lash together and use for their escape. And in the nineteenth century a Japanese traveller, Mr Hata, had been aboard a steamer passing Taiwan and drawn a sketch of a bamboo raft far out to sea, sailed by an old gentleman sitting in what looked like a bamboo hut on the stern.

But that was all the pictorial evidence I could find, and when I went to Taiwan to do my research it seemed that I was too late.

Taiwan had rafts all right, many hundreds of them, and still operating in the same section of coast facing across to China. But in the past twenty years there had been two far-reaching changes. Firstly, the rafts were now propelled by engines. Masts and sails were no longer used. Second, the rafts were not made of bamboo but from large plastic drainage pipes carefully curved to imitate the shape of the traditional bamboo raft. Bamboo, I was told by a cheerful Taiwanese raftbuilder on the beach, was too difficult to obtain, rotted quickly, and was not strong enough to carry large engines. Indeed some of the plastic tube rafts were fitted with engines so powerful that I suspected they did duty as very good smuggling platforms, low-slung, fast and difficult to detect on radar as they ferried contraband to and from the fishing fleet in the Strait. But at least I was encouraged by the fact that the shape of the bamboo raft was good enough to have been copied in modern material, even down to the characteristic upcurve of the bow. What I needed was to find somewhere that still used genuine bamboo rafts, and the people who knew how to make them.

Then came a lucky coincidence. Another friend, the curator of the Exeter Maritime Museum in England, happened to telephone to tell me about his plans for the museum's collection of traditional native vessels. He had recently visited Vietnam to purchase a bamboo basket boat, a strange little basin-shaped vessel like a large pudding bowl. Had he seen any sailing rafts? I asked him on the off chance. To my astonishment and delight he answered, Yes! He had seen them still used for fishing at a small coastal town called Sam Son about one hundred miles south of Hanoi in what was once North Vietnam. He also warned that it might be difficult for me to get permission to visit the area, because Vietnam still had very little contact with the non-communist world. On his visit the authorities had been suspicious of Western visitors who asked to travel outside the main tourist spots. Undeterred I wrote off to the Vietnamese Ministry of Culture, explaining that I wanted to see traditional Vietnamese boats, and after a two-month wait received a visa. Thus in October 1991 I found myself flying from Bangkok up to Hanoi aboard an aging Russian-built airliner of Vietnam Airlines, not knowing what to expect in a country that was one of the poorest in Asia. Sitting next to me was an earnest Japanese about thirty years old. He explained that he

7

worked for a large Japanese company but studied insects as a hobby. Vietnam interested him as the entomology of the country had really not been looked at since it had been a French colony in the 1950s. He had saved up his money and his holiday time to make a visit. As he finished speaking, a large cockroach fell from the luggage compartment above his head, and plopped on to his lap. 'Your first genuine Vietnamese bug,' I could not resist noting.

At Hanoi's airport I stood in line with the other passengers, mostly diplomats and their families and, here and there, Vietnamese returning from foreign delegations and dressed in the cheap cotton raincoats and incongruous pork-pie hats favoured by nationals of the Eastern Bloc. We waited to have our visas minutely examined by security police with green uniforms and humourless expressions. The airport building was shabby and unimpressive, so functional that it was obvious that Vietnam had no spare cash to smarten up its impression on arriving foreigners. My gaze wandered to the glass partition separating the incoming passengers from the dusty baggage area where we would pick up our luggage. Standing just the other side of the grimy glass was a short, chubby Vietnamese man of about thirty-five years' age. He was dressed in a wrinkled yellow plaid shirt which hung outside ill-fitting trousers. On his feet were flip-flop sandals with no socks, and in one hand he held a cigarette which dripped ash on the floor. He had a thin straggly moustache, slight acne, and his bulging eyes gave him a somewhat frog-like expression. He was scanning the incoming queue. With a sinking heart I noticed that he was holding up a piece of torn cardboard with my name scrawled on it. I waved to him, and the chubby face broke into a smile of welcome that revealed a mouthful of brown and irregular teeth. His name, I learned as soon as I had cleared the formalities, was Truc, and he had been sent by the Ministry of Information – disconcertingly he always pronounced it Military Information – to be my guide. Few people could have made a less favourable impression or turned out to be such a stalwart ally. Over the next eighteen months Truc was to evolve from being my official guide and minder for the Ministry into my colleague, ally, Mr Fixit, and firm friend. In a society still shackled by regulations and bureaucracy he was astonishingly impudent. He was afraid of nothing and nobody. He bullied, sweet-talked, cajoled, or brazened his way through every situation. And his sense of humour was never far away. We could be tired, exhausted, dirty and fed up after some particularly gruelling episode trying, say, to obtain an official permit, and Truc would see the funny side of the situation, throw back his head, and give a great chuckle, exposing those dreadful teeth. As he ushered me out to a ramshackle Russian-built car parked under a straggly tree with the Ministry driver asleep across the back seat, he explained to me that Truc was the name of a species of bamboo. How suitable.

We trundled off on the forty-mile drive from Noi Bai Airport to Hanoi itself, more than an hour's drive southward across the alluvial plain of the Red River. It was then about five or six o'clock in the evening, and it was obvious that the road was a main highway even though it was badly potholed and only one and a half lanes wide. It was busy with bicycle traffic and an occasional truck grinding along at much the same speed as the cyclists and belching out black fumes. The trucks were so ramshackle that it was amazing they could move at all. Their chronically delapidated state was emphasised by the frequent broken-down vehicle at the side of the road, propped up on piles of stones that gave the breakdown a permanent appearance. Sometimes the driver or a mechanic could be seen hard at work hammering, bending or welding some makeshift repair in place. It was very evident that there were no supplies or spare parts available. Vietnam, I knew, was still subject to an economic embargo imposed by the United States, and it was obvious that the country was desperately short of even the simplest materials. Yet the first impression was how everyone seemed to be getting on calmly and industriously with their work, even though they had very little in the way of tools or material. The road was raised up on an embankment, and on each side the rice paddy-fields stretched away, precisely divided by their little earth dikes. On the land the peasants were working steadily, hoeing clods of earth to break them up, or using a scoop like a large shovel suspended on a tripod to bring up water. The operator, usually a woman, swung this device backward and forward, rythmically dipping up the water from the irrigation ditches and throwing it up on to the field. All was orderly and neat. There was no rubbish on the sides of the road, no bad smells, and when we drove through the little villages of the neat brick-built two-storey houses, the roadside stalls were carefully set out with displays of cooked foods and snacks, vegetables, piles of bamboo mats, and even some consumer goods — at one spot was a gleaming white display of lavatory pans.

Meanwhile Truc chatted amiably, though his English was sometimes

Countryside, near Hanoi

difficult to follow. He had a wife, he told me, who was a translator in a government statistics office. They had met at English language college, and had a three-year-old son, on whom Truc clearly doted. But it seemed that Truc was not quite clear why I had come to Vietnam. No one at the Ministry had informed him. I said that I was interested in seeing bamboo sailing rafts, and had been told they could still be found in a place called Sam Son. Truc's face brightened. Yes, yes, he knew exactly what I meant. By chance he, his wife and child had spent their summer holiday at Sam Son. We had reached the city, and Truc directed the driver to his own house. Wait a minute, he told him, and dashed inside. Moments later he reappeared holding the souvenir he had brought back from Sam Son for his small son – it was a small, crudely made model of a bamboo sailing raft with two masts and red sails. It seemed that I was on the right track.

Hanoi itself appeared to be caught in a time warp. Largely due to the trade embargo, Hanoi had missed out on the thirty years of international aid and development which had changed most cities in Asia beyond recognition. On Hanoi's outskirts stood the standard ugly Soviet-style apartment blocks, but the centre was still much as the French had left it forty years earlier, though extremely run-down. The main avenues were shaded by splendid African mahogany trees, and lined with French colonial mansions with small front gardens, peeling green-painted shutters, and buff coloured walls stained with tropical mould. But what really gave the feeling that time had stood still was that there were virtually no cars. The Vietnamese could not afford to import them. So the avenues of Hanoi were filled with rivers of bicyclists pedalling sedately along the broad, flat highway, without any of the noise and stink of cars and trucks found in most Asian capitals. The most strident noise was the beep-beep of small motor-scooters which were becoming increasingly popular. They weaved their way past the slower-moving pedal-driven rickshaws in which, to complete the feeling of time warp, sat Vietnamese wearing khaki pith helmets, still standard headgear and made at Number One Hat Factory on the outskirts of the city.

The markets and older residential areas of the city were equally unscathed by modern trends. There the houses were all squashed together, rarely more than two storeys, with red tile roofs, and television aerials sprouting everywhere and set on bamboo poles rather than metal rods. Again the desperate shortage of materials and the home-made nature of the goods was evident. In one street people were hand-making bicycles out of tubing, welding the bits together and then painting them. In another street electrical components were offered for sale, but the selection displayed on stalls or set out on the pavement was so out of date as to be useless – huge heavyweight East German parts of ten or fifteen years' vintage, coils of salvaged wire flex, electrical parts that would fit refrigerators or air-conditioning units that had long vanished from use in the West or the booming countries of South-East Asia. The alleyways of the market area were not wide enough for cars to go up and down, so once again there was mostly bicycle and motor-scooter traffic. People ducked in and out from doorways to sit out in the street and gossip, and cook on small charcoal hearths set up on the broken slabs of the pavement. They sat on tiny stools the shape of oversized cotton reels, stooped over tables eating – they always seemed to be eating – bowls of noodles and soup while all around them the bicycle bells tinkled and the motor-scooters beeped, not to clear the way but just to let people know the riders had arrived. Again the place was surprisingly clean considering how cramped it was. Each evening, Truc explained, a gong was banged to announce the arrival of the hand-drawn rubbish cart, and people placed their garbage out in neat little piles to be collected.

Truc had said he would drop me off at my hotel, and the car stopped outside what looked like just another of the small houses in the street. It was located on a corner between an ironmongers which sold hand-beaten galvanised buckets and a shop displaying coloured powder for making your own paint. I was shown up a narrow back stair to a small white room with a very hard bed in one corner. Off the room was a bathroom with a bucket, a shower tap and a cement floor. The electrical fittings mingled every sort of voltage and plug shape, whether

Market, Hanoi

Continental European, British, American, or Soviet-style. All the wiring was exposed and frayed, and small lizards ran across the ceiling.

Downstairs in the front room I was surprised to find myself sharing the supper table with the only other foreign guest, a Frenchman, an accountant from Dijon. He had wanted to come to see what Vietnam was like, he told me, due to the French colonial connection. The Vietnamese Embassy in Paris had refused him a visa to travel on his own, so he had come to Bangkok where he had been able to arrange a solo visa through a travel agency. Two or three bar girls arrived while we were having our meal, and had to be fended off. They were obviously recruited by the sleazy young man, apparently a nephew of the owner, who made the hotel bookings while his sisters and cousins passed their time painting their nails and reading TV magazines in the front room. Suddenly from outside came the distinctive and startling hoot of a steam engine. I went outside to look. The railway line ran right across the narrow street, and along it slowly chugged a genuine steam locomotive, looming over the crowd of bicyclists who had stopped and dismounted to let it pass. The combination of the dark evening and the great grey-and-black engine puffing steam over the heads of the crowd, made me feel that I had strayed into a 1930s black-and-white film.

Next morning Truc and I were delayed for several hours while he went to the Interior Ministry to persuade them to issue an official permit for me to travel to Sam Son. Then we set off in the same rickety car that had picked us up from the airport. This time our route was south, out of the city, along Highway One, the road linking the northern capital Hanoi with the southern city of Ho Chi Minh, which most people still inadvertently called Saigon. It would have been impossible to drive quickly. The rice harvest had recently been collected, and the farmers were taking advantage of the passing traffic to spread rice stalks on the road surface so that the wheels of the cars and lorries knocked off the last grains. Again the grandly named Highway One was only a one-and-a-half-lane road, so this resulted in some close shaves as our car swished over the carpet of rice stalks and weaved between the suicidally inclined farmers and their wives who kept scuttling out to re-adjust their harvest, their heads and hands inches from the passing wheels. Once again there were the broken down lorries, the occasional car and jeep, and sometimes a cart pulled by a water buffalo which wore iron shoes that clinked on the tarmac road surface. At least nine-tenths of the traffic was bicycle. In fact, bicycles were used for serious transport of goods. Twice we passed columns of at least a hundred men and women, dismounted and moving at a determined trot pushing their bicycles alongside them. Each bicycle was neatly loaded with a bulging sack of grain or a great bundle of brushwood to be chopped up and used as fertiliser. The ant-like tenacity of these extraordinary mobile columns was heightened by the fact that the majority of the men and women were not panting, as they pushed their heavy loads, but smiling.

It dawned on me that no one seemed to be idle. There were no loafers, no bystanders just gazing around, no one merely sitting beside the road and watching the passing scene. Everyone seemed to be working or at least hurrying from one place to another, and usually carrying something. There was an air of industry and purpose which I found very impressive. And once again the acute shortage of materials was noticeable. Highway One, the most important road in the whole country, did not even have its own bridges. It shared them with the rickety railway line which ran parallel to the road. So whenever we came to a river, the road traffic was diverted up on to the railway track and had to cross on the railway bridge, driving along the metal tracks.

It took four hours to cover approximately one hundred miles from Hanoi to the point where a side road branched off to bring us into Sam Son. It was dusk by the time we got there, and our car turned into the compound of the offices of the People's Committee of Sam Son. The offices were closed for the evening, and there were no lights and no one to greet us until a fit-looking man in his late forties or early fifties swung into the carpark on a moped and dismounted. He was wearing a track suit. Truc introduced him as Mr Khiem, the Chairman of the People's Committee. I liked Mr Khiem at once. He was far from being a stuffy bureaucrat. Indeed, he apologised for being late, saying that he had just come in from playing football with the local team. He had a square, intelligent face and a quiet manner which exuded self-confidence. During the American war as it was called, the local party apparatus had sent him to be educated in Moscow, and from there Mr Khiem had gone on to spend three years studying agriculture in Cuba before coming back to Hanoi for another university degree. Mr Khiem was no party stick-in-the-mud. He was energetic, open-minded, and very keen to develop the economy of his little township by whatever means possible. What is more, he was the son and grandson of fishermen, and when I

asked about bamboo fishing rafts he had all the information at his fingertips. Yes, bamboo sailing rafts did still exist at Sam Son. It was the last
large concentration of rafts in all Vietnam. There were perhaps three or
four hundred of them scattered up and down the nearby coast, though
the greatest number was at the village of Long Spine Mountain, on the
edge of Sam Son itself. Each raft was normally owned and operated by
a couple of men, and just before daybreak they sailed out on the early
morning breeze to about a mile offshore, fished until about noon, then
rode in with the afternoon onshore wind. Their catch was usually very
small, just enough to feed the fishermen's families with perhaps a handful of small fish or shrimp to sell to the market women who came down
to the beach. In the morning Mr Khiem would arrange for me to meet
some fishermen, and perhaps go out on one of the rafts.

Truc and I spent that night in one of Sam Son's half-dozen ugly and
half-finished seafront hotels. They were built of concrete to Soviet
design, and were already crumbling and streaked with stains as they rotted before they were complete. Between them were much more
charming guest-houses with red tile roofs, and tucked here and there,
the simple two-room houses of the raft fishermen, often serving double
duty in summer as cafés and restaurants. I woke up next morning to find
very few people on the broad streets because this was the winter season,
and no one came to Sam Son in the wet, grey, cold weather. The hotels
were all empty and damp, the little shops shuttered and quiet, but there,
out to sea, was a sight that took my breath away. The horizon was speckled with the triangular sails of literally hundreds of sailing rafts. Small
though they were, each raft carried three sails so it looked as if the
entire surface of the sea were covered with sails, moving and interweav-
ing in a gliding minuet. None of the rafts carried even the smallest
outboard engine but depended solely on wind or oars to move, and
they hovered back and forth on their fishing pattern like a feeding swarm
of butterflies. Most of the sails were off-white, but here and there a fisherman had sewed a panel of blue or red into his sails, and these made
bright splashes of colour in the fishing fleet. Never in my life had I seen
so many working boats under sail, and I doubted whether there was a
similar spectacle anywhere else in the world.

By noon the fishing fleet had begun heading for shore, and I could see
why the bamboo sailing rafts had survived at Sam Son. The beach was
long, flat and shelved so gently that no normal vessel could have come

Sam Son

ashore without running aground. But the bamboo sailing rafts needed less than a foot of water to float, and came gliding right into the shallows. At a distance the rafts were so low-slung that they were sometimes invisible between the ripples, and it looked as if the fishermen were literally standing on the sea. When the raft bumped on the sand, the fishermen could step ashore only knee deep in the water. There they were met by their families who helped them carry their nets, masts, and boat gear to huts set back among the pine trees that fringed the beach. Then six people would take up their positions around the beached raft, slip ropes under it, which were attached to shoulder yokes, lift the raft bodily out of the sea, and carry it at a trot up the beach to place it above high watermark.

I walked over to inspect one of the beached rafts. They were elegant and simple in design. Eighteen large bamboo poles were lashed together side by side to make a platform, considerably longer than it was broad. Scorch marks along the bamboos showed that they had been heated in fire to give the characteristic upward curve of the bow. The three masts were set in rough blocks of wood tied to the upper surface of the platform, and everything was lashed in place with what looked like bamboo string. There was not a single nail or piece of metal to be seen. The most interesting features were three narrow slots cut in the body of the raft. Down through these slots the fishermen slid the long narrow retractable keels, known as leeboards or dagger boards, which gave the raft its grip on the surface of the sea. These sliding leeboards, according to Professor Needham, were one of the significant cultural characteristics which appeared to link Asia with the New World. Leeboards were an invention found only among the native craft of East Asia and the Pacific coast of South America on opposite sides of the Pacific Ocean. Either the two cultures had developed leeboards independently, or perhaps one group had copied from the other. Maybe a sailing raft from Asia, or even in the other direction, had brought the technology across the great ocean.

With Truc's help I bombarded the fishermen with questions. Where did they get the bamboo for their rafts? It came from the jungle about one hundred miles inland, and was a very special type of giant bamboo suitable for raft-building. What did they use to tie the rafts together? Usually strips of bamboo skin, which first had to be boiled in lime to make it more pliable and to preserve it. But sometimes they used lashings of rattan, a jungle plant which threw out long tendrils that made natural bindings. Then came my key question: how long did they think a bamboo raft would stay afloat? The fishermen looked doubtful. They couldn't really give me an answer from their own experience, because they themselves hauled their rafts out of the water every afternoon. They knew the bamboo would float for at least three months, and guessed that it might last longer. But equally important was the strength of the bindings. Every three months the fishermen had to take their rafts to pieces and relash them using fresh bamboo string or, nowadays, nylon fishing-line. Then what did they think about the notion of sailing a large bamboo raft right across the Pacific Ocean? The fishermen looked astounded. Then, perhaps because they were reluctant to seem faint-hearted and were proud of their strange vessels, they replied, Why not?

I spent the next two days walking up and down the beach at Sam Son, measuring sailing rafts, collecting lengths of bamboo string and scraps of bamboo as samples, watching the fishermen repairing their boats, asking more questions, and writing down notes to carry back to Colin Mudie. He was the naval architect in England who had designed my three previous replica vessels: a leather-covered skinboat which had been used in 1976–77 to sail across the North Atlantic to show that Irish monks could have reached America a thousand years before Columbus; an eighth-century Arab trading ship the planks of which were sewn together with coconut rope and which had been sailed from Muscat on the Arabian coast to China in 1980–81 to retrace the early Arab trade routes which had given rise to the stories of Sindbad the Sailor; and the copy of a small Bronze-Age rowing galley in which twenty oarsmen had rowed and sailed in 1984 from Greece to Georgia on the coast of the Black Sea, to retrace the route of Jason and the Argonauts. This time I would be asking Colin to produce a design which was completely different: a raft that would be capable of crossing 6,500 miles of ocean, the equivalent of sailing from Europe across the Atlantic to North America, and then back again.

Finally Truc introduced me to two fishermen who were willing to take me on a trial trip aboard a fishing raft. I accompanied them as the two fishermen, each wearing no more than a T-shirt and cotton shorts, waded out through the shallows pushing their raft until they were thigh-deep in the water. Then all three of us clambered aboard, and the two

Fisherman at Sam Son

men began to work the long flexible oars that slowly drove the raft towards the line of breakers lying between us and the open sea. As we approached the breaker line, a normal boat would have pitched and tossed awkwardly on the wave crests. But the bamboo raft ploughed forward smoothly. Instead of being lifted in the air by each wave, the raft merely absorbed the wave top which washed right through it. The sea-water flowed up through the cracks between the bamboo poles, and the wave crest travelled right *over* the raft. It was a strange sensation: on the one hand the surface of the raft was actually underwater and all three of us had wet feet; but on the other hand, there was really no feeling of the movement of the sea, no rolling and pitching. And when we had passed beyond the line of breakers, and hoisted the three sails, the sensation was even more curious. The upcurved bow of the raft poked clear of the water, and so too did the side bamboos of the raft, which were slightly raised. But the main surface of the raft was level with the surface of the sea, or actually underwater. I watched a tiny fish, no bigger than a min-now swim in one side of the raft, find a path between two bamboos, make its wriggling way right across the raft, and swim out the other side and back into the ocean.

The two fishermen were completely at ease on their semi-submerged work platform. They adjusted the flimsy sails made of discarded sugar sacks, and slid the leeboards up and down according to the angle of the wind, while their raft pulled a fine meshed trawl net through the water. They seemed quite content to catch no more than a cupful of minute shrimp. These shrimp, I later learned, would fetch a premium price for sale in Hanoi and give them enough cash to buy a day's food for their family. When they ate their lunch it was no more than a handful of cold rice carried in an ingenious watertight container made by slicing off the top of a section of bamboo and fitting it back on as a cap. Another bamboo tube held their drinking water. After a few hours we headed back for the beach, sailing until we were once again in the breaker line, then steering the raft with the oars to keep it straight to the waves which once again rolled right through the raft, washing halfway up our legs. The fishermen paid little heed to the water, which was warm even in October, and I noticed how their semi-aquatic way of life had produced powerful muscular shoulders from handling the oars, and broad, almost prehensile, feet which gripped the wet surface of the bamboos.

As I walked back up the damp sand of the beach to where Truc was waiting for me, I came to a firm decision: the country where I should build my ocean-going raft to test Needham's theory of trans-Pacific raft voyages was Vietnam. It lay within the Chinese culture zone; the people were hardworking and reliable; and at Sam Son were fishermen and raft sailors who had the unique skills and knowledge to construct the vessel. If Mr Khiem would agree, I would come back to Sam Son as soon as I had a proper design for an ocean-going raft, and we would proceed with the next step of the project.

2

BUILDING IN VIETNAM

'Rafts are notorious,' Colin Mudie warned me, 'for stability problems at high angles of heel, and for the difficulty of righting a large raft which develops great initial stability when upturned.' Put bluntly, the Vietnamese sailing rafts had been reassuringly stable, but there was a dangerous penalty: when a raft reached a certain angle of heel, it flipped over suddenly, and once capsized, was virtually impossible to turn back the right way up. And, of course, if the capsize happened in the wide ocean, then the crew was in real trouble. I had gone to see the naval architect at his home in Southern England, taking with me the sample lengths of bamboo from Sam Son, as well as strips of the bamboo string used for lashing the fishing rafts together. Colin relished any technical challenge that was out of the ordinary, and he deployed a remarkably wide range of skills and interests. A leading designer of sail training vessels, he also had an encyclopedic knowledge of historic and traditional sailing craft so he had produced design plans for anything from a replica seventeenth-century trading ship to a Chinese junk. Now he was ready to make a preliminary design of an ocean-going sailing raft based on the data I had gathered from Sam Son and Taiwan, as well as references to early rafts and sailing vessels in the Chinese records. As a precaution he and his wife Rosemary would also write and run a computer study of the raft's theoretical stability when carrying various loads. Colin had a profound respect for the centuries of natural design and development which must have taken place among native peoples in the evolution of their own watercraft. So we agreed on a step-by-step approach that would closely involve the raftbuilders of Sam Son.

Colin would first produce his preliminary design study, from which I would arrange to have built an eighteen-inch-long model of the raft, precise in every detail. I would take this model to the fishermen in Sam Son, and ask them to construct a small version of the raft, half the width and half the length of the final vessel. By this exercise we hoped to learn something of the building techniques needed to construct a vessel considerably larger than the small rafts of Sam Son, and also use the smaller version for sailing trials. After Colin had incorporated any additional details in his final design, I would proceed to the building of a full-size raft of ocean-going dimensions.

'What sort of length did you have in mind?' Colin asked me.

'About sixty-feet. For a crew of five or six people,' I answered.

Colin did a quick sum. 'From what you observed of the Sam Son fishing rafts, that seems about right. I would guess that your ocean-going raft is going to be in the order of sixteen to eighteen metres long and needs three layers of bamboo to provide the required buoyancy for the crew and all their kit.'

As yet I had given little thought as to precisely who should be the crew of the raft. My only firm idea was to try to include a fisherman from Sam Son who knew how to handle and work with bamboo and could teach the techniques of raft sailing using leeboards. He would have to be willing to leave his village and sail not just a couple of miles offshore but thousands of miles into the ocean, spending up to six months cooped up in the company of foreigners who did not speak his language. Selection of the other crew members could wait until I had the main raft under construction. So I was surprised when, on returning home to Ireland, I received a phone call, and a woman's voice, speaking with a foreign accent, asked if I was looking for crew for a sailing expedition in Asian waters. At first I had trouble identifying the accent.

'I am sorry to trouble you,' the voice began very politely. 'Would it be possible to speak to Mr Tim Severin?'

'You're already speaking to him.'

There was a slight pause, of surprise. 'Oh, so sorry, I had thought I would be talking to his secretary. My name is Nina Kojima, and I am calling from Tokyo.' How on earth did this person know I was planning the raft expedition? I wondered to myself. But it was chance. 'I was given

your name by the captain of a Japanese sail training ship,' Nina continued. 'I am an artist, and my dream has been to sail as crew member on
an expedition and make drawings and paintings.'

'Well, as it happens, I may be going on a Pacific voyage,' I said cautiously. 'But the expedition won't start out for at least a year, and the
conditions will be very difficult. The vessel – it is a raft – has not even
been built yet.'

'I have been learning to sail, and would be willing to study and prepare some more,' Nina continued firmly. Later I was to learn that Nina
was not a person to be put off. She was highly determined and by the
end of the telephone conversation I found myself agreeing that if Truc
could get her a visa, she would meet me in Vietnam, and make some
drawings at Sam Son so I could see the quality of her work, while she
would find out more about the China Voyage.

We met in Bangkok Airport in early June, preparing to board the
same flight to Hanoi. I knew that the small Japanese woman standing by
the check-in desk had to be the artist of the telephone call because she
was holding a brown canvas rucksack from which protruded the end of
a roll of artist's drawing paper. Nina was just under 5 feet 2 inches tall,
slightly built, and very casually dressed in a long and rumpled white shirt
with a pen clipped in the neck band. The tail of her shirt hung outside a
pair of patched and baggy cotton pantaloons. The trousers were blue
with white star patterns, and ended at mid-calf to reveal small neat
brown feet in sandals. These shapeless trousers, I later learned, were
extremely old-fashioned – the sort of working trousers worn by
Japanese village women forty years earlier or grandmothers in Tokyo. I
introduced myself, and as we waited for our flight to be called, I tried to
guess Nina's age. It was nearly impossible. Nina had a round face, pale
skin and short-cut hair. She could have been in her late teens, twenties,
or perhaps early thirties. What really confused any calculation was her
manner. She had a completely unselfconscious way of talking and gesturing, and seemed to be living in a slightly forgetful and innocent
world. She gazed with open curiosity at the other passengers, dropped
her passport, temporarily mislaid her ticket, forgot her rucksack and had
to go back to get it, kicked off her sandals as soon as we got to our seats
on the plane, and craned her neck to look out of the aircraft window. To
her everything seemed to be curious and interesting, and she was utterly
unconcerned how she appeared to other people.

The reason for this slightly Bohemian manner became apparent. Nina's father, she told me, was also an artist who had liberal ideas about bringing up his only child. He had allowed his daughter to grow up completely free of restraint. When Nina was a small child he had taken her along with him when he went painting, given her drawing materials to play with and make her own sketches, and let her develop in her own way with none of the usual strict conventions of Japanese upbringing. Understandably, Nina had then found formal Japanese schooling rather a struggle, although she had studied English successfully. It had taken her several extra years to get through art college, and then she had worked variously as an interpreter and guide, and appeared on Japanese television in Teach Yourself English programmes before finally settling on what she really liked to do – namely to draw and illustrate for magazines and books as a freelance artist. She did not tell me then, but it was a precarious way of making a living. To purchase her ticket to Vietnam she had been obliged to take extra work as a waitress in a sushi bar.

A weary-looking Truc met the two of us at Hanoi, apologising for his tiredness saying that he had been escorting a North Korean delegation around Hanoi for the past four days. But he had managed to telephone Mr Khiem, the Chairman of the Sam Son People's Committee, and Mr Khiem was keen to help my project. He had arranged for a team of fishermen to be on standby to build the test raft, and we would travel down next morning by train. We went to Hanoi Station at 6 a.m., and Truc had to spend half an hour persuading the railway security police that I really did have official papers to travel by train. The police seemed to take no notice of Nina. When we got into our carriage, we had to sit patiently for another hour on hard wooden slat benches while the starting time was delayed by signal breakdowns and the late running of more important train services. Finally the train began to move off, and nearly left without Nina. She had stepped out on to the platform to do some sketching, became oblivious to her surroundings, and was standing there drawing the slow-moving train, having forgotten that she was meant to be on it. Truc, who had been slumped against the carriage window half-asleep, realised the situation and leaped out to grab Nina and bundle her aboard before she was left stranded.

This little incident would not have occurred, I realised, if Nina had not looked as if she could have been Vietnamese. Whereas I was obviously a Western foreigner and would have been stopped by the railway police if I took photographs or made drawings, Nina was ignored on the assumption that she was a local person. In fact, this confusion was to arise many times over the next few months. To me Nina looked very Japanese. But her idiosyncratic peasant clothing and Asian appearance led many Vietnamese, who had never seen a Japanese before and thought they were all wealthy and dressed fashionably, to think she was from somewhere in Vietnam. They were baffled when they discovered that Nina did not speak a word of Vietnamese, and they would repeat themselves again and again, speaking to her slowly and clearly while Nina smiled politely and shook her head.

'They keep trying to make you understand because they think you are from one of the minority hill tribes somewhere near the Laos border,' chortled Truc, 'who speak their own tribal languages.'

The train ride was even more tedious than going by car to Sam Son, and midway there was a similar case of mistaken identity which showed Truc in a new light. As the train trundled along, a drunken policeman came staggering and lurching down the aisle, saw Nina and myself, and dropped into the seat opposite us, rudely pushing away the occupant already sitting there. The policeman was sweating heavily, semi-stupified, and carrying a gun. He leaned forward and tried to engage us in drunken conversation. Awkwardly we looked out of the window, or smiled politely, wishing he would go away. But he only became more insistent, and began fumbling and pushing at us. A railway conductor appeared, saw the uniform and the gun, and obviously thought it wiser not to intervene and disappeared. We were rescued by Truc who had again been trying to catch up on his sleep farther down the open carriage. To my astonishment the easy-going, chubby Truc suddenly burst upon the scene, grabbed the drunken policeman by the lapels, though he was a head shorter than the man, and hauled him to his feet, before pushing him along the aisle to the farthest end of the carriage where he slammed him into a seat. Then I saw Truc reach into his back pocket and produce a plastic card which he shook in the man's face, while he yelled at him in a fury. The policeman seemed to shrivel.

'Thanks very much, Truc. That saved us,' I said when he reappeared. 'What was that you showed him?'

Truc laughed. 'My press card,' he said. 'It's got a nice big red stripe on it, so I pretended I was a high party official. He was too drunk to notice the difference. I felt I was like a referee showing the red card at a

Beach netting, Sam Son

football game,' and he threw back his head to laugh and show those brown and black teeth.

When we arrived in Sam Son we found a very different scene to the quiet, rather bleak seaside town that I had visited in late autumn. It was now summer, and the holiday season had begun. Holidaymakers came

down from the work cadres of the factories and offices of Hanoi, and spent a week or two enjoying the beach and sea. They packed into the shabby state-run hotels or took rooms at the small guest-houses. The long sandy beach which had been empty in winter except for a few upturned boats, now had a line of at least a hundred little portable kiosks of bamboo matting which sold soft drinks and hot green tea, or rented out inner tubes from truck tyres. These were painted with white numbers and made simple bathing rings for the visitors. There was a curious side-by-side activity as the fishermen continued to go about their usual business of launching rafts, hauling nets up the beach, and gathering seaweed, while the city families walked around them, splashed in the shallows, or sat in deckchairs gazing at the horizon. A favourite excursion for the visitors was to stroll all the way to the south end of the beach, past the fishermen's quarter, then climb the long flight of stone steps which led up the temple on the rocky hill. The temple, with its red tiles and carved dragons on the ridge line was set among papayas and pine trees, and was the home of Sam Son's protective god. Even in strictly communist Vietnam the great temple drum boomed out every few hours to scare away evil spirits and claim the God's attention. Below the temple hill, at the far end of the beach, a dozen elderly workmen were waiting for us. They were the work crew Mr Khiem had assigned to build the test raft.

Mr Khiem had nominated the oldest fishermen in the community because of their experience, but also, I guessed, because it gave the semi-retired veterans some paid work. They were an entertaining and very motley gang. The oldest, Mr Luong, was in his eighties, and looked like one of those model Chinese fishermen carved in ivory or bone who stands on a rock with his fishing rod. He wore a frayed conical straw hat, a faded red smock and fisherman's trousers rolled to the knee. His wizened face sprouted the long straggly wisps of a white mandarin moustache and beard. Another man, Mr Luoc, whom I nicknamed 'the comic', was about ten years younger, bespectacled and always clowning around to get laughs. To my surprise I discovered that he devoted at least half his time as an assistant to the priest at the temple on the hill. His elder brother, Mr Nhieu, who was also on the work squad, was a former vice-chairman of the People's Committee, but clearly had been put out to pasture for being such a hopeless organiser. Mr Nhieu carried a notebook everywhere with him, and wrote copious official notes. But he could never understand what they meant when he came to review them, so he stood there scratching his head, and turning the pages and getting more and more frustrated and perplexed. Unfortunately, Mr Khiem had put him in charge of the work squad, so our progress was frequently held up while he tried to reach a decision. Nothing could have been more disastrous when trying to direct the efforts of a dozen elderly men because, of course, each of them had his own long-held opinion of how any job should be done, and was quite sure that his own method was the only correct one. Also, being elderly, they were very ready to voice their opinions and denounce the ideas of their fellows. I came to understand why the townsfolk of Sam Son said of their fishermen that, 'They have stomachs like the sea, and voices like the wind.' It meant they ate a great deal, and always shouted at one another at the tops of their voices even when standing only a yard apart. The effect was unnerving, and at first I thought the old men would come to blows. But it was only their way of discussing how they should set about copying the little model raft that I had brought with me.

In fact it took them a very short space of time – only three weeks – to build the test raft ready to launch. Despite their age they were remarkably nimble. To simplify matters, they decided to build three of their normal-size rafts and then stack them vertically to give the three-layer buoyancy that Colin Mudie had calculated. They began by shaving the shiny outer skin off the bamboo poles with iron machetes, and fire-bending the poles to the curve they required for the eventual profile of the raft. Formerly this bending had been done by holding a firebrand of twigs under each bamboo at selected points, while applying tension to the bamboo so that the fibres contracted and the bamboo took up a permanent curve. Nowadays, however, a burning bicycle tyre was used instead of a twig firebrand. The curved bamboo poles were then taken down to the sea to be cleaned of soot by scrubbing with sand and seawater, and laid out on a building frame like a large bedstead that the old men had erected on the beach. There they lashed the bamboo poles side by side to a dozen crosspieces of light timber, tying them in place with strips of bamboo skin which they had boiled in a solution of lime. The old-timers worked in pairs, one man lying on his back on the sand underneath the building frame, while his partner perched on top of the raft and poked the strip of bamboo down to his colleague between the bamboos. The fastening was then pulled up tight while one man beat on the bamboo pole with a wooden mallet to vibrate the pole and its lashing as tightly as possible to the adjacent bamboo. The hammering and pounding made a terrific noise, as if the old men were tuning dementedly a giant xylophone.

Watching them work, Truc and I learned several valuable lessons. The principal one was that when we came to build the main raft, we would have to find a different construction sequence. It was all very well to build the test raft in three separate layers, but when we came to lash the three layers on top of one another, the old men found it almost impossible to tie them together securely. It was too difficult to pass strips of bamboo right through all three layers and pull them sufficiently tight. Also, the bamboos in each layer did not exactly overlap one on top of the other, so the slots of the leeboards had to be made by cutting holes through the body of raft which weakened it. Another lesson was in man-management. The sight of three rafts being stacked on top of one another was so unusual that it attracted raft fishermen from all up and down the beach. When they had finished their day's work they would saunter along, to stand and stare, smoke cigarettes, drink glasses of tea, and offer advice. And, of course, the moment they offered any advice, the old men building the raft put down their mallets or rolled out from under the raft in order to reply to the criticisms and discuss possible modifications. They were thoroughly enjoying their new-found importance and their conversations, always conducted at a roar, brought all progress to a halt. Truc and I decided that the full-sized raft would have to be built inside a fenced-off compound to keep any onlookers at a safe distance, otherwise it would never get finished. Over the gate to the

Building the test raft

compound Truc proposed hanging a sign which read 'No Admittance! No Visitors! No Advice!'

Meanwhile Nina was having the time of her life. As we had agreed, she sketched and made paintings of the raft-building, but she was just as intrigued by the way of life of the Sam Son fishermen and their families. In her peasant's trousers and loose shirt Nina would wander up and down the beach sketching fisherwomen hauling nets, men putting to sea in their boats, or whatever caught her wide-eyed attention. It was easy to know where Nina was, even among the crowds of holidaymakers, because she was always the centre of a tight swarm of children. They clustered around her as she stood and sketched, peeking at her work, and asking to be allowed to use a pencil or a brush pen. Naturally Nina allowed them to do so, and as the days passed, the children adopted Nina as one of their own. When they came to know her better, the older children began fending off the younger ones so that Nina could work with less disturbance, or they brought her cups of tea, a fisherman's straw hat for shade, even on one disastrous day a locally made ice cream. Nina in her innocence ate the ice cream and, of course, it played havoc with her digestion. At the end of the day a child would literally deliver Nina back to Truc and myself, Nina riding along perched on the back wheel of a bicycle while her child-guide stood on the pedals to turn them.

In his role as our official guide Truc had warned Nina and me that we should stay near the raft-building site and not go wandering unescorted into the town. This, he said, was for 'security reasons' imposed by the Sam Son police and military department. Of course, Nina either forgot or ignored the injunction, and the children frequently led her off by the hand to take her to their homes or show her some scene they thought she might like to sketch. The extent of Nina's illegal wanderings became apparent when she and I were eventually taken on an escorted tour of the inner town. As we passed down various lanes in the officially out-of-bounds area, children or their parents seemed to pop out of every second or third house to call out 'Nina! Nina!', and beckon her in.

No harm was done and no one seemed to take these transgressions very seriously until the day Nina found her way three or four kilometres down the coast to a cove used as a small harbour. It was a picturesque little place, and Nina began to make sketches. Unfortunately, being a harbour, however insignificant, it was also the base for a detachment of the Vietnamese Frontier Guard who promptly detained Nina on suspicion of espionage. Truc and I knew nothing of this until a message reached us late in the evening to say that Nina was under arrest. Rolling his eyes to heaven at Nina's mishaps, Truc asked me to bring Nina's Japanese passport and accompany him to the Frontier Guard barracks. There we found Nina a mixture of puzzlement and impatience after being detained for five very boring hours. She was quite unable to understand why she was not allowed to leave. We explained that she had wandered into a Forbidden Area, and begged her to be patient while Truc settled down to a lengthy and tactful discussion with the senior officer at the post. Nina was a foreigner, Truc explained, and she did not understand the regulations. She had made a genuine mistake, and sincerely apologised. Even the suspicious commander of the frontier post found it difficult to believe Nina was really a spy when Truc turned the pages of her sketch pad and showed him pictures of old fishermen tying bamboo poles together, children's portraits, pigs, and villagers on bicycles. Yet it took another two hours to coax him into releasing Nina into our custody, with a promise that we would not let her wander again. Nina, of course, was furious and could not understand what all the fuss was about.

We did return to the cove some ten days later, but this time with advance notice from Mr Khiem, who told the Frontier Guards our intention. We had launched the test raft, and the little harbour was the only place to moor the raft in safety while we conducted sailing trials. I also made sure of paying a courtesy call on the commander of the guard post before we set out to sea with a scratch crew composed of Truc, two Vietnamese fishermen, and old Mr Nhieu, the note-taker. The latter insisted on accompanying the vessel as he was officially in charge of the local labour force. But he had no confidence whatsoever in the seaworthiness of a three-layer raft. Though I had promised him we were only going a few hundred metres offshore, Mr Nhieu showed up with a reserve supply of food and several litres of drinking water in case we were swept out to sea for a week. As it turned out, our three-layer raft was even more stable than the normal fishing rafts. When we deliberately capsized it, the test raft would not flip over until it had reached an angle of almost eighty degrees. That was extremely satisfying, and compensated for the disappointment that, try as we might, we could not get the raft to sail faster than one and a half knots, barely walking pace.

A carpenter from Sam Son who had prepared the wooden crosspieces for the test raft was one member of the test-raft crew. I had noticed him on the very first day I came to Sam Son because the man looked so much like the stage villain in an Italian-made Western film. He had a narrow, haunted face with prominent cheekbones that gave him a sinister, wolfish expression, emphasised by the black hat he wore. He was a tremendous worker, single-handedly keeping pace with the raft-lashing team as he shaped the various wooden fittings using only a meagre set of three chisels, an old bow saw, and a lump of wood for a hammer. This carpenter was in his late thirties, and patting his chest, pointing at me and then at the horizon, he had indicated that he would like to go on my journey. Now, as he helped sail the test raft, I saw that he was also a very capable sailor, and was just as active and enthusiastic about his work. Truc told me that the carpenter's name was Loi which meant 'Profit'. He was married, had three children and, yes, he was very keen to go on my expedition, though he had never even travelled as far as Hanoi. Watching Loi scrambling about the test raft expertly adjusting the sails, knotting ropes, and using his club hammer and chisels to make the timber joints fit better, I suspected that I had found the Vietnamese member of my sailing team.

Also, I had seen for myself how bamboo needed expert handling. Botanists have classified several hundred different species of bamboo, but only the raftbuilders knew exactly what species of bamboo should be used for which job. For instance, one type of bamboo provided the flexible skin used for lashing, another type was used for the locking pegs which held any carpentry joints together, a third for mast or spars, and so forth. The list went on and on, and, of course, by far the most important species of bamboo was the one which the raftbuilders called *luong*. It was the giant bamboo which provided the long poles used for the body of the raft, and was particularly buoyant because the bamboo stalk had thin walls and large internal air chambers. The botanists had named it after the Vietnamese province of Thanh Hoa where Sam Son was located, and it grew in the jungles close to the border with Laos, a hundred miles inland. The caution I had been given time and time again, whether from well-wishers or from critics, was that bamboos would never stay afloat long enough to cross the Pacific Ocean. The hollow poles would crack and absorb water, or be eaten by ship worm, or grow waterlogged and lose their strength, or, for whatever reason, sink. I decided that if I was going to trust the lives of several men to a bamboo raft, I should visit the jungle and find out more about the plant on which we would depend.

The jungle was yet another area off-limits to foreigners, so Truc had to obtain special permission from Hanoi, and also from the provincial government of Thanh Hoa, to go there. Also, the mountain people who harvested the bamboos were not ethnic Vietnamese, but came from a Thai-speaking minority tribe. So it was lucky that Mr Khiem had on his staff an army captain who was native to one of the mountain villages. This man was willing to escort us into the jungle, act as our interpreter, and introduce us to his people. There was no doubt that the captain was racially different from most of the Vietnamese I had met. He had a flatter, more Chinese-looking face, very smooth and hairless so that his deep-set eyes lacked eyebrows or eyelashes. When he smiled, the eyes disappeared almost completely into slits. In build he was much shorter and broader than the Northern Vietnamese, and rarely had I met such a tough-looking individual. He could have been moulded from compacted rubber, and seemed completely impervious to heat, cold, or discomfort.

During seven hours of jolting travel in a jeep he sat as relaxed as if he had been in an armchair, while the vehicle bounced and thrashed its way over badly made roads through foothills planted with sugar cane and then along a stony track up into the mountains. His only luggage was a plastic zipcase containing a single sheet of paper which was our official permission to travel, a cheap torch, and, tucked into his waistband, a pistol. Although it grew cold and began to rain, he had neither extra clothing nor raincoat to put over his thin khaki shirt, nor did he seem to need one. The most impressive display of his toughness was when the villagers at a roadside hamlet recognised him and invited us in for refreshment. We were offered a choice of green tea or a clear liquid which looked like water, but one sip told me that it was alcohol about as strong as fortified wine. The captain casually gulped down three full tumblers of the stuff, and returned to the jeep as if he were striding out on a formal parade.

By late evening we had finally reached his village which could have been a setting for Shangri-La. A shallow river had scooped a fertile valley out of the limestone mountains. Wisps and tendrils of pale grey mist floated round the steep sides of the valley, which were clothed in dense green tropical forest except at places where a cliff face or a huge boulder showed a patch of grey rock, hung with vines and lianas. Occasionally the skeleton of a leafless flame tree towered above smaller shrubs. The cliffs around the valley caught and echoed every sound, and once the engine of our jeep had stopped, there was no sound except for the crowing of cocks, the sound of someone chopping firewood, and the calls of children playing. The houses were tribal longhouses, massive wooden structures raised up on stout posts with buffalo and pot-bellied pigs snuffling and squelching in the mud beneath them. Their steeply pitched roofs of palm thatch had neither chimneys nor smoke holes, so the blue-grey smoke from the cooking fires oozed up through the pale brown thatch or curled up around the long eaves so that the longhouses seemed to be steaming gently. Each longhouse had its own garden planted with areca, papaya, banana and cassava, and here and there was the distinct sunburst cluster of the leaves of the Pandanus palm. There was no electricity, no piped water, no plastic or metal that I could see, just the hamlet of native houses looking as if they had been there since the beginning of time. Inside they were equally in harmony with their environment – just a single huge room spanned by massive, smoke-blackened rafters, generous windows to let in light and air which could be closed with light bamboo screens in bad weather, and a floor made of

Floating bamboos downriver

split bamboos well polished with use. This meant that the interior of the longhouse was very clean. Any dust or dirt was simply swept through the cracks and fell on the livestock below.

Next morning we explored the forest. The clumps of giant bamboo were easy to see because they were so tall, forty or fifty feet high, that they sprouted up over the general level of the greenery, and their tops appeared as pale silvery tufts waving in the breeze. To reach them we first had to wade through the pale jade waters of the shallow river, then scramble up a narrow footpath up the mountain slopes. Foresters passed us, small wiry men carrying machetes and, in one case, a cross-bow for shooting birds. Suddenly there was a strange whooping cry above us, echoing through the forest. The army captain pulled me abruptly to one side off the path. There was a distant rumbling and crashing, which was intensified and reflected by the mountain slopes. The noise seemed to be coming closer. Suddenly from above us a twenty-foot-long heavy log burst into view, careening down the path like a bobsled. It bounced and thundered past us as we shrank back into the bushes, and disappeared downslope in a cloud of leaves and twigs, crashing onward towards the river. It seemed that our footpath served double duty as a log slide, and the cry was a warning for travellers to stand clear.

The heavier timber of the forest was cut and shifted by men, but harvesting of the bamboos was mostly done by the tribal women. Five of them accompanied us, and they were stunningly beautiful, with lovely golden-brown skin and long sleek hair gathered back and set off with a bright red or pink flower. They carried themselves with the grace and elegance of the truly fit, as they made their way up the steep path dressed in loose white blouses and long, tight black skirts decorated near the hem with a band of silk embroidery in brown, dark blue, red and yellow. Around her waist each woman wore a cummerbund of brightly coloured silk and a broad silver decorated belt which set off her slim figure and tiny waist, and also gave her a swashbuckling air, for the belts served a practical purpose. In them was tucked her working tool – a long, razor-sharp machete.

When we reached the first bamboo clump, the women began to clear away the undergrowth, sweeping away the smaller bushes and vines with slicing strokes. In their bright colours, they looked like an exotic group of forest creatures grazing their natural habitat. Then they began to cut down the bamboos, chopping through the stalks of the towering plants with a few well-placed strokes so that the tall bamboos tumbled to the ground. This was harvesting, not clear-felling, because the women were careful to cut down only the mature bamboos which grew from the clump roots half-underground, and they avoided damaging the short spikes of the new bamboo shoots which were poking up through the soil. The bamboos grew like enormous stalks of grass rather than like trees. Each year the roots of the bamboo threw out shoots which thrust upward at astonishing speed, growing their full height in just two or three months. For making rafts, I was told, the bamboos should be two years old because they were still young and supple enough to be fire-bent. For house-building or scaffolding work it was better to use the stiffer three-year-old stalks. The cutting teams harvested more than 11,000 bamboos each year, and left them on the banks of the fast-flowing headwaters of the river system. The freshly cut bamboos were lashed together in bundles which were steered downstream by professional raftsmen. It was a dangerous and sometimes fatal job. At high water when the rivers were running strongly, the unwieldy rafts were swept under overhangs, and sometimes their steersmen drowned. At one spot so many raft-riders had lost their lives that it was called the Cave of Ghosts.

Colin Mudie's design for a 60-foot raft needed about 220 prime quality bamboo poles, each 30 feet long. Also I required 36 pieces of curved timber cut from naturally crooked branches, to make the crossbeams of the full-size raft. The captain promised that he would arrange for men from his village to search the jungle for exactly the right shapes of timber. They had plenty of time because the women would not be cutting the bamboo poles for the raft for another four or five months. Why was that? I asked him. Because if I needed the best quality bamboo then the only season to cut it was November or December. This was when there was the least amount of sap in the bamboo stalks. The captain picked up a short length of bamboo which had been felled less than a minute before. Sticky sap was oozing from the cut end, and already half a dozen flying insects had settled on the juice to feed. One particular insect, he explained to me, was deadly for bamboo. It settled on the cut bamboo, fed on the sap, and laid eggs which became tiny larvae that burrowed right through the walls of the bamboo, and literally ate it into a honeycomb. If I built the raft with infected bamboo the vessel would turn to

Tribal longhouse

powder within weeks. As we walked back to his village, he casually broke off a piece of old dry bamboo from a garden fence, showed me some tiny pin holes in the surface, and then cracked it open. The bamboo wall looked like a piece of furniture that had been ravaged by woodworm. It would have taken only three or four weeks for the hungry larvae to do this damage, he said. The destruction of the bamboo is so fast that when a bamboo hut is badly infected by the insects you can sit inside and actually hear them chewing. At the time I thought he was exaggerating, but I was to discover that he was telling the truth.

That evening I discovered another, very pleasant use for bamboo. The captain's family organised a communal feast in their longhouse. Pigs were slaughtered, ducks carried in flapping and quacking, and two large fires were stoked up on the massive stone slabs which served as hearths in the interior of the longhouse. While the meat barbecued and the cooking pots steamed, the captain explained to me the use of a large earthenware jar. It was about three feet high, wide-necked, and had a capacity of about twenty gallons. It was filled with what seemed to be dark woodshavings or bark chippings. Stuck into the shavings were half a dozen long, slender tubes of bamboo. They looked like oversized drinking straws, and this is exactly what they proved to be. When the meal was almost ready, two women went down to the river and filled a stout bamboo tube, which they used as a bucket to bring water back to the longhouse. The water was then carefully poured into the jar, until it was brim-full. The captain explained that he, as the host, and I, as his chief guest, should begin the evening festivities by sucking on the hollow bamboo tubes. To make sure that we each drank properly, he would hold over the jar the hollow horn of a wild cow also filled with riverwater. The end of the horn had been drilled with a drainhole which he blocked with his thumb. As the two of us drank, the captain would move his thumb, so that the water drained from the cow's horn into the jar. Evidently it was important for the two of us to suck up water through the bamboo straws fast enough so that the water level in the earthenware jar did not overflow.

One pull at the drinking tube told me what I had suspected: the jar now contained alcohol, the same drink we had been offered at the road-side halt. But there was no escaping the social obligation. While about thirty of the captain's family and friends cheered and clapped encouragement, we shared the first cow's horn of native brew. Then another group took over, and another, and another, until everybody in the long-house, including women and children, was taking regular turns at the drinking straws and the evening became merrier and merrier. There seemed to be no limit to the amount of alcohol the jar would produce. As the level in the jar went down, more water was brought from the river and, try as I might, I never did discover exactly what was in the earthenware jar that turned water into alcohol instantly. 'Jungle herbs and cassava root chips', was all I was told.

The drink was cool, pleasantly tangy, and definitely intoxicating. This was an advantage when the meal was served. Trays laden with all sorts of bowls were laid out on the longhouse floor, and we squatted round in groups. Again, as guest of honour, I was expected to start the proceedings by sampling the special hors-d'oeuvre. It arrived in a small bowl and wobbled evilly. It looked like dark cherry jelly. 'What is that?' I enquired, and was told that it was the blood of the ducks I had seen earlier. The blood had been carefully drained off when the birds were slaughtered. The ducks' feet were boiled, chopped up, and while hot, dropped into the bowl of raw duck's blood as a garnish. Once again there was no way of avoiding one's social duty. Trying to eat globs of congealed duck's blood using only chopsticks left me looking like Count Dracula with red streaks down my chin, while I reminded myself that goose liver paté was also eaten raw.

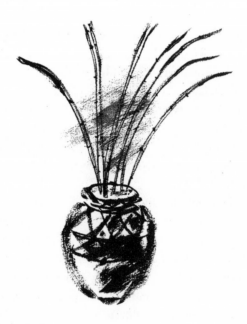

Cassava Wine tub

3

LACQUER AND
BAMBOO BEETLES

The ocean-going raft – when it was finally built – was going to need a name, and from reading Professor Needham's book it seemed appropriate to call the raft after Hsu Fu, a Chinese mariner sent by the first Emperor of China to explore for islands in the Pacific. Hsu Fu set out twice, and he and his companions never returned from the second trip. Early historians of China surmised that this was because Hsu Fu must have found a land so pleasant that he saw no reason to return to China. Apparently, they did not consider that Hsu Fu and the 3,000 people who accompanied him may have drowned.

Hsu Fu's story comes from an impeccable source and has strong circumstantial evidence to support it. His two voyages of exploration are mentioned in the *Shiji,* the great classic of Chinese annals completed in 91 BC by the eunuch Sima Qian, Grand Historian of the Han dynasty. Sima Qian devoted nineteen years to compiling a definitive account of the rise and career of the despotic First Emperor of China, Qin Shihuang, now best known for his extravagant tomb containing an army of nearly 6,000 terracotta warriors to form an honour guard for the emperor in his afterlife. But in 219 BC, the year of Hsu Fu's first voyage, the Emperor believed he could arrange matters so that he did not die, but would live for ever. He was then forty years old and had enjoyed such an unbroken chain of successes since coming to the throne at the age of thirteen that he had developed megalomania on a grand scale. He had fathered at least twenty children, miraculously survived a very well-planned assassination attempt, and his armies had overrun all

45

neighbouring states until they expanded the borders of his inland king-dom to the shores of the China Sea. Now he believed that immortality also lay within his grasp. This ambition was encouraged by the magicians, soothsayers and necromancers who clustered at the Imperial Court. They pandered to the Emperor's belief, shared with most of his subjects, that the human world was populated by spirits and visited by gods and goddesses. Long current in Chinese folklore was the notion that there existed a miraculous plant from which could be extracted a drug that extended natural life. Qin Shihuang devoted considerable resources and effort in trying to track down this miracle plant for his own use. He sent investigators to the west and south to search the deserts and mountains where, according to a parallel folkmyth, lay the legendary home of the gods. Here it might be possible for the Emperor's envoys to obtain the Peaches of Immortality, food of the gods, which had taken 3,000 years to ripen.

A better chance of locating the life-prolonging elixir lay in the oppo-site direction, to the east. Somewhere in the far ocean, according to folklore, were the three Blessed Isles – Pheng-Lai, Fang-Chang, and Ying-Chou – whose mountains were covered in terraces and towers of gold, and hollowed out with a labyrinth of caves and grottoes of jade. There all the animals and birds were pure white, and no one who ate the fruits of those islands ever grew old or died. These Blessed Isles were extraordinarily difficult to reach because they were either free-floating and changed position, or they were hidden in mists, or they were attached to the backs of great turtles. In any case, the discoverer would have to avoid fire-breathing guards who patrolled them. Not in the least deterred by these barriers, the Emperor Qin Shihuang, recounts the *Shiji,* 'sent out Hsu Fu by sea to search for magical beings and strange things. When he returned, he invented excuses, saying: "In the midst of the ocean I met a great Mage who said to me, 'Are you the envoy of the Emperor of the West?' to which I replied that I was. 'What have you come for?' said he, and I answered that I sought for those drugs which lengthen life and promote longevity. 'The offers of your Qin King,' he said, 'are but poor; you may see these drugs but you may not take them away.' Then going south-east we came to Pheng-Lai, and I saw the gates of the Chih-Chheng palace. In the front was a guardian of brazen hue and dragon form lighting the skies with his radiance. In this place I did obei-sance to the Sea Mage twice, and asked him what offerings we should present to him. 'Bring me young men,' he said, 'of good birth and breeding, together with apt virgins, and workmen of all trades: then you will get your drugs.' " Qin Shihuang, very pleased, set three thousand young men and girls at Hsu Fu's disposal, gave him the seeds of the five grains, and artisans of every sort, after which he set sail. Hsu Fu found some calm and fertile plain, with broad forests and rich marshes, where he made himself king – at least he never came back to China.'

Soothsayers' advice was heeded by modern fishermen, just as much as it had been followed by bygone emperors. The raftbuilders of Sam Son always consulted the priest of the temple on the hill before they embarked on any major project. The priest would examine his books of Chinese astrology and select a suitable lucky or 'gold day' to begin the work. For the start of the building of the full-sized raft he picked the day on which the fishermen of Sam Son commemorated their common ancestor, an unnamed sailor of the distant past, who, they claimed, had founded their village and then vanished 'on the sea'. By coincidence the priest had chosen Christmas Day, and although 25 December brought wretched weather, cold and grey with the rain squalls sweeping along the flat exposed beach, the fishermen of Sam Son showed up to make a token start. Shivering in thin cotton jackets, scarves pulled over their heads, and protected only by a single sheet of plastic tied around them with string, they worked an hour or so to get the enterprise started before they slunk off to their houses. I did not fret about the delay, because by now I had absolute confidence in the men I was working with. Whether foresters in the bamboo jungle or the fishermen of Sam Son, when the Vietnamese I was working with said they would do a job on such and such a day, they kept their word. Three hundred and fifty giant bamboos had already been delivered from the jungle, as the tough captain had promised. More than enough for the job in hand, the bamboos were now stacked on the beach, looking resplendently green and shiny with their outer skin still on them, and of such good quality and size that the raftbuilders patted them approvingly and pointed out to one another the biggest of the poles, 30 feet long and up to six inches across. When there was a hold-up in the final shipment of crooked branches for the crosspieces, the captain personally rode on the lorry bringing the timber down from the mountains, and threatened a luckless official with his pistol in order to get the consignment through.

On Christmas Eve, I also introduced a new face on the beach at Sam

Son. Nick Burningham was the 'engineer' the raftbuilders had asked for. They were worried by the responsibility of building a raft so much larger than their usual vessels, and had requested that I find an expert who could direct them. Nick was the ideal person for the role. He had been strongly recommended to me by a former shipmate, a maritime archaeologist who had sailed with me on my Arab expedition, the Sindbad Voyage, and who now lived in Australia. There he had met Nick who had worked as a museum curator in the Northern Territories of Australia and was a specialist in the preservation of native watercraft. Nick had built, traditional sailing boats in eastern Indonesia and sailed them to Australia, and had a vast fund of knowledge about traditional boatbuilding. Even better, from my point of view and probably in the opinion of the raftbuilders of Sam Son too, Nick looked the part of the seasoned mariner. In his late forties he was tall and spare, with a ruddy skin and bright blue eyes. He habitually wore a battered sailor's cap on the back of his head, and sported a fine curly grey beard which made him look older than he really was. He was a figure out of a Conrad novel as he strode up and down the Sam Son beach, taking measurements, marking timber and bamboo, and illustrating his instructions with fine sweeping gestures. He also had a great sensitivity for literature, a wry sense of humour, and could match any of the fishermen when it came to enjoying the local rice brew.

His introduction to Sam Son was well timed. On Christmas Eve he and I were invited by some of the fishermen to share an evening's drinking. They offered us a tea-coloured drink described by the label on the bottle to be whisky made in Taiwan. But they then confessed that the bottle had been half-empty so they had topped it up with 'local spirit'. The resulting mixture was lethal, smelled terrible, and I retired after just an hour, to be thoroughly ill. Nick, however, held his own, and finally departed the party astride a borrowed rickety bicycle with a drunken fisherman riding on the back wheel. Nick negotiated the short ride back to the lodgings where we stayed, but the fisherman tumbled off face-down in a puddle and was so intoxicated that he nearly drowned. Nick's reputation was assured. When the next day dawned with its awful weather Nick reported that the most hardened of our work team were drinking beer and rice wine for breakfast, and beckoned him to join them.

Once again the first job was to skin the giant bamboos. Machetes were used as drawknives to shave away the hard, shiny outer layer and to scrape off the projecting ridges of the bamboos so they could be lashed together more tightly. Now there were nearly forty workers, all fishermen, and although they included the Methuselahs who built the test raft, there was also a new contingent of younger, stronger men. When I asked what had happened to the test raft I had left at the cove of the Frontier Guards after the sailing trials, I was shown the stockade which enclosed our building area. It was made of a lattice-work of bamboo lathes. The test raft had been dismantled and chopped up to make the fence. Nothing in Sam Son, it seemed, was ever wasted. Even the shavings of bamboo skin were hoarded for fire-lighter, and this was a lure to the urchins who prowled the perimeter peering in through the fence. When the elderly and grouchy guard whom Mr Khiem had appointed to look after the enclosure was looking the other way, the children would poke long home-made rakes through the fence and hook out the shavings, running off with armfuls of them whenever the guard spotted the thieves and gave chase. Eventually a better solution was found when the quickest and boldest urchin was put on the labour force, and paid a daily wage to chase away his erstwhile companions.

The danger of insects laying their eggs on the fresh cut bamboos still worried the raftbuilders, even though the poles were autumn felled and had the minimum amount of sap. So as soon as the bamboos were skinned, the fishermen coated them with a natural insect repellent. They made it from the bright green leaves of Japanese lilac, thrown into a pit and pounded into rough paste, and then mixed with seawater and lime to make a vile-looking yellow-green liquid. This was then painted on all 350 of the poles, and seemed to be effective. Now came the crucial bending of the poles to the required curve. The 30-foot poles were not long enough to run the full length of the 60-foot raft, and would have to be joined end to end. It was important that the joints should not all occur in the same plane, so Nick had worked out a variety of bends. These were now put into the bamboos by the fishermen, using their burning brands of bicycle tyre. When the first batch of bamboos was being bent, something kept going wrong. One after another the bamboos broke, or their walls collapsed inward, and they had to be thrown away. At first the fishermen thought the trouble was that the bamboos were too green, and they waited two more days for the poles to dry out. This improved matters, but still the raftbuilders were not satisfied. They were not bending the bamboos as accurately as they would have liked. They held a conference among themselves and decided that the trouble was the breeze which came in from the sea every day about noon. This wind made it difficult to focus the flames of the burning tyres on precisely the right spot. They sent Truc to explain their difficulty.

'They say that they cannot bend the bamboo correctly under such conditions,' Truc explained. 'The wind makes the flame flicker too much.' My heart sank. Was this just an excuse to give up the job before they had scarcely started? But Truc had more to report. 'They ask if you would allow them to change their working hours. The wind only begins in late morning, and they suggest that if they begin work earlier in the day they can get the day's quota done while the air is still calm.'

'How much earlier?' I enquired.

'They want to begin at four in the morning and promise to complete the job on time.' It was the first occasion I had heard of workers volunteering to begin before sunrise. Next day before dawn, I went to the beach and found what looked like a scene from Hell: thirty men were hard at work in pairs inside the stockade, one man crouching down and holding the flaming torch under a bamboo pole, while his companion pulled down the free end to induce a curve. The blazing flames, the soot-blackened hands and taut faces, the firelight glittering off the eyes of the workers, and the dense plumes of smoke drifting up into the night sky against the moon made a powerful impression.

The next step almost undermined the whole project. I had taken very seriously the warnings about shipworm eating the bamboo. Teredo, or shipworm, can have a devastating effect on the hulls of wooden ships at sea. Very similar in action to the bamboo parasite, the free-swimming teredo larva enters the wood through a tiny hole, then feeds by chewing along the length of the plank, opening up long galleries that riddle the timber until it collapses. I was uncomfortably aware of the sad fate of a replica Chinese junk, named *Tai Ki* which had been built in Hong Kong twenty years earlier and set sail to cross to America on the identical track that I now proposed. *Tai Ki* had literally been chewed to pieces in mid-ocean. No one knew whether the destructive teredo had entered her timbers in Hong Kong harbour or while sailing. But the result had brought to an end one of the bravest and most exhausting attempts at crossing the Pacific in a historic vessel. *Tai Ki's* crew had worked day and night to winkle out the larvae and plug the holes, until after sixteen weeks they gave up the battle. By then great chunks of the planking had fallen away, seawater was flooding into the junk's hold, and her crew had been wise to abandon ship midway across the Pacific. It was a gallant effort, destroyed by small white grubs much the same size and shape as those found in a rotten apple.

So I tried to discover if there was a traditional protection against shipworm attack. In Sam Son no one could advise me. Their rafts were taken out of the water daily which would have discouraged the infestation with teredo. However, I did come across several references to the fact that the Chinese used an oil, called tung oil, pressed from the fruit of a tree, which was said to be both a preservative and a natural antifouling. But I was wary. The unfortunate crew of *Tai Ki* had put their faith in several coats of tung oil, to no effect. Then, off a backstreet bookstall in Hanoi, Nick bought the reprint of a book written in the French colonial era which described traditional Vietnamese crafts. It mentioned the use of natural lacquer to seal the hulls of boats. Lacquer was one of the most versatile and famous products of ancient China, so I wondered if it also discouraged teredo. Truc inadvertently provided a possible answer. He told me that lacquer was still grown in Vietnam and South China. The sap of the lacquer tree oozes out when the tree is cut and is collected in the same way that rubber is gathered. Truc remembered how, while doing his military service, he and some of his companions had itched and scratched and puffed up when their platoon strayed near some lacquer-trees. Lacquer resin, I realised, was one of nature's toxins. From Truc's description, it seemed the tree put out a natural defence probably against insect attack. If so, lacquer might also ward off shipworm.

I decided we should paint all the bamboo poles with raw lacquer before we tied them together. The Frenchman's handbook had a little sketch which showed the cross-section of a collecting basket full of lacquer sap. The skin of clear lacquer floating at the surface was used for artwork and fine lacquerware. It was the sludge of thick lacquer which settled at the bottom of the basket that was used for painting the hulls of boats. With Truc's help I obtained the 150 kilograms of lacquer we needed, and brought it to Sam Son. It was supplied in plastic bags, carefully wrapped up and tied at the neck with string. I thought nothing of it as we opened the first plastic bag, poured out a cupful of the lacquer, which looked like thick engine oil, and tried painting it on a length of bamboo. Truc standing nearby, explained that he preferred not to come closer as the last time he had touched fresh lacquer his arm had swelled up and a doctor had to give him an injection to control the allergy. I felt only a mild itching. Nevertheless, I asked Truc to warn the raftbuilders to be careful.

Next day the raftbuilders began the task of painting the bamboos, and the results were dramatic. Five or six of the fishermen swelled up like balloons within hours, and also had to have injections. The others, one by one, showed the same symptoms over the next few days, and complained of itchy faces and skin rashes, though most of them kept working. Only two men out of forty showed no allergy, and they eventually took on the entire job of painting, wearing face masks and gloves. Even Nick, who took care to avoid contact with lacquer as far as possible, was to develop a violent skin rash and sores and complained of dizziness. I was puzzled because in all my researches I had never come across a reference to the lacquer sickness, and wondered if I had made some sort of elementary mistake. It was Nina who told me otherwise. Oh yes, she said brightly. When she had been at art college in Japan, there had been classes in lacquer work. Students who took the course were laughed at because their faces swelled up and they walked around with their heads in bandages. This was quite normal, and their professor had said there was no cure, but no long-lasting effect either. After long exposure some people developed an immunity, but the best course was to avoid direct skin contact with the lacquer and wear masks, aprons and long gloves when working with it. This still did not explain why the workmen were affected so badly. Later Truc found out that the fishermen had reverted to magic to try to protect themselves. When they started work in the morning, each man would stick a finger into a jar of lacquer and lick it, saying, 'Lacquer I am not afraid of you. You cannot harm me.' The result, of course, was catastrophic. As Nina said, the last thing to do ever was to touch lacquer directly. I just hoped that any hungry shipworm which nibbled the lacquer would be similarly smitten.

Fortunately the allergenic effect largely disappeared as the lacquer dried and set, leaving the giant bamboos with a handsome sheen the colour of dark honey. Once more we set up a raft-building frame, but this time much longer and wider than the one we'd used for the test raft. And instead of building three layers separately and joining them together, we constructed the raft from the centre outwards, tying the bamboos in place with lengths of rattan instead of bamboo skin. The raftbuilders were happy to use rattan, the jungle vine often used for furniture-making. Formerly they had used rattan for raftbuilding but it had become too difficult to get and was more expensive than the local bamboo skin. Now Truc arranged for bundles of rattan to be brought down from the coast north of Hanoi where the sailors still used it for making ropes and cable. As thick as a pencil, the rattan was split down its length and used like stiff cord to tie the bamboos to one another. Finally, the rattan lashings were given a preventive coat of lacquer

Fastening the hull bamboos

painted on by the 'iron men', the only two workmen who did not suf-fer from lacquer sickness.

Progress on the raft was astonishingly rapid. By early February the raft looked like the backbone of a giant herring with a spine of bamboo and projecting ribs of crossbeams. Just three weeks later the main body of the raft was completed, and the work squad had used up 46 kilometres of rattan and tied more than 3,000 knots. Yet even with so many lashings holding it together, the raft was very flexible. If you climbed up on the raft, and jumped up and down, the whole 60-foot-long structure, weigh-ing perhaps 4 tons, quivered and flexed like a giant bamboo fishing-rod. It was what Colin Mudie the designer had intended: only by flexing with the waves would the raft withstand the power of the sea. I just hoped that all that flexing and twisting of the hull would not burst the 3,000 rattan lashings.

Accommodation for the crew was proving a headache. The raft was sure to be a very wet place to live. Water would come from every direc-tion. There would be rain from above, spray from the side, wave crests sweeping right across the low structure, and of course solid water surg-ing up from below as the larger waves passed between the bamboos of the hull. If ancient sailors had crossed the oceans aboard big bamboo sail-ing rafts, how had they compensated for the fact that the waves washed right through the structure? No one could have lived for any length of time on a platform where every large ocean wave washed up to your ankles or even your knees. Under those conditions any crew would soon perish from exposure. I had read that when small bamboo rafts had been used as river ferries in Taiwan, the passenger kept dry by sitting in a wooden washtub tied to the deck while the crew worked barelegged. Why not use the same idea on the ocean-going raft, but on a larger scale using light tubs made from woven and tarred bamboo lathes? Every day at Sam Son I watched Vietnamese fishermen paddling out to sea in their little basketboats, the bowl-shaped coracles looking like half a wal-nut shell which skittered and bobbed crazily on the wave tops. It occurred to me that here was a design we could adapt for the raft's accommodation. If the large sailing raft carried on its surface two or three bamboo baskets, tarred to make them watertight, then these would provide refuges for the crew. And, of course, in one of the famous yarns about Sindbad the Sailor, he had escaped from a shipwreck by sailing off in a wooden washtub. Perhaps by substituting tarred baskets for washtubs I could do the same, though it did sound uncomfortably like trying to go to sea in a sieve.

So the workmen wove three shallow baskets, coated them with sticky black tar, and tied them to the raft's upper surface. Two baskets were designed to be the bases for the cabins, while the third was left open as an elementary cockpit where the crew would steer and work the vessel.

My first idea for the cabins themselves was a spectacular failure. I asked the workmen to make them of the same tarred basketwork, but that scheme had to be abandoned when the 'cabins' failed to hold their shape, and sagged forlornly until they looked more like semi-deflated bladders dripping with tar. We were now getting very near launch date, and time was running short, so the quickest and easiest solution was to build a couple of low thatched huts standing inside the deck baskets. Workmen bicycled off to their local supplier of building bamboo, and came pedalling back balancing bamboo poles on their shoulders to lash together to make the framework of the huts. A couple of old men appeared with bundles of dried palm leaves, which they first soaked in seawater and then folded and tied to a light framework of split bamboos to add on as walls and roofs. A final layer of bamboo matting finished off the job. The whole, hasty process took no more than two days, and at the end of it a pair of rather dumpy thatched huts sat in their basket bases looking as if they had been transplanted from the deepest jungle. For some reason the ridge of one hut curved upward in a normal hog's back, while the other dipped downward like the back of a Vietnamese pot-bellied pig. Looking at this distinctly un-maritime arrangement, I wondered just how well the thatched huts would stand up to the punishment of the ocean, and if they would stay attached to the mother raft. If not, then the two thatched huts on their black basket bases would sail off looking remarkably like twin Noah's Arks.

We were scrambling towards a launch deadline because, naturally, the temple priest had already selected a particularly auspicious day for the raft to be dragged down the beach and put in the water. The day he had picked was 16 March, which that year was the day to commemorate the local god, Doc Cuoc. The name meant 'One Foot' and the god's story was that he had come down from Heaven to defend the village when it was attacked by enemies. The attack came from land and sea at the same time, so Doc Cuoc had taken his sword and sliced himself in half verti-cally. One part had fought on the sea, and the other on land. In the

innermost room of the temple, almost invisible under gilded idols, statues of Buddha and smoking clumps of joss-sticks, was the rock on which Doc Cuoc had landed. Its surface was marked with the imprint of a single foot.

Launch day for the raft was planned to be a very major celebration for the entire community, and the priest's choice this time proved better than the cold miserable day when we had begun work just twelve weeks before. March 16 dawned bright and sunny, the first really good day of the year. By first light I was at the fisherman's hut where about thirty women of the village were peering in mirrors to put the last-minute touches to their festival costumes, and to adjust make-up and hairstyles. They were dressed in Vietnamese loose trousers of silk, and flowing tunics of yellow brocade and crimson. They would carry the offerings to the temple – trays of sticky rice and fruit, arrangements of flowers, and as the centrepiece, the flattened face of a very large porker which the workmen had eaten at a celebration supper the night before. The pig's face had been boiled and scrubbed, peeled off and split, and now lay pink and glistening on top of a large mound of rice, its snout shining wetly. It must have been almost a yard across, from ear to ear. As the red sky of a perfect dawn changed to bright blue, it was time to start on the half-mile walk to the temple. There were two warning taps on the big drum which would lead the way, and the women took up their positions in two lines, each balancing a tray of food or a flower basket on her head. I noticed that the younger ones wore lipstick, but the lips of the older women were a much more powerful red, stained by betel nut they had been chewing. Behind the big drum came the band of four musicians dressed in loose black tunics and black pillbox hats. They played classic Vietnamese instruments as they walked – a small drum, a short, sweet-sounding flute, and a quavering two-string violin. The fourth instrument was a hollow piece of wood like a large clam shell on which the player clattered two sticks to make a sound like castanets. Being proprietor and captain of the new vessel, I was officially the person making the offerings to Doc Cuoc, so I, too, was placed in the column. Like the bandsmen I also wore a little black pillbox hat.

Our procession moved along the back of the beach and past the raft waiting to be launched. The bamboo stockade had been torn down, ready for the launch, and the raft looked strangely naked and vulnerable as if newly hatched. The large stack of giant bamboo which had once

Procession to the temple

been piled on the beach had vanished, absorbed into the raft. The last two spare poles were now stuck in the sand as flagposts, flying the Vietnamese and Irish flags side by side. I was a little melancholy to know that I would soon be leaving this place which, for the past eighteen months, had been the centre of my attention. The procession passed the little beach hut where a fisherman's wife sold glasses of tea, fruit and cigarettes, and fire crackers in purple paper for pilgrims to the temple. Here our raftbuilders had gambled over cards during their lunch breaks, or left their bicycles while they were at work. Beside the hut was an easel on which the local beach photographer displayed photos of tourists he took with his ancient camera and developed in the washbasin at his home. Now the easel was covered with group portraits, pictures of the raftbuilders who had posed for a memento picture on the final day of construction. All of them were wearing brown cotton tunics because of a promise I had made on the very first day of construction. Bamboo and tar and – as it turned out – lacquer would ruin their clothes, and I had given my word that every man would receive a new workshirt and trousers when the job was done.

The procession reached the foot of the long steep flight of stairs leading up to the temple. The women adjusted the trays and loads on their heads to balance them more securely and began the climb while the music kept playing. The drum had been taken on ahead, and must now have been installed in its regular position inside the temple, for I could hear its deep boom, boom, boom. The noise was deafening as we reached the little courtyard and stooped to enter the main room of the temple. It was perhaps forty feet by thirty, and half in darkness due to the crush of people who blocked the light coming in through the doors. There were no windows, just heavy smoke-blackened timbers holding up the tiled roof above us, and in front the long altar on which the women placed their trays of offerings until there was scarcely an inch of space left between the gifts and the previous offerings of vases, bags of sweets, statuettes, and glasses filled with sand and stuck with smoking joss-sticks. On each side of the altar stood six-foot-high wooden carvings of cranes, the birds of the gods, standing on the backs of turtles, the symbols of longevity and wisdom. Beside them were the effigies of two furiously scowling guardian demons, painted black and grimacing with red tongues and staring white eyes, each one armed with a sword.

A very old lady, one with very bright betel-stained lips, began the proceedings by reading out a long quavering announcement – 'It's the report to the Gods,' Truc whispered in my ear. In honour of the occasion he was dressed uncharacteristically in a smartly cut suit and looked like a successful young and podgy stockbroker. A sudden tremendous clanging stroke on a brass gong made me jump, and was answered by the big drum. Back and forth the drum and gong thundered at each other, until it was time for the priest, a small elderly man in grey tunic and trousers, to read out a whole series of incantations. He read from a school exercise book prepared not in the usual roman script used by the Vietnamese, but from a text written in Chinese, for Chinese was the language of the temple. Each time his high quavering voice stopped, the interval was filled by a sudden burst of the clatter sticks on the wooden castanet, a jaunty trill of the flute, or a thunderous roll on the huge hanging drum. Smoke rose from the joss-sticks and made my eyes water. I could now see that most of the flower displays had roses at the top and chrysanthemums at the bottom, and between them splayed thin wooden skewers on which cigarettes had been spiked. The gods appreciated smoking, it seemed.

The leading lady of the women's procession now advanced towards the altar with a little dancing walk, dropped on her knees, and held out her arms in supplication. She took a sprig of green leaves of some sort of herb, rubbed them together, then placed them in a saucer on the altar. She returned to the ranks of ladies, and they all went through a slow and complicated ritual presentation of gifts – bundles of purple joss-sticks, little blue-and-white china flasks of rice wine. Each item was carried in solemn procession into the room at the back of the temple and placed near Doc Cuoc's footprint. Finally it was time for the priest to make an appeal for the safety of the raft, its crew and captain. He read from sheets of yellow paper placed on a portable lectern, and I could just distinguish my name in the stream of Chinese.

'He's reading out your c.v. for the gods,' whispered Truc.

The yellow sheets were signed with a fine fat red seal, and when the priest had ended his recitation, the oldest lady gave a high wailing cry and the sheets were taken to a brazier and set alight so the smoke of their message should be carried to the gods. By then I had stepped outside to get some fresh air, away from the stifling smoke and heat of the temple. I stood on the balcony and looked down at the beach, over the tops of the papaya trees surrounding temple grounds where dragonflies were hovering in the heat of the first fine day. Far below, the raft lay waiting between lines of coloured bunting, and beyond it extended the long line of Sam Son's beach with the cheap hotels, the upturned black blobs of the basketboats, and a few fisherwomen gathering seaweed in the shallows of the falling tide. I found myself wishing for a smooth voyage – Doc Cuoc was, after all, a half-god of the sea, and anything which might help the project would be welcome.

Everyone went back down the steps to where all forty raftbuilders stood expectantly beside the raft, ready to push the vessel down to the sea. No one had ever launched such a large raft off the beach before, and Nick had asked for rollers to get the raft across the soft sand. But Sam Son was such a poor community that all that could be found were some rusty metal waterpipes. Mr Khiem's deputy scrambled up on top of the main cabin roof where the temple drum had now been hoisted. He called to the workmen, and they put their shoulders to the raft in anticipation. A rattle on the drum, then three loud thumps, and the first heave. The raft did not budge. Try again, and this time the raft moved four feet to the thump of the drum. Again, another shove and a few more feet. Nick and I laid out tow ropes to the bow of the raft, and cajoled bystanders to lend a hand. There was a huge crowd looking on, including the ladies of the procession who had come on down to enjoy the show. Slowly the raft inched forward, and the day grew hotter and hotter. The workmen's new brown costumes were soaked with sweat and they were losing heart. Then the raft fell off its rollers, and had to be lifted up with lorry jacks and repositioned. I could feel the enthusiasm ebbing away as the workmen became more and more exhausted. Muttering began, and it seemed that only half the labour force was now trying to move the boat. The others hung back, looking surly. Truc, normally so good natured, was shouting angrily at Nina who was sitting on the raft and sketching the scene.

Moments later Truc came to me. 'It's Nina,' he panted. 'The workmen say the raft will not go down to the sea with a woman on board. They believe it is bad luck. Nina has to get off. But she refuses. Please tell her!' Truc pleaded.

Tempers were getting frayed. I went across to Nina and asked her to climb down. She was very angry. 'But you gave your permission. I will only get off the raft if you order me as captain!' she blazed.

'I'm sorry. Maybe it's superstition but the men won't work unless you get off the raft. You have to get down.'

Nina glowered, then climbed down and stormed off. The men assembled for one last effort. The waterpipes were now battered and bent and in a tangle under the raft. But all we needed was to get the raft below high-water mark where the advancing tide would lift her off. Boom! Boom! Boom! The drum coordinated one last heave, and the raft slid the final fifteen yards along the sand in a single lurching rush. The waterpipes twisted and bent like spaghetti, and metal scraped against metal so that it seemed the raft gave a great grinding bellow. Finally the raft came to rest, sitting just below the tideline.

It would be sunset by the time *Hsu Fu* floated, and most of the crowd lost interest and wandered away. Nick, Truc and I waited for the sea to come and collect the raft. This was a time for quiet reflection, as the tide ripples slowly advanced over the damp sand until they began to lap against the lowest of the three layers of bamboo in the hull. When was the last time the same bamboos had been in water? I wondered. Probably when they were floated downriver by the mountain people of the bamboo jungle. And the last time a large ocean-going raft waited to go to sea like this? It was impossible to tell, perhaps two hundred years, maybe five hundred. The advancing tide was nudging the raft, and *Hsu Fu* began to give little tremors as though awakening from a deep sleep. The daylight had faded and the branches of the trees around the temple on the hill above us were black against the sky when *Hsu Fu* finally lifted clear of the sand, and became a living vessel.

Hsu Fu waiting to go afloat, launch day

4

TRIALS AND DEPARTURE

The sea nearly snatched away *Hsu Fu* in the first few hours. The fishermen feared that an undertow at the launching site would push the raft onto the rocks beneath the temple headland unless we shifted the vessel as soon as she was afloat. But the fine weather of the launch day vanished. At dusk a rising onshore wind began to drive big rolling waves up the sand, and *Hsu Fu* tossed and heaved on the surf, tugging at her home-made anchors. By midnight the wind had strengthened to gale force, and in the darkness there was high drama. The men who had put such skill and effort into building *Hsu Fu* were not going to let the raft be destroyed. More than a hundred men appeared from the fishing village, black shapes in the darkness who took hold of the coarse ropes that secured the raft stern-on to the beach. By brute force they began to pull the raft sideways away from the danger. But the ropes were rotten, and time and again they snapped though they were as thick as a man's wrist. The fishermen of Sam Son knotted and spliced and made repairs in the vital ropes and kept pulling the raft sideways inch by inch until the volunteers were reeling with exhaustion. After three hours *Hsu Fu* was hauled out of immediate danger, but only just. All that night, and the next day, and the night after that, the gale lashed the coast, and the raft wallowed among the rollers, held by those suspect ropes while relays of lookouts huddled on the beach under mats and plastic sheets to keep an eye on her, ready to raise the alarm if the raft broke adrift.

Mr Khiem had contacted the captain of a police patrol boat who was willing to tow *Hsu Fu* to the sheltered waters of Halong Bay, north of

Hanoi, where masts and sails would be fitted. Obviously the bargain was highly irregular, but I asked no questions, and paid the 300 dollars in cash that was asked. The patrol boat was an ancient tub and had so many rust holes that you could see daylight clear through her superstructure. But the crew seemed competent, and I could not imagine a better way of avoiding official difficulties over shifting the raft from one Vietnamese province to another than to have it towed by the very people responsible for patrolling the coast. Two men were needed to travel on the raft in case anything went wrong during the tow, and immediately Loi the carpenter volunteered. As soon as the wind eased, he and another man from Sam Son went out to *Hsu Fu* while Truc and I shuttled back and forth using a basketboat as a ferry to take out supplies for their journey. The rusty police boat arrived, the towline was made secure, and *Hsu Fu* set off northward trailing along behind her tug. As Truc and I headed back to shore in the little basketboat, there seemed to be a light drizzle in the sky over the stern of the raft. It was Loi, alternately standing up in the cockpit with his hands clasped in prayer in front of him and calling on his gods for protection, and leaning forward to burn offerings of sacred purple paper over a small flame. The drizzle was the ash of his burned offerings floating up into the sky. Suddenly my horizon was filled with white water as a roller came cresting under our cockleshell and tipped the little basketboat end over end flinging me, Truc and the boatman into the water. We waded ashore coughing up salt water and drenched to the skin. On the beach Truc, who had never before been on any boat, collapsed against me.

'It's done!' he said. 'The raft is built and on its way. There were many times when I thought we would never succeed.'

Halong Bay was the hope of Vietnam's fledgling tourist industry. Romantic sugarloaf mountains of the type familiar from Chinese art surround a broad shallow gulf, and dozens more of the strange rounded hills thrust up as weirdly shaped islands in the middle of the calm waters. When a mist hung over the bay the scene was a Chinese scroll painting in real life. I had chosen Halong for the next step of the project because here on the border with China the fishermen still used fan-shaped Chinese junk sails on their fishing boats, and I wanted to rig *Hsu Fu* with classic Chinese sails. At Halong three months earlier Truc and I had ordered three traditional junk sails to be made by Mr Ching, the sailmaker. He was not a man to be hurried because Mr Ching employed his

Basket boats at Halong Bay

wife, sisters and neighbours' wives to make sails the old way – every seam stitched by hand. What is more they used the strongest thread available, and in Vietnam that meant the cotton panels were sewn together with pure yellow silk. Each of the three sails was then treated with a special liquid to discourage mildew and rot. This liquid was made by chopping up the roots of an inedible yam which looked like stringy, tough beetroot. The yam pieces were then simmered in water with the sailcloth for ten or twelve hours. The sails were removed, dried, and then simmered again until each sail had been treated four times. They emerged a lovely dark tan-red, the colour of Chinese sails since the earliest pictures of junks at sea.

Mr Ching and his three sons had also gone in their fishing boat to one of the remote Halong Islands to find the trees to make masts for *Hsu Fu*. They had selected chestnut trees, which surprised me because chestnut was not a timber normally used for making masts. But I said nothing, for I was very much in their hands. Mr Ching was a sailor of the old school, a small, very quiet and rather shy man about fifty years old, who knew his business and was set in his ways. When Nick proposed an improved way of setting the masts in place, Mr Ching baulked at the suggestion. Mr Ching's sons were our main labour force and obeyed their father to the letter, so I thought it best to let Mr Ching use his time-honoured system. It was the only time that Nick lost his patience and flared up to complain that his advice and work were being disregarded. His agitation was a sign of how deeply committed he had become to the raft's success. *Hsu Fu* was Nick's creation just as much as the work of the raftbuilders or Colin Mudie's design, and now Nick's job as 'engineer' was nearly done. Soon he would have to return to Australia to his museum work, but leaving the raft was a wrench. So when we hoisted *Hsu Fu*'s sails for the first time on a trial sail, I insisted that it was Nick who took the helm as we glided across the glassy calm waters of Halong under the gentlest breeze.

It was a tranquil introduction to the long and perilous route which I hoped would soon take *Hsu Fu* from her Chinese departure point in Hong Kong, across the Straits to Taiwan, and then in a great arc northeast to the main islands of Japan. From there we would embark on the greatest test of all: the 4,500-mile crossing of the North Pacific, heading towards North America to see if a bamboo sailing raft, normally considered to be a vessel restricted to coastal waters, could survive a trans-oceanic voyage.

I now had a bamboo raft, but almost no crew. Perversely, while everything had gone so well with the raft-building, a series of mishaps had delayed the assembly of a crew. One volunteer had been obliged to withdraw a week before he was due to come out to Halong, because his doctor diagnosed a potentially dangerous health condition and told him he had to stay within twenty-four hours' reach of a modern hospital. Even Loi, who was as keen as ever to join, was having problems in getting a passport from the Vietnamese authorities, who did not issue passports as a matter of right. Also Loi still did not speak a word of English. Ideally, I still needed to find a doctor, a photographer, an artist, and a shipwright. From that list my automatic first choice was the artist Trondur Patursson, who lived in the remote Faeroe Isles between Scotland and Iceland. Of Viking stock, Trondur was the finest traditional seaman I had ever met, and had sailed with me on three previous voyages. But he could not join me until he had completed several commissions. Nina was eager to take his place as a shipboard artist but

Sailing trials in Halong Bay

she was too slight to be of much help in the heavy work of running the raft. After long discussions I agreed with Nina that, now *Hsu Fu* was successfully launched, she would return to Tokyo for a few weeks and resume her work as an artist for magazines and books. She would then rejoin the raft team in Taiwan, after we had taken the raft there from Hong Kong and learned how to sail the vessel. From Taiwan she would sail with us up to Japan, making drawings of our landfalls and life onboard. It was a relief to know that Nina would be available to be our interpreter with the Japanese authorities, but in the meantime there was only one other person who had definitely signed up for the trip, and was definitely available: the ship's doctor, Joe.

Joe Beynon had lodged details of his qualifications at the Expedition Centre of the Royal Geographical Society in London where a register is kept of people keen to go on expeditions. What caught my eye when I looked through the register was that Joe was not only a doctor, but also a photographer. To combine both skills in one member of a small crew was a bonus, and I contacted Joe to arrange an interview. He arrived by bicycle from his job at the hospital – looking very fit and Anglo-Saxon with tousled blond hair, blue eyes and fresh face. In fact, he looked so much younger than his twenty-eight years that it was difficult to believe that he had completed his medical training. Joe also revealed a ready sense of humour and was so easy-going that I knew at once that he would get along well aboard the cramped conditions of the raft. In fact, Joe was so obviously a good team member that I was prepared to accept his one obvious failing – he had never sailed before in his life.

He would take a sailing course, Joe promised me, and also study for a radio operator's certificate so that the raft could be licenced to carry a satellite radio. The hi-tech wizardry of satellite radio had been a key factor in my decision to attempt the China Voyage. Even if the bamboo raft stayed afloat longer than most critics expected, the northern part of the Pacific Ocean could be extremely stormy and treacherous. If there was an emergency, say the raft capsized or began to break up, then it would be vital to alert the outside world and give a precise position so the shore-based authorities would know exactly where to find us if a rescue attempt was possible. Of course, I hoped that such a crisis would never happen, but I was equally determined that the expedition should be equipped with every modern safety device. The satellite radio was central to the whole strategy of safety. It was small enough to fit into a briefcase, and could be powered by a car battery charged by solar panels or a small windmill. The radio was not designed for voice communication, but operated through a small computer and keyboard so that written messages could be sent to a communications satellite and fed into the normal telephone network. In effect the radio would allow *Hsu Fu* to send fax messages anywhere in the world. I planned to use the radio to send a daily position report from the raft to a shore station which would monitor our progress. If nothing was heard from us, then the shore station would alert the rescue authorities. Nevertheless, the Pacific is so huge that if *Hsu Fu* foundered in mid-ocean an aircraft would take five or six hours to reach the spot from the nearest point of land, and a ship would take three or four days. So, in addition to the satellite radio, the raft would need a sophisticated radio location beacon and flares, and each crew member must have a modern survival suit. An inflatable life-raft was also on the list of safety gear, though it was the item least likely to be used. *Hsu Fu* was, after all, a raft, and unless she broke up catastrophically or the bamboos sank, she was a life-saving platform in her own right.

Safety equipment was a very major expense. Publishers' book advances and personal savings had paid most of the cost of building the raft, but by the time *Hsu Fu* was launched, there was very little money left and I still had other items to buy, like cooking gear and food. Unexpectedly, the satellite radio helped to solve the cash crisis. The manufacturers of the satellite radio, Trimble Navigation, had agreed to lend me the set when I contacted the Mariners' Museum in Newport News, Virginia, and asked if the museum would be interested in acquiring the raft to display after the voyage and, if so, would it help towards its building costs. The answer was no, the museum did not have enough space to exhibit the vessel. But there was another, interesting suggestion: perhaps we could arrange for a satellite link between local schools in Virginia and the raft. The proposal was that school classes would send in questions to the museum, which would relay them to me by satellite. I would then answer the questions from the middle of the ocean. It was exactly the sort of interaction I approved of. To share the experience of the voyage with classes of schoolchildren thousands of miles away was an intriguing prospect, and the museum liked the educational potential of the project well enough to make a grant which meant that the project could go forward.

The ability to communicate with the outside world proved to be the key to other, vital sponsorship. Hong Kong Telecom, the telecommunications company of Hong Kong, made a grant to the costs of using satellite time, and the most generous offer of help came from another communications company, DHL Worldwide Express. They agreed to ship all the expedition's gear to Hong Kong without payment, and offered to act as our communications centre during the voyage. If all the equipment worked properly, our daily messages could go from the little satellite radio in its watertight case, up through the atmosphere to a maritime communications satellite hovering in the sky, back down to earth and then to Hong Kong, where DHL staff would send it on. In the months ahead that link would prove a lifeline.

Thus the Vietnamese phase of the project ended on an optimistic note when, on 10 April *Hsu Fu* left Halong as deck cargo on another elderly Vietnamese vessel, this time a small freighter plying the route between Halong and Hong Kong. Nick returned to Australia, Nina to Japan, Truc went to Hanoi with Loi to help him get his long-delayed passport, and I headed for Hong Kong to meet Joe. I had allowed three weeks in Hong Kong to fit out the raft with the safety equipment, conduct a few more sailing trials, and stock up with food supplies for the voyage.

Temporary mooring space was found for *Hsu Fu* among the glossy pleasure yachts of Aberdeen Harbour where the boatboys carried portable telephones or electronic pagers hooked on their belts, and huge floating restaurants blazed with neon signs and gold lettering. Here Joe and I tried to cope with the last-minute details of paperwork and take on stores while various crew members trickled in. First we waited for Loi to arrive. When he showed up, he was stunned by the high-profile opulence of Hong Kong compared to Vietnam's austerity and poverty, but adapted very quickly and took up residence on the raft. Then we waited for Rex, our fourth crew member. Like Joe, Rex Warner was from London, and his qualifications were excellent – sailing and navigation instructor, experience on a number of maritime expeditions, 40,000 miles at sea on his own classic wooden boat, and so forth. He had heard about the China Voyage from a radio interview I had given, and was very keen to join, if only on approval. His difficulty was that he was returning from an expedition to celebrate the 400th anniversary of Columbus's first voyage to the New World, and was stuck halfway across the Atlantic. So the messages kept coming in, telling of head winds, calms, more head winds, severe gales – and his boat did not have an engine. It all added up to the fact that Rex never got to Hong Kong in time to join the raft before we set sail. Eventually he made his way to our first landfall and joined from there.

In the meantime, however, an unlikely-looking crew member came aboard. Mark Reynolds was in his late twenties, tall and very thin, with shoulder-length hair held under a knitted skullcap. He wore a woven bangle around one ankle and dressed in a loose shirt and flapping Thai trousers. A fringed cotton shoulder bag hung over one shoulder and he was the very image of a hippy or New-Age traveller. Originally from a farm in Yorkshire, he had travelled the world studying, of all things, drumming techniques, before finishing up in Hong Kong where he lived on one of the outlying islands with his Japanese girlfriend. There was no way of knowing that his shoulder bag contained lovingly cared-for wood-working tools, and that he was a gifted carpenter and ropeworker. What is more, he had a passion for junk-rigged sailing vessels.

Mark had learned about the China Voyage quite by accident. Normally he never read a newspaper or listened to the radio. But one Sunday he needed to replace a light bulb, and because the Chinese village shop was shut, he took the public ferry across to the main town of Hong Kong. When the passengers left the ferry at the terminal, Mark noticed a photograph of a junk-rigged vessel on the front page of a discarded newspaper lying on the floor. He picked it up, saw the picture of *Hsu Fu* and read about the China Voyage. The next day he came down to Aberdeen Harbour and found his way out to the raft. He chatted with me for a few minutes, offered to help with setting up the rigging, and by late afternoon I had invited him to join the crew. Initially he was cautious, and agreed to come only as far as Taiwan. As it turned out, Mark was to be a key member of the team all the way to Japan. It was, as he said, a curious situation that he had gone out of his front door to buy a light bulb and found himself on a half-submerged vessel in the China Sea on the way to Tokyo.

The newspaper report about the China Voyage also produced an offer of help from the Hsu Fu Association of Hong Kong. I was completely baffled. I had never heard of the Hsu Fu Association and had no idea what it was until I found myself in the plush surroundings of the Mandarin Hotel taking tea with an elderly and clearly prosperous Hong

Kong Chinese businessman and several members of his junior staff. Mr Zai Chung Ling's business card informed me that he was the Managing Director of Wishing Long Hong B & M Supplies, of Always Wide Investment Ltd, of Hong Kong Chinese Graveyard Enterprise Ltd, Fook Hing Funeral Service Ltd, as well as Chairman of a bullion company, a commodities company and a finance company. But pride of place on his visiting card was the fact that he was Managing Director of the Hsu Fu Association of Hong Kong, and a picture on the card showed a tall, distinguished Chinese mandarin dressed in traditional Chinese robes and a mandarin's hat. Clearly it was a portrait of Hsu Fu himself. Through an interpreter Mr Ling explained that he had first come to Hong Kong as a young immigrant from mainland China and started in the business of supplying building materials. On a trip to see customers in Japan he happened to visit the town of Shingu where there was a shrine to Hsu Fu, who had supposedly landed in that part of Japan during his explorations for the First Emperor. Over the following years Mr Ling's business had flourished, and he had gone many times to Japan, always making a point of visiting Hsu Fu's shrine in Shingu. Soon he had taken Hsu Fu as his personal god and made an annual pilgrimage.

Here was a new twist to the Hsu Fu story. As a Westerner, I had thought of Hsu Fu as a long-dead mariner whose voyages into the Pacific symbolised early Asian exploration. But in the Orient Hsu Fu could also be a spiritual and religious icon, a figure to be revered. Mr Ling had devoted much of his life to studying the story of Hsu Fu, and was not alone in this homage. There was, he told me, a Hsu Fu Association in Japan, another in Taiwan, and one in China. The Hong Kong Association had been in existence for twenty-five years. At this point he introduced another member of his group. He was visiting Hong Kong from the mainland, and was the Secretary of the Hsu Fu Society of China, which had 20,000 members. I was intrigued. To Mr Ling, Hsu Fu was a religion; to the visitor from China it seemed that Hsu Fu was the focal point of a contact group reaching overseas from mainland China to Hong Kong and Japan, as well as bringing together thousands of people in China. Yet again, in Taiwan, Hsu Fu was an honoured ancestor to those who claimed descent from him and were members of the same clan or provincial organisation. Mr Ling and his associate from China were keen to have me appreciate that the Hsu Fu story in the *Shiji* was genuine. Hsu Fu was not an imaginary figure, but a real person who had served as an official at the court of the First Emperor. In 1984 Chinese historians had identified Hsu Fu's home village in the province of Shantung. Records of his family had been preserved, and the researchers had been able to trace direct descendants of the great mariner, still living in the area. They were descendants to the seventy-third generation. With the help of the Hsu Fu Association the government of China had erected a pavilion in honour of the great mariner.

Mr Ling also offered me practical help. He would pay, he told me, for a *feng shui* expert to preside at our departure from Aberdeen Harbour. The *feng shui* expert would call on the spirits to favour our venture. I thanked him for his kindness and told him that, being Hong Kong, our business sponsors had already engaged a *feng shui* consultant. But I would be happy to accept Mr Ling's other suggestion that when we set out, we would carry a banner announcing that our voyage was in honour of Hsu Fu and linked with the Hsu Fu Association.

Naturally the day of our formal departure from Aberdeen was another 'gold day' in the Chinese calendar, selected by the *feng shui* expert as propitious for the undertaking. The expert proved to be a rather matter-of-fact woman of late middle-age, who came down to the wharf and set up a table at the harbour's edge. There she tinkled a little brass bell to attract the attention of the spirits, said prayers for our safety, burned paper offerings, and conducted a ceremony remarkably similar to the one we had already seen in Sam Son. Then we cast off and proceeded out of the packed harbour of Aberdeen, not to go directly to sea but to find an anchorage off the small outlying island of Po Ti where we could complete our last-minute loading of stores and wait for a favourable wind. I intended to learn from those medieval Arab travellers who, when they left on the long pilgrimage to Mecca, began with a very small step. Their first day's journey was never more than a mile or so from their town. There they stopped and made camp, so that everyone could discover what they had left behind . . . and run back home to get it. *Hsu Fu* was setting out on a voyage of perhaps 6,500 miles so it seemed a wise example to follow.

Our low-key departure meant that Joe, Loi, Mark and I could be joined by a fifth volunteer. Geoffrey Dobbs was a successful Hong Kong businessman who ran a small company trading with China, and his brother had sailed with me on two previous expeditions. Already Geoffrey had been generous in helping us prepare *Hsu Fu*, lending us the services of his two Chinese boatboys who looked after his pleasure yacht *Hard Times*, and it was *Hard Times* which now towed us out to the anchorage at Po Ti. As the day of departure grew closer, it was clear that Geoffrey was more and more tempted by the chance of a brief passage aboard the raft, if only to swap stories later with his brother. In theory the first sector of the voyage would be a 120-mile crossing to Taiwan which I estimated would take a week or ten days at most. Geoffrey calculated that he could spare that time away from his office. It would only be a brief absence. As it turned out, we were both wrong.

We marked time at Po Ti Island for a day hoping that the north-east head wind would change in our favour. But all it did was slacken to a gentle breeze, and offer us a chance to head diagonally out of Hong Kong waters, using the first few miles as badly needed sailing practice. All of us, except for Loi, felt like novices as on 17 May we hoisted anchor, hauled up the elegant red sails, and set course. Loi rushed around the raft as though he were sailing single-handed, trimming the sails and adjusting, using leeboards to stop the vessel sliding sideways across the water. But *Hsu Fu* now weighed seven or eight tons with all her stores and water, and did not behave like a nimble Sam Son fishing raft. She lumbered sedately across the harbour approaches, as Loi tried raising and lowering the leeboards to different positions. We trudged across the main shipping lane with tankers and coasters hooting irritably at us to get out of the way. We failed to clear the farther islands which guard the entrance, and had to turn back to Po Ti. But by the time we reached Po Ti, our clumsy handling of the sails meant that we had actually lost ground and were farther back than when we had started. So we turned the raft around again, and sailed slowly back across the channel.

Once more the passing shipping hooted and swerved. Once more we failed to make any progress and had to turn around. Now it was dark, and we were sailing by the light of Hong Kong's amazing night skyline, glittering with the lights of hundreds of skyscrapers, apartment blocks and advertising hoardings. All around us moved the navigation lights of the ships entering or leaving Hong Kong's bustling harbour. Hour after hour we half-sailed, half-drifted back and forth, getting nowhere and fumbling with the ropes in the darkness. Dawn saw us still among the big ship moorings, washing back and forth with the tide. This was getting to be embarrassing, and when the wind shifted a trifle and let us steer southward, I thought it wiser that we should slink out of Hong Kong even though we would be heading at right angles to our intended course towards Taiwan.

'Consider this a shakedown cruise,' I optimistically told the patient crew. 'We're getting to know the raft, and finding out how to live aboard.'

They looked suitably understanding.

Loi and Mark put their sleeping bags in the forward cabin; Geoffrey, Joe and I installed ourselves in the aft cabin. Neither cabin offered standing headroom. In fact, they were little more than oversized dog kennels, in which you could only kneel or lie down. Nor were they waterproof either from above or below. A brief shower of rain produced dribbles and trickles of water through a myriad of holes in the thatch, and whenever a large wave washed through the raft, we heard the water sloshing inside the basket base. It seemed the basketwork was not as watertight as intended. But at least we kept ourselves reasonably dry as there was a false floor of bamboo lathes keeping us off the puddles. The air temperature was in the seventies, and when the sun came out it was really very pleasant to pick one's way about the raft, adjusting ropes, stowing the food supplies more securely, and generally looking after the vessel. *Hsu Fu* may have been a plodder, but she was remarkably easy to live on. The stability of the raft was astonishing. She didn't tip or sway so you lost your footing or had to grab for a handhold. When the first big ship passed us and sent a massive bow-wave rolling towards us, Mark called out a warning to hang on. But the wave simply came, washed into the bamboos, and passed on. *Hsu Fu* barely rocked. It was all very comforting.

Cooking and food were, of course, the topics which occupied everyone's private thoughts. What would the food be like? Would there be enough of it in our daily ration? What items would go bad quickly and should be eaten first? I had put Geoffrey in charge of the food stocks and his job was to issue the day's quota. Cooking would be done on a rota system with everyone taking a turn. Each of us wondered how good the others were as ship's cook, and hoped that no one was a real disaster with the pots and pans. Loi began the rota, partly because he insisted but also because he at least knew how to control our two cookers. These were very simple devices – two small paraffin burners in square tins which gave a modest flame. They worked like hurricane-lamps and had cost the grand total of three dollars in Hanoi market. I bought them on the principle that anything so simple, however modest, would be unlikely to go wrong. It was a happy decision. The two cookers were to last for six months, performing reliably even when drenched by waves breaking into the cockpit. You simply shook off the seawater, waited a few moments, and lit them again.

Cooking on them, however, required a bit of practice, as Joe soon demonstrated. In his good-natured way he volunteered to cook supper, following on Loi's very passable lunch of rice and fish. Geoffrey as quartermaster issued Joe with three kilos of rice, a couple of dried cabbage, and some dried pork. The rest of us waited to see what would happen, trying not to make our interest too obvious. But it was difficult to ignore the cook's activities as the two stoves sat in a wooden box at one end of the basketwork cockpit, the only place for the crew to gather and relax.

'How much water do I put with rice?' asked Joe. Mark and I glanced at one another quizzically.

The preparation of the meal seemed to take for ever. It got dark. Joe continued to fumble around, and kept asking Geoffrey for extra items from the food stores. Finally he announced the meal was ready, but with a slightly shamed tone. There was a noticeable burned smell hanging over the cockpit.

'Ahem,' announced Joe, who suffered from slight asthma and had a trick of clearing his throat before speaking. 'Do you want to have the rice first? Or the soupy thing? Or do you want to have both together?'

The 'soupy thing' proved to be a bizarre broth of oranges, nuts and carrots. After the initial shock it didn't taste too bad, and we were ravenous by then. But the main course of cabbage and rice was a mud-coloured porridge of vegetable served on a mound of rice which was thoroughly burned.

'Anyone want any more?' Joe asked after four hungry men had quietly emptied their rather small bowls. Each person tried to make his excuse sound a little different. 'I'll have some later', 'Perhaps in a while', 'I think I'll have my coffee first.' But Joe was not deceived.

'Perhaps I should throw the rest overboard?' he suggested with a good-natured grin. 'Any objections?' Everyone burst into laughter. 'Put it down to my cunning,' said Joe. 'It was so bad that I hope I will not be asked to cook again.' In fact, Joe was to develop into a fine cook using the same small stoves, but his phrase 'soupy thing' remained the catchphrase for any really appalling meal throughout the rest of the voyage.

On that first evening the real lesson was how well everyone coped with the situation, obviously determined not to let the foul meal mar the good atmosphere among the crew. As we sat drinking our coffee, I could hear Loi, who had volunteered to clean up, chuckling softly to himself as he used the point of his machete to chip away burned rice from the bottom of one saucepan, and burned cabbage from the other.

So *Hsu Fu* left Hong Kong like a drunk staggering a weaving course away from his host's home after a late-night party, and each crew member began to establish his personality. Geoffrey, for example, managed to keep remarkably clean, shaving every day and washing his clothes to try to rid them of the sticky tar spots which transferred from the basket-work cockpit. Day by day Mark became even leaner than before, and acquired a very nautical air, with bare feet and naked to the waist, hair down to his shoulders, and his Thai trousers rolled up to the knees. Joe's fair northern skin suffered from bruises and rashes, his feet swelled with sunburn, and he was very taken aback to find how easily he tired – a sign of seasickness which was to pass after a week. Loi, meanwhile, thrived. For him, being aboard the raft was a dream come true. He was thrilled and excited about everything – about Hong Kong, the big raft itself, the modern sailing clothing he had been issued, all the foreign goods and knick-knacks. Unexpectedly he suffered from sunburn, and had never used suntan lotion before. He rubbed the ointment on his eyelids, and the sweat brought it down into his eyes so he squinted terribly as Joe patiently tried teaching him the limited vocabulary needed on the raft: 'Rope, knife, big bowl, small bowl, lemon, orange, milk, leeboard', a microcosm of the important items on a small ship in a large ocean.

As usual with a new vessel at the start of a voyage, there was a long list of adjustments to be made. So Mark contentedly spent hour after hour sorting out the cat's-cradle of ropes which controlled the three junk sails, and Loi busied himself with lashing and relashing various parts of the structure. We had brought 3,000 extra lengths of spare rattan from Vietnam, but at the pace Loi was using it up I wondered how long our reserve stock would last. Geoffrey and Joe sorted out the chaos of last-minute loading. Nearly all our food stocks had been purchased in the Chinese markets of Hong Kong so there were bags of rice and dried noodles, bottles of soy sauce, blocks of bean curd, leaves of dried seaweed, and packets of dried shrimp and squid and tiny fish like whitebait, together with mysterious stone jars of pickles and condiments whose Chinese labels left us none the wiser. Most of the food fitted into eight plastic tubs of the type much favoured by the Aberdeen Harbour boatmen and women. These second-hand tubs had been used for shipping bulk foodstuffs from China to Hong Kong, and now made stout watertight containers to protect our food from the waves washing through the raft. We were not trying to imitate the living conditions of early Asian mariners by wearing ancient clothing and eating only ancient foodstuffs, but it was still ugly and anachronistic to see so much plastic on the bamboo raft. At Mark's suggestion we designated one of the barrels as a rubbish tub so that at least we could try not to throw our unwanted waste overboard.

The sea itself was now a bright, clear light blue, a welcome change from the murky yellow-grey waters close to Hong Kong. Peering down through the slots for the leeboards we could see that we had been joined already by an escort of pilot fish, about two dozen of them, nimble creatures each about thumb-length and very smart in yellow and black bands so they would not have looked out of place in an aquarium. They swam within a few inches of the raft or darted into the cracks between the bamboos. Below them moved several pale mauve, almost transparent fish about eight inches long, flickering here and there in the shadows, so insubstantial as to seem like ghosts. I wondered if a child's dip-net would catch them – already the crew were thinking about fresh fish for supper. Loi was trailing a big hook with a plastic fluorescent squid as lure on a stout fishing-line, but he hadn't had a single bite, and the only fish of definitely edible size was a small shark, about three feet long, which had taken up station deep down under the slow-moving raft and stayed there, scavenging.

In short, the first slow-moving days of *Hsu Fu*'s ambitious voyage required patience and good humour, but there was plenty of both, and a genuinely happy atmosphere established itself as everyone made a determined effort to establish good relations with one another. We set ourselves to learn how best to live side by side in the cramped conditions, and were even able to joke when we made the alarming discovery that the raft carried a potentially lethal cargo – bamboo beetle.

At first I couldn't believe it. After all the care we had taken to cut the bamboo in autumn, then paint it with the juice of lilac leaves, it seemed impossible that the raft was infected. But the evidence was there before me each morning as I woke up in my sleeping bag in the little cabin and looked upward. I could see a faint trickle of bamboo dust falling through the sunbeams. On top of my sleeping bag lay a light powdering of the same dust, as fine as ground oatmeal; and whenever anyone walked along the cabin roof, the natural walkway down the length of the boat, the whole cabin shook and sagged, and the light shower of bamboo dust became a thicker mist which came drifting down through the sunlight. I thought back to what had happened during the construction and it did not take long to work out the error. It was when we had abandoned the idea of basketwork cabin tops, and I asked the workmen to build small thatched cabins. In their hurry they had simply bicycled back to their village and brought the first bamboos that came to hand to make the cabin frames. The bamboos they used were infected with parasites, and now the speed of destruction was alarmingly fast. The butt-ends of the cabin bamboos which protruded into the cockpit looked firm and solid on the day we set sail, but three days later were so soft and spongy that you could poke your finger into them like the fresh marrow in a shinbone.

When, with the help of a Vietnamese-English dictionary, I discussed the situation with Loi, our resident bamboo expert, he did not seem too worried. He gave me to understand that the bamboo beetle would soon be killed off by the sea air. Then he and Joe spent a couple of days replacing the infected bamboo with fresh pieces taken from our stock of spare material, simply banging the new lengths in with a mallet so they lay alongside the riddled material. Wouldn't the bamboo beetle transfer from the old bamboo to the new, and eat that as well? I asked Loi. But he shook his head. I hoped he was correct. We could live in rotten and rickety cabins, but if the parasites migrated into the giant bamboos of the main hull, then our trip was doomed before it had really begun. So on the very quietest nights during those first few easy-going days, when there was not a ripple or splash of the ocean nor a single slight creak of the sails, I would lie awake and listen, and satisfy myself that what I had been told was true: you could actually hear the powder-post beetles eating.

5

ACROSS THE
TAIWAN STRAIT

I t would be imagined that the strange sight of a bamboo sailing raft, apparently emerging from another millennium, half-submerged and under three junk sails, would have attracted the attention of local shipping. Quite the reverse was true. On the second night out of Hong Kong we blundered into the middle of a fishing fleet working close inshore. All around us small fishing boats were wheeling and stopping as they set and retrieved nets. Banks of powerful arc-lights blazed out over the water to attract the fish to the surface, and there was a constant clatter of diesel generators. For more than an hour *Hsu Fu* drifted slowly through the congregation of boats, suddenly appearing in a pool of light, then passing out into the shadows. Often we were no more than fifty feet from a fishing boat. But no one paid the slightest attention, except – once – we were greeted with a volley of oaths in Cantonese, undoubtedly telling us to clear off. Nor was there any greater interest in broad daylight when a line of four, medium-sized fishing boats came past us next day, obviously inbound for Aberdeen Harbour. They passed a hundred yards away and never so much as changed course to take a closer look. As each boat drew level, we could see half a dozen of the fisherwomen whose job was to clean and gut the catch, sitting on the side rail and watching us intently. Each woman wore the distinctive coolie hat of her trade, so they looked like a row of extras in a Chinese opera. As each boat drew level, we waved cheerfully. But no one waved back, the fishing boats kept a dead straight course for home.

'Oh well,' said Geoffrey with a shrug. 'They probably think we are mad or Vietnamese boat people. This is Asia.'

A totally different craft came over the horizon soon afterwards. It headed directly towards us at full speed behind a great white foaming bow-wave. This was no fishing boat. It was travelling much too fast, and had the blunt lines of a small warship.

'Royal Hong Kong Police patrol boat,' said Geoffrey cheerfully. 'Probably coming to take a look.' But when the vessel came closer we saw it was flying not the Hong Kong flag, but the red-and-yellow ensign of the People's Republic of China. The inspection took on a decidedly menacing air. The big patrol boat cut its engines as it drew level, and the grey-painted military hull sank down into the water. It wallowed along-side, its big engines growling. On the bridge stood a dozen men in uniform, two or three had binoculars. All of them were staring down at us and scanning *Hsu Fu* intently. I took a look through my own binocu-lars. The bridge crew of the Chinese patrol ship were grim faced. No one was smiling. I held up a small walky-talky set, and pointed to it – an international signal that I wanted to converse on VHF. But nothing. *Hsu Fu* still had her sails up, there was a light breeze, and we were making barely one knot over an oily sea. An officer on the bridge made an angry gesture. We presumed he was an officer because he was wearing shoul-der boards on his uniform shirt. He made a brusque T-signal with his arms. It was obviously a command to heave to.

'Drop the sails,' I called to the crew. They obeyed very promptly. Everyone was feeling very nervous. Were we breaking some law? Were we on the point of being arrested for blundering into Chinese waters? The expressions of all the Chinese officers were so unfriendly that I anticipated, at best, some uncomfortable moments trying to explain exactly what we were doing, and that maybe we would be brought into the nearest port for further investigation. We carried a small inflatable dinghy on board, and I asked Mark and Joe to pump it up, ready for me to cross over to the patrol boat with our papers. Just at that moment a small fat man bobbed up among the line of hostile faces. He looked more like the ship's cook than an officer, as he was wearing a grubby white T-shirt. Luckily it seemed he was also the ship's joker. He took one look at us, yelled something incomprehensible at the top of his lungs, and then burst into a great screech of laughter and almost fell overboard with his mirth. Whatever he said – probably an insult –

took the tension out of the situation. The bridge officers visibly relaxed. The one with the shoulder boards made another gesture, this time waving us off curtly. It seemed that whatever it was they wanted before, the patrol was now ordering us to get out of Chinese waters immediately.

Had I been able to get aboard the Chinese patrol ship I had intended to ask if they would send a message to Hong Kong. Our little satellite radio was acting erratically. On the first two days of the voyage I was able to make it work and called the DHL office in Hong Kong to report our position. But the next day I had failed to make any connection with the satellite. Officially Joe held the radio operator's licence, but, in fact, I was responsible for communications as Joe had his photography to attend to, and I had operated the ship's radio on all my previous expeditions. Now, try as I might, I could not solve the problem. Mark repositioned the radio aerial, lashing it to the top of the little mizzen-mast where it sat looking like a large white Easter egg, but the signals still failed to get through. Later I discovered that the culprit was the battery. The radio ran off a twelve-volt battery charged either by a windmill or from a set of solar panels strapped to the cabin top. This battery was stowed in the cockpit and exposed to wind and spray, so it was of a special type, waterproof, sealed, and filled with a gel instead of liquid electrolyte so it would not spill in rough seas. In fact, the battery was faulty, sometimes delivering insufficient power to run the radio. To compound the problem, a drop in battery power corrupted the software programme which controlled the radio itself.

The Chinese Navy, it was clear, was not available for passing on a message, and nor, two hours later, was a passing container ship. It went by us at a distance of about two miles, and was clearly bound for Hong Kong from the huge Taiwanese trading port of Kaoishung. Once again I switched on the little walky-talky and called up the unknown ship using the international channel. There was no reply. I tried again. This time a heavily accented voice answered, 'Who are you?' By now the vessel was close enough for us to read the name — *Arce*. 'Hello *Arce*, this is the sailing raft *Hsu Fu* out of Hong Kong and bound for Taiwan. Please can you send a safety message for me? Our radio is broken.' Another long pause. 'I no see you.' Then silence. The container ship went on its way. No one was interested.

'Better wait until we see a European ship,' said Geoffrey, 'maybe

Danish Maersk Line. I use them quite a lot in my business, and they sail regularly between Hong Kong and Taiwan.'

Sure enough, about an hour later, a large container ship appeared, following the same track between Taiwan and Hong Kong as if there were a groove in the surface of the sea. It had MAERSK written on the hull in huge letters. This time my call on the walky-talky was answered instantly by a very matter-of-fact Danish voice. Yes, they were bound for Hong Kong, and yes, they would ask their shore agent there to telephone DHL to report that our radio was out of action, all was well aboard *Hsu Fu* and we were proceeding as planned for Taiwan. Twice more in the next twenty-four hours we were able to hand on the same message, once via a German ship of the Hansa Line, and once in the darkness to a ship visible only by its navigation lights from which a punctilious-sounding voice signed off with the words – 'This is a Japanese ship.'

I was sure that at least one message would get through (indeed all three of them did) and, oddly enough, losing the radio brought a welcome sense of release. It helped concentrate the mind on what we should be doing aboard the raft at the start of the journey. Daily radio reports were all very well for safety, but they distracted from the immediate reality of our situation. We needed to focus on learning to sail the raft properly and also to begin to come to terms with the fact that the sea was not just around us in the conventional sense of a yacht or motor-launch, but actually washing right through the raft so that we were much more on the interface between weather and waves than was the case on any other vessel we had experienced. Of course, I was very anxious that we should solve the radio problem and make the safety link work properly, but for the moment the absence of the radio link sharpened the sense that we were alone on the sea, and that it was up to us whether we managed or lost control of the situation.

Extreme fatigue was our immediate burden. The last few days had been hectic and exhausting. There had been the inevitable rush to get final items aboard before we sailed. Time also had to be found to say our thanks and farewells properly to friends, well-wishers and benefactors. In the background were the nagging worries about the raft – was it safe? had we thought of all the items we needed? would the weather turn against us? and so on. It all added up to the fact that by the time we set out from Hong Kong, the crew were physically and emotionally drained. Actually, leaving port had brought a new rush of energy. The excitement and the sense of adventure gave a boost so that each crew member was hyperactive and eager, busily attending to the small chores of mending, adapting, and easing all the complex functions of the new, untried raft. But that boost of energy had lasted about forty-eight hours, and then the accumulation of lack of sleep, unaccustomed surroundings and strange diet, and frequent hard physical labour, began to make itself felt. As captain, I feared that unless the crew had at least a couple of quiet calm nights to catch up on rest, we would start making mistakes through tiredness.

But we got very little rest. On the night of 24 May Joe, Loi and I were on watch in the cockpit when the uppermost spar on the mainsail snapped. It was a dark night with just a glimmer of stars and a light and fickle wind which frequently changed direction. *Hsu Fu* was edging over a black gentle swell when the mainsail silently swung across from one side of the raft to the other like a massive heavy fan, and we clearly heard a sharp cracking sound high above us. Against the sky we could see that the upper edge of the mainsail was no longer straight, but hung like a broken wing. The sail was crippled.

'Accidents like that always happen at two in the morning,' I sighed, 'but the wind is too light to do any further damage. We are too tired to do anything useful now. Better to tackle the problem in daylight.'

After breakfast we lowered the damaged sail to the deck, feeding out the ropes through brand-new blocks which squeaked and screeched in protest. The stout bamboo pole, four inches in diameter, which Mr Ching had supplied to hold the upper part of the sail had snapped in half. We cut free the sail, and for four hours Loi and Mark squatted on the bamboo roof of the main cabin shaping a new spar from a stout length of spare bamboo and lashing on the sail. Loi was in his element, shaving down lengths of rattan to make lashings to hold the sail to the spar, wrapping the rattan in place, then seizing the free end with his strong teeth like a pair of pincers and pulling it taut with his neck muscles straining. Finally the replacement spar was ready, and all the crew gathered by the main halyard to haul our new creation to the mast top. We were feeling rather proud of ourselves, content that from our own resources we had managed to get over the little difficulty. All together! — and we heaved away smartly, raising the sail in smooth folds like a Venetian blind unfurling. Heave now! Heave! — and the top of the sail rose and rose until it reached the correct height, hung there splendidly

Building the raft on the beach at Sam Son, Vietnam. Note the cabin frame in the foreground. (*Tim Severin*)

Mr Luoc, 'the comic', firebends a giant bamboo for the raft's main hull. A total of 220 bamboos were needed, and each had its own special curve. (*Tim Severin*)

Above: Fishermen at Sam Son lashing together the bamboos for the main hull.
(*Tim Severin*)

Opposite: Hsu Fu at sea, with Mark at the foremast top. (*Joe Beynon*)

Below: Launching *Hsu Fu* down the beach at Sam Son. (*Tim Severin*)

Above: Mealtime in the basketwork cockpit. (*Joe Beynon*)

Opposite: Joe sunbathing on the roof of the cabin beside the solar panels which powered the satellite radio. (*Rex Warner*)

Below: The first catch of the voyage – a dorado, caught by Mark and Loi. (*Joe Beynon*)

Hsu Fu drifting on the swell off Taiwan. (*Joe Beynon*)

Loi adjusting the set of the mainsail
in bad weather. (*Joe Beynon*)

Mark slacking off the mastshrouds
in bad weather. (*Joe Beynon*)

The 'grave' of Hsu Fu, Shingu, Japan. (*Joe Beynon*)

Approaching Shimoda in fog, at one of the world's busiest shipping crossroads. (*Joe Beynon*)

1

2

3

4

The Crew

1 Tim Severin. (*Joe Beynon*)

2 Joe Beynon. (*Rex Warner*)

3 Loi. (*Joe Beynon*)

4 Rex Warner. (*Joe Beynon*)

5 Trondur Patursson. (*Joe Beynon*)

6 Nina Kojima. (*Joe Beynon*)

7 Mark Reynolds. (*Joe Beynon*)

5

6

7

for a moment, and then there was a loud clear bursting pop, and the new spar we had laboured over all morning broke clean through. No one said a word – all of us were consciously putting on a brave face. But Loi and I were the only ones who knew that the broken spar was a length of spare *luong*, the giant bamboo selected for the raft's main structure. If that was all the strength there was in a piece of *luong*, how sturdy was the undulating body of the raft itself?

Patiently Loi and Mark set about constructing another spar. This time, because we had no more *luong* of a suitable length, they lashed together three shorter, thinner lengths of bamboos in a bundle and that seemed to do the trick. As they worked, Loi kept glancing back towards the fishing-line we had been trailing since our departure from Hong Kong. It still hung slack. There must have been fish in these waters, otherwise the fishing boats would not be in the vicinity. Yet we had not seen anything except for our little pilot fish, and the escort shark which had now been replaced by a larger four-foot version. Then, at about 5 p.m. a patch of water off the bow of the raft suddenly erupted. A school of small tuna, about eighteen inches to a foot long, came jumping and skipping out of the water. Normally one would have expected these fish to be frantically avoiding a predator attacking them from below, or perhaps leaping in pursuit of their own prey. But no, the tuna seemed to be totally unconcerned. They leaped up and down, flinging themselves a few inches clear of the sea, then falling back in the same spot, then jumping out again jauntily. For all the world, it looked as if they were dancing. The first group was joined by another shoal of dancing tuna of the same size and behaving in exactly the same strange way, but this time a few metres astern of the raft. Soon a third group of tuna appeared and began to splash about in the same lunatic pattern, as though they were impelled by a strange mania. This bizarre display continued for about ten minutes and then, abruptly all the fish dived and disappeared.

'Looks like a rain dance,' I said to Mark, and nodded towards the southern horizon. 'Maybe the fish detect something about the change of air pressure ahead of bad weather, and that makes them behave so strangely.' There, south of us, heavy clouds were gathering.

A deluge of tropical rain fell on us an hour later. The water poured from the sky as though a fire hydrant had been opened. It was impossible to see more than twenty yards in any direction through the thick grey curtain of falling water. The raindrops, fat and rapid, splattered down. They rebounded off the woven mat of cabin tops, spraying out horizontally. Trickles of rainwater dripped into the cabins and soaked any clothing that was not safely stowed in watertight kit-bags. The silent radio stayed firmly closed in its briefcase. The lovely dark red sails turned a soggy maroon, and Mr Ching's special anti-rot treatment leached out as blood-red runnels. In the cockpit everything was sodden – crew, cookers, ropes, pots and pans. Two buckets hanging on the stern gathered a couple of inches of rainwater in a few moments. The rain cooled the surface of the sea so that the wave crests which swirled through the raft were noticeably colder than before. When the rain was at its fiercest there was a sensation of being almost totally enveloped in water, the sea around us and beneath us, the saturated air above us, and a fine wet mist which filled our lungs.

With the rain came a southerly wind, moderate at first but then steadily increasing until it built to gale force. For the first hour we welcomed the wind because it filled *Hsu Fu*'s sails and drove the raft through the water at a steady pace, which was what we wanted after so much time spent nearly becalmed. But soon the wind was too strong for safety; the chestnut masts began to bend and groan alarmingly in their maststeps, and we had to reduce sail. In theory, this was one of the great advantages of the Chinese junk rig. By slackening a single rope, the great Venetian blind would begin to slide down the mast and automatically fold itself into a neater, smaller shape. But the cotton sail was sodden with rain, and the force of the wind pressed the cloth against the mast so that it jammed and stuck there. Loi, Mark and Joe had to climb up the sail, using the bamboo battens like a ladder and jump up and down so that their weight and movement forced the sail down.

Panel by panel we reduced sail as the wind increased in strength. Finally we had removed all the sails and *Hsu Fu* began to ride out her first full gale.

It was an unforgettable experience. All the drama of heavy weather was there: the wind howling and shrieking through the rigging, the crazy flapping of loose canvas, the rattle of ropes thrumming against the wooden mast, the sea churned into twenty-foot-high waves which came rolling down towards the raft with their characteristic menacing rumble. Now it was dark, and our world was a dimly seen circle of indigo water, foam-streaked and turbulent. Here was the classic setting for a small boat fighting to survive the powerful attack of the sea. But there was one thing which was totally and completely different – the calm response of *Hsu Fu*. In every other small boat I had ever sailed, we would have been clinging to handholds or bracing ourselves against the lurch and heave of the vessel. Small items would have slid off the cockpit bench and fallen to the floor. A hot drink would have had to be held carefully so that it did not spill with the swooping lurch of the vessel, and there would have been the regular alarming judder of waves pounding into the side of the hull. But *Hsu Fu* was nothing like that. The raft simply rose and dipped calmly with each passing wave. The raft stayed level. There was never a sudden lurch. You could stand a coffee cup on the cockpit floor, and even at the height of the gale the level of the liquid did not slop over the rim. The cup itself did not slide anywhere. *Hsu Fu* was an amazingly stable platform. It was a maritime version of the Chinese proverb of the bamboo which survives the hurricane because it bends with the wind, while the great trees resist stiffly and are destroyed. The same was true of our bamboo raft. *Hsu Fu* did not resist the waves but simply soaked up their power into the open structure of her bamboo hull. Each wave charged into the body of the raft, its foaming crest swirling around the cockpit and cabin baskets, and then carried onward and out from the opposite side of the vessel. *Hsu Fu* merely rocked gently at the onslaught. It was as if the strength of the sea had turned to the proverbial water. *Hsu Fu* felt completely and utterly *safe*.

To an experienced sailor the vessel's unorthodox behaviour took some getting used to. For the first three or four hours there was still a tendency to see a large wave approaching out of the darkness and tense oneself, waiting for the impact. But when there was no sudden thump, and after this had happened fifty or a hundred times you began to relax and accept that the raft was an easy-riding platform and there was no reason to take special precautions. The cockpit crew, including Joe who had never been in a gale before in his life, began to relax. Conditions were too noisy and turbulent for anyone to be able to get any sleep, so everyone stayed up, sitting in the cockpit, cocooned in oilskins which glistened in the torrential rain that continued to sweep across us in heavy squalls. There was nothing to do except wait for the gale to cease while we let *Hsu Fu* drift with the wind. Indeed the atmosphere became so relaxed that one almost forgot that the raft was actually riding out a gale that would have been very uncomfortable on a conventional yacht. The only reminder of the size of the waves was when a wave crest smacked squarely into the side of the cockpit basket and broke over the crew. This happened to Mark as he was holding half a cup of coffee, and he glanced down to find his cup full to the brim with seawater. It was almost a shock to realise that there were actually big waves out beyond the flimsy rim of woven basketwork.

We did have one bad fright, however. It was about two hours after dark, when the moon was completely obscured by the monsoon clouds. We had just finished our evening meal of a bowl of soup and some biscuits. Cooking anything more ambitious was a waste of time. With so much rain falling into our food it would have been cold and watery in an instant. All five of us were sitting on the slat benches of the cockpit trying to shelter from the full force of the wind. No one was talking because the noise of the wind and waves made normal conversation impossible. Abruptly Loi raised his head, listening. I noticed his look of alarm, and scrambled to my feet and stared forward, also listening intently. I heard what had caught his attention – the heavy thump of a big ship engine. The visibility was atrocious, perhaps forty yards, and I could see nothing. Yet the ship had to be dangerously close if we could hear its engine above all the fury and noise of a gale. For perhaps half a minute we strained to identify the source of the engine noise. All of us realised that there was nothing we could do, no evasive action we could take. *Hsu Fu* was being driven sideways by the gale, and we were helpless. Loi gave a cry and pointed. For a heart-stopping moment we saw a great black shape driving past us, directly ahead, and so close that we had to look upward to see the red speck of a navigation light high above us. It was the steel side of a large merchant ship travelling through the murk at fifteen to twenty knots and about thirty yards away from our waterlogged raft. The ship would be running on radar to avoid obstacles, but *Hsu Fu* was so low in the water that her radar echo, even with a radar reflector we had hoisted to the mast for just such conditions, must have been obscured among the clutter of the waves. There was not the slightest chance that the ship had seen us or knew that we were there, almost under her bow. The massive dark shape glided past, so close that we could detect the beat of the great propeller vibrating through the hull of the raft, and then the ship vanished in the darkness in a few seconds. It had been a very close shave.

All that night the foul weather continued, and the next morning the monsoon sky remained so dark and overcast that it seemed that day had never dawned. Little by little the wind eased until we could hoist a few panels of sail and begin to move forward. But the high waves persisted, and *Hsu Fu* moved across them twisting and flexing and creaking. The sound of the raft in a seaway was also unique – a constant groaning and creaking of bamboos rubbing against one another and working against the rattan lashings, the swirl and gurgle of water seething up between the cracks in the bamboos, and another distinct sound at the stern where the cut-off ends of bamboos projected like organ pipes and the water gurgled and boomed into their open ends. Overlying these background noises were dozens of individual squeaks and grating noises from the super-structure where everything was in motion, rubbing or sliding or bending with the flexing of the raft.

Nothing was stationary. *Hsu Fu* rippled and bent with the waves, or twisted in a spiral motion so that her three masts swayed in different directions at the same time and looked as if they belonged to three com-pletely different vessels. The raft had to flex to survive, but there was a serious penalty: the constant movement produced tremendous abra-sion. Ropes, basketwork, sails, mast fastenings, cabins, spare bamboos, food containers, everything was rubbing against its neighbour, and wear-ing away. So the ropes broke, holes were worn in the cabin roofs, and the corners of the basketwork frayed. And when you stepped out of the bas-ketwork cockpit and on to the body of the raft, you had to be very careful where you put your feet. The gaps between the main bamboos were opening and closing with the movement of the vessel, and if your foot slipped between two bamboos it could be crushed. When a rope accidentally slipped down between two bamboos, it was immediately nipped and chewed right through, as if it had been seized by a fierce dog. This never-ending flexing of the raft was to dominate our everyday lives all the time we were on *Hsu Fu*.

Handling the raft required very little attention. It only needed two men working in unison to raise and lower the junk sails to suit the wind strength. One man, if he was deft, could adjust the leeboards the way you wanted. Then you set the twin rudders to the correct angle, fixing them in position on a wooden pin rail, and after that the raft ran forward on course as if computer-guided. But looking after the wear and tear was a full-time job. Morning, noon, and evening someone had to go round the raft, making an inspection tour to check every rope for chafe, to tighten up lashings, to see that the moving bamboos were not grinding holes in one another. The speed of chafe was astonishing. When we hoisted sail after that first gale, we found that the canvas had been rubbing ever so slightly on the moving cabin top to which it had been lashed for safety. On a normal boat nothing would have happened. But on flexible, bending, shifting *Hsu Fu* the canvas had been nibbled away in less than twenty-four hours. The mainsail had holes in it as if it had been attacked by giant moths.

A gale so early in the voyage was a bonus. It had given us confidence in our vessel, and over the next three days the crew began to knit together more closely as a working team, now they were assured of the raft's seaworthiness. Mark and Loi were the key members. Both of them possessed the practical skills of ropework and carpentry to look after the raft properly and to teach the others. The immediate priority was to stitch together canvas door flaps for our kennel-like cabins to stop the spray flying in, and more canvas panels to hang around the sides of the cockpit to give us better shelter while on watch. So the entire crew sat on the main cabin roof armed with heavy needles and thread. Mark stitched the heavy canvas so neatly that he had clearly had a lot of practice.

'Where did you learn?' Joe asked him.

'Oh, I sewed myself a Red Indian-style tepee in Hong Kong,' Mark replied, 'and lived in it in a Chinese garden until the town authorities made me take it down.'

Joe's stitching was rather ragged, and Geoffrey the other novice on board, teased him good-naturedly.

'Don't speak too soon,' Joe warned him cheerfully. 'Remember, if you get hurt, I'm the one who'll be stitching you up.'

The banter was an excellent sign that the crew were very willing to establish solid cooperation and friendship based on mutual tolerance. Joe, for example, had a voracious appetite. As a schoolboy, he confessed, the family of one of his schoolfriends had forbidden their son to bring him into their kitchen because he always left the larder bare. Now when he woke up every morning, he emerged from his sleeping bag with the same worried question – 'Has there been breakfast yet?', just in case he had missed it. Geoffrey who controlled the food stores, jokingly accused Joe of prowling the raft at night while on his watch, trying to burgle the stores barrels. Geoffrey himself was unrecognisable as the well-turned-out business entrepreneur of Hong Kong. He had lost weight, gained the beginnings of a tan, and as soon as the sun came out, spent most of the day stripped to the waist reading the fattest, thickest novel he had been able to buy. Burly and well over six feet, Geoffrey made Loi look tiny. The skinny Vietnamese fisherman-carpenter must have weighed less than eight stone, with bandy legs and sticklike arms gangling in each direction. Yet it was Loi who ate the most, happily finishing up for his breakfast any food that had been left over from the night before, even when it was soggy, cold spaghetti. Loi was constantly eager and enthusiastic to work, except when it rained. He hated working in the rain, perhaps because he felt cold, and would prefer to leave the job until later, but that was impossible because *Hsu Fu* demanded never-ending repairs. Only Loi's lack of English worried me. I was concerned that he would begin to feel lonely and isolated if, as the weeks went by, he still could not converse with the rest of the crew. But for the moment there seemed no problem. Loi was chirpy and smiling, and raised a cheer from all the rest of us when after a week at sea he used his first English word, saying 'good-night' before heading for the forward cabin.

Mark shared the forward cabin with Loi, and I hoped that the two of them would get along together. Mark was so important to the running of the raft that I wanted to be sure he kept in good spirits, but I feared it could be difficult. His lifestyle was based on independence and rejection of authority and structure, so the discipline of living and working in the cramped conditions of a raft was sure to prove a strain. Matters came to a head early on. I had asked the crew to gather every day at eight so we could discuss the day's programme ahead. This meant that even the night watch who had just finished four hours on duty, had to stay up instead of heading for their well-earned rest. The first day Mark arrived on time, but the day after that he showed up ten minutes late, and then on the following day wandered into the cockpit twenty minutes after everyone had sat waiting for him. It was not deliberate tardiness, just that Mark normally lived his own life the way he wanted to, got up when he felt like it, came and went as he pleased, had no regular job, and this liberty was very important to him. He was also someone who was sensitive to imagined slights, and the last thing I wanted to do was to lose his trust. But it was better to deal with the problem frankly.

'Mark,' I told him firmly in front of all the others after they had sat waiting for him to appear, 'it is important for everyone to be on time, and be here at eight. It's not a matter of time-keeping for time-keeping's sake. But because this is the time when we can all be together as a team, find out what everyone else is doing, and discuss the best way of running the raft.'

Mark took the rebuke reasonably. 'I'm really sorry,' he said. 'I didn't mean to cause any problem. And I didn't realise what the time was. I don't wear a watch, and half the time my clock is buried in my luggage. Five minutes before breakfast please be sure to give me a shout, and if I don't appear, shout even louder. I'll be there.'

The others, aware of Mark's thin-skinned temperament, relaxed. And Mark was as good as his word: for the sake of *Hsu Fu* he adopted rigorous time-keeping.

The three days following the gale were bright and sunny, ideal for sewing canvas and minor chores, but not for sailing. We made ourselves more room in the cockpit by sorting out the clutter there. The two cookers in their wooden box now sat at the forward end of the cockpit where they were handy for brewing up hot drinks, but a little awkward for Joe, Geoffrey and myself who had to climb over the cooker box to enter our cabin. Everything else – the day's issue of fresh oranges, a jar of coffee, another of sugar, a tin of powdered milk, the eating bowls and our chopsticks – we pushed under the benches. Our cooking spices, garlic and ginger and the rest, were kept dry in one of the Sam Son bamboo stowage tubes, and each morning Geoffrey filled a small tub with the day's food rations drawn from the main storage barrels. One whole morning was spent removing all the useless packaging and wrappings from our food stores, so that it would stow more compactly. All the reject packaging was put into the special rubbish barrel in case we needed it for some other purpose. Old tins and silver foil, for instance, would become home-made fishing lures, though we still had not had any luck with fishing. Several times we had glimpsed the silver and blue flicker of a large leaf-shaped fish loitering beneath *Hsu Fu* about six feet down. It would come swimming out hungrily to inspect any vegetable peelings the cook-of-the-day threw overboard. But always the fish turned back, rejecting the offering, even when Mark tried coaxing it with a rotten carrot carefully carved to look like a minnow.

Hsu Fu's gentle pace better suited the small and meek species of wildlife who were attracted to the sanctuary of the raft. A small land bird had taken refuge on the cabin roof during the gale. The bird had the slim forked tail of a house martin or a small swallow, a white breast and black head, and a dark red face as though a garden robin had made a mistake when applying its make-up. For two or three days our visitor was decidedly sorry for itself, its crest and neck feathers all ruffled and out of sorts. We gave it food and water until it perked up. By that time the bird was reluctant to leave its new-found home and had become a regular member of *Hsu Fu*'s humble animal world. Let the tuna dance or – as happened one sunny afternoon – a school of dolphins rush past energetically – *Hsu Fu* had more modest companions. Her forest-green skirt of weed, which had grown with amazing speed in the warm waters of Aberdeen Harbour until some fronds were two feet long, now sheltered a colony of raft fish; the hitch-hiking swallow never ventured more than twenty yards away before curling back on the wing to land on whatever spot took its fancy; and even our community of powder-post beetles still stolidly munching through our bamboo cabin poles were passengers suited to a slow pace of life. And what other vessel could boast a genuine deck spider. We knew we had one aboard because at dawn we would find glistening spider's webs hung between the side bamboos and the cabins. It seemed a pity to disturb them as we went about our daily chores.

At night *Hsu Fu* eased forward under a sky bright with moon and stars, and then abruptly tinged with menace by towering cloud banks which came drifting out of the south. The memory of the recent gale was too fresh to ignore the possibility of a soaking deluge of a rainstorm chilling the skin, the need to climb into oilskins already wet from the last gale, and the risk to masts and rigging. To me there was a world of difference between the haunting romance of clouds sliding across the face of a bright moon when seen from land, and the same clouds watched by the careful helmsman squinting to see if sudden squalls lurk in the dark shadows beneath them. So I would call upon the crew to reduce sail, just in case. Perhaps I was being too cautious. But whenever *Hsu Fu* was hit by a sudden gust of wind, I could hear the sounds of fragile and untested materials: the heavy creak of stressed bamboo or the sudden groan of cordage and spars absorbing the quick onrush of wind. The boat seemed to be crying out in pain, like an arthritic suddenly called upon to use weak muscles. So my principle was always to go as gently as possible, reduce the risks, and give *Hsu Fu* the best chance. I was conscious that we were still at the very outset of our voyage, and had much to learn. We were not in an ocean race, nor were we mountaineers who had set out to climb to a summit. We were on *Hsu Fu* to taste what it would have been like to sail on an ocean-going raft 2,000 years ago, and perhaps to discover whether such a vessel could have crossed an ocean. It was the voyage itself, not the end point, which mattered.

6

S WEPT A WAY BY THE B LACK S TREAM

The Kuroshio or Japan Current, its waters dark and warm, gathers its strength among the Philippine Islands, pours past the island of Taiwan, and then curves towards Japan before spewing out into the North Pacific Ocean and dissipating to become the North Pacific Current. What is unusual about the Kuroshio is not so much the volume of water that is transported, though that is huge, but the way the current confines itself to a narrow band. The current is seldom more than four hundred metres deep, and branches and eddies split off and travel their separate ways through gulfs and straits, but the main thrust of the Kuroshio is remarkably concentrated. Off the south coast of Japan the current stays within a corridor only fifteen to twenty-five miles broad. Off the east coast of Taiwan where the current can attain a speed of five knots, the width is even less. For that reason the Japanese name for the phenomenon is peculiarly apt: Kuroshio means 'the Black Stream', and the Kuroshio is just that – a powerful river in the ocean.

With *Hsu Fu* taking two weeks to plod across the Taiwan Strait and May drawing to a close, I took another look at the chart. My original plan had been to cross directly from Hong Kong to the nearest point of land on the south-west corner of Taiwan. This short crossing would be a test run. But now, with the raft travelling more slowly than I had planned, I began to have second thoughts. Our eventual destination in Taiwan was a small harbour in the extreme north, not far from Taipei where we had been invited by the Taiwanese Yachting Association. To get there we would have a long haul against a back eddy of the Kuroshio if we stayed on the west side of Taiwan. A better route seemed to be to go around the southern tip of the island, find the main north-going flow of the Kuroshio, and be carried briskly to our destination by the current. This, anyhow, was what Robert Wu, Vice-Chairman of the Taiwanese Yachting Association, had recommended when I had met him in Hong Kong before the start of the China Voyage. It was evident that two to three knots of the Black Stream would more than double *Hsu Fu*'s average speed. I was pondering this alternative when my mind was made up for me by a passing freighter. I had called on the little walky-talky to ask if the merchant ship would report *Hsu Fu*'s position to Hong Kong, and was told that there was such severe weather in the Taiwan Strait that even 40,000-ton ships were avoiding the area.

So we set course for the Bashi Channel past Taiwan's southern cape, and at once our luck improved. For a start we caught our first big fish, an important moment on any voyage. It hooked itself on Loi's trailing line. We had been towing the line with its bright pink imitation squid lure for so long that when Geoffrey called out, 'Look at that fish jumping! Isn't it spectacular!', we glanced back in the direction he was pointing without realising what was happening. A splendid fish, green and gold and about four feet long was jumping and somersaulting in the air far behind us, the sunlight flashing off its scales. Then someone noticed the bright pink flash in its mouth.

'It's hooked!' Mark cried jubilantly, and ran to the stern to start hauling in the line. The fish put up a terrific fight, thrashing and plunging as Loi and Mark pulled it closer, and lunged away powerfully when it detected the presence of the raft. We held our breath as Loi carefully pulled in the last few yards of line hand over hand. Mark crouched on the slippery bamboos at the stern, holding a makeshift loop of wire to slip over the fish's tail. Once, twice, and then again Mark tried to lasso the thrashing fish, and failed. Each time it flipped away in a surge of foam. But it was firmly hooked, and the fourth time it came within reach, Mark dropped the wire loop, grabbed the fish by the tail with his bare hand, and yanked it flying through the air to land in the cockpit where it flapped and thrashed in fury, spraying blood and scales everywhere. It was a dorado or dolphin fish, a voracious predator which feeds mostly on flying fish. It had a long, flat muscular body and a high, blunt, hatchet of a forehead with round staring eyes which gave it a prehistoric yet savage look. Loi butchered it eagerly, first cutting off inch-thick steaks which we fried in soy sauce and oil and were delicious. The rest – the liver, head, backbone, guts, and gills – he boiled with rice for supper. It was insipid and full of bones.

'Hope we don't have to have it for breakfast,' muttered Mark through a prickly mouthful. But to Loi the meal was a huge success.

We could tell we were approaching the coast of Taiwan by the amount of pollution floating in the water around us. The rubbish was every-where – broken boxes, scraps of plastic sheet, lumps of styrofoam packaging, old shoes, plastic bags, even metal boxes which should have sunk but somehow kept afloat and joined the rest of the trash circulating in a thin scum of dirty foam. Late in the evening of 1 June we glimpsed the low grey coastline of Taiwan, and with the wind in our favour crept past O-Luan, its southern cape. A mile off the headland a military guard-ship was on duty, presumably watching against smugglers or hostile vessels from mainland China. The guardship approached us, circled, then resumed station clearly not interested. Nor did it answer to a radio call. As *Hsu Fu* sidled up to the Black Stream which ran past the cape, I had a mental image of our raft as a country bumpkin who had just come to town, sees a moving pavement or an escalator for the first time, and hesitates before stepping on the moving surface. But the wind was from the south, nearly gale force, and there was no holding back. *Hsu Fu* was pushed squarely on the Black Stream.

The Kuroshio sweeping past the point of Taiwan flows over reefs and shallows which cause the water to heap up in strange billows. Over the top of these undulations the gale was now building strange waves which carried *Hsu Fu* rising and swooping in a rollercoaster ride. The wind was from dead astern, the most dangerous direction because the fan-shaped sails could flap from side to side and smash themselves to pieces. After three or four hours we heard the foresail yard crack in two just as the mainsail had done earlier. But there was no time to repair it as we dared not lose the thrust of wind and current. In less than eight hours we were swept fifty miles up the east Taiwan coast, a greater distance than in the previous three days of sailing. It was exhilarating progress, all the more spectacular because on our left the tall cliffs and steep mountains of Taiwan's east coast rose in ridges of black and purple against gunmetal clouds building up over the land. It was risky navigation because *Hsu Fu* was dangerously close to land. Our vessel was a clumsy raft, not an agile yacht, and a change of wind direction would drive her helplessly on to a lee shore.

We were very much on our own. Our friends of the Taiwanese Yachting Association had said they would come to look for us, but it was impossible for them to know precisely where to search because we had no radio to give an up-to-the-minute position. And the weather did not help. By mid-morning the monsoon rain was once again drizzling from an overcast sky, and visibility was atrocious. Out of the murk appeared a large squadron of warships. They appeared and disappeared in the mist and were too far away to have seen us. It was the Taiwanese Navy on patrol, circling the island, radar scanners whirling, grey warship after grey warship, maintaining a vigil against the mainland Communists that had been in place for forty years in an atmosphere of tension and suspicion. These were disputed waters, and there was very little commercial traffic on this coast. We had seen two small coasters the previous night, and one large Japanese car-carrier which had confirmed by radio that there were strong gales in the Taiwan Strait on the other side of the island. It seemed that the decision to go around Taiwan was paying dividends.

Our sail-handling was now more expert. Even with *Hsu Fu* swaying on the waves which came surging up from astern and seethed up through the bamboo deck all the way down the length of the raft, we managed to execute tricky manoeuvres neatly. We lowered the broken foresail, mended it with fresh bamboo battens, and rehoisted it. Everything went like clockwork, and when we had to change direction, an awkward manoeuvre with a strong following wind, we could have been sailing a big raft all our lives. Under Loi's direction we lifted the two forward lee-boards and hardened in on the foresail to increase downwind speed. Judging the moment finely, we swung the foresail from one side to the other, and a moment later pushed across the little mizzen-sail using it like the steering tailplane of an aircraft. As *Hsu Fu* altered course, the big red mainsail swung majestically across, and our raft was sailing off on the opposite tack. We never even touched the rudders.

By noon on 4 June the helpful gale had faded, and was replaced by a head wind from the north, which for the next two days forced us away from the coast and out to sea. It was a grey, wet, nondescript sort of day, with a perpetually gloomy sky and spatterings of rain so that we had to wear oilskins all the time. The oilskins grew clammy and soggy on the inside from our condensing sweat. It was not cold, and we all went barefoot. But the constant damp and rain meant that the cockpit floor of pressed bamboo strips was spongy and soggy to the touch.

I was sitting beside Mark on the main cabin roof, helping him stitch a repair in the mainsail, when I noticed the distant speck of a ship on the horizon. It must have spotted us on radar for the vessel was headed directly at us, and moving fast.

'Maybe it's our friends from Taiwan looking for us,' I said, 'though it's coming from the wrong direction. Anyhow it is obviously heading to intercept us.'

As the stranger came closer, we saw that it was a military-style vessel of elderly design. It was low and narrow, with a shallow draught very unsuitable for the conditions, so that it was pitching heavily. Whatever navy owned it, they must have had a small defence budget to have sent such a vessel, more suitable for inshore work, out into deep waters.

'Could be the Taiwanese Coastguard coming to check on us,' said Geoffrey, hopefully. But I was puzzled. Closer at hand, the strange ship looked even odder. It was very badly looked-after, and was shabby and rust-streaked. Though it was clearly a patrol vessel it carried no flag, except for a small scrap of dirty plain red cloth, nor did it have any warship numbers painted on its hull. The only equipment which seemed to work was its radar which was spinning away briskly, and its engines which drove the ship very fast.

'What's the Taiwanese Navy flag?' I asked Geoffrey.

'I don't know,' he replied, 'but the Chinese Navy has its own special ensign.'

'I don't think any navy would want to lay claim to that shambles,' I said. 'I've got a nasty feeling that they don't belong to any Navy.'

The lean, dirty patrol vessel was now level with us. There was no fishing gear nor any big guns, just a long, low, uncluttered deck. On the battered bridge stood a group of men scanning us through binoculars. None of them wore uniform. There were half a dozen more men clustered on deck by the foot of the bridge, none of them wore uniform either. They all inspected us intently. We waved cheerfully. No one aboard the suspicious vessel made a move. One of the men on the bridge raised a speaking trumpet to his mouth. He was about to call an order, then changed his mind and lowered the loudhailer.

'What on earth are they doing out here?' asked Joe. 'They are far out, the wrong side of Taiwan.' The strange, rather sinister vessel was neither commercial nor military.

The same thought crossed our minds.

'They are probably pirates,' said Geoffrey. 'Even in Hong Kong waters commercial ships are boarded by crews from mainland China, sometimes in uniform, sometimes not. They loot the vessel of things like TV sets and luxury goods and then leave. If there's any resistance, they shoot the crew.'

'Well they won't find many TV sets aboard this bamboo raft,' commented Joe. And the pirate, if that is what he was, revved up his engines and began to turn away. Ten minutes later it was a grey lurching speck on the horizon, cruising the sea to make another interception.

We had now been at sea for nineteen days, double the length of time originally planned for the first sector. Of course our food was running low. Geoffrey checked to see how much longer our stock of food and drinking water would hold out at our present rate of consumption. He found we had eaten 8 kilos of noodles, 5 kilos of rice, 10 kilos of bran and dried fruit, and 40 onions. All the Chinese cabbages had turned rancid and slimy within the first week, and after two weeks the last of 120 oranges had gone rotten. There were 6 remaining lemons. We had no other fruit or vegetables. Also our food preferences were obvious: we preferred coffee (5 jars) to drinking tea (160 tea bags), and craved sweet food – we had finished all 10 packets of sweet biscuits and eaten 6 kilos of sugar, which was more than our consumption of rice. We appreciated dried seaweed, dried bean curd, and dried shrimps (all gone), but steered clear of the little finger-length dried fish which were too salty.

Our eating habits were reflected in the amount of fresh water we drank. Every time we ate food which was too salty or spicy, our water consumption had gone up from 16 litres per day for the 5-man crew to 18 litres. Our attempts to save fresh water by mixing in seawater when cooking rice or noodles had not had much success. We saved fresh water in cooking, but tended to drink more water afterwards, particularly when we got the cooking mixture wrong. Fat noodles, for example, could be boiled in a 50:50 mixture, but fine noodles and rice needed only the slightest touch of seawater or they became far too salty. Geoffrey concluded that we had enough water to stay at sea for at least another twenty days, and though we were down to our last pack of sugar, our last tin of powdered milk, and last jar of coffee, these were luxuries and it would be another couple of days before it would be necessary to impose severe rationing on basic foodstuffs such as rice and noodles. Geoffrey himself said nothing about his own predicament. He should have been back in his office at least a week earlier. Without a radio he had not been able to tell his staff what was happening, and if he said he was being scrutinised by pirates off the Taiwanese coast they would probably have thought they would not see him again.

For the rest of that day *Hsu Fu* lay becalmed on a scummy brown sea, though whether the colour was the result of pollution or natural organic material in the water, it was hard to tell. I took the chance to inflate the little rubber dinghy and row off to see the raft from a distance. She was a truly unusual sight, just three masts with limp sails appearing above the low oily swell, an occasional glimpse of the cabin tops, and – very rarely – the half-submerged hull as if she were waterlogged driftwood. At fifty yards, if you listened carefully, you could hear the gurgle and splash of water washing and booming through her bamboos.

The next night, equally calm, a brilliant full moon appeared over the mountains of Taiwan and engraved them black on the horizon even though Taiwan was forty miles away. Banks of clouds moved slowly across the face of the moon, and in their gaps a lunar eclipse was revealed, bit by bit as if in time-lapse photography. When the moonlight was at its brightest, it penetrated deep into the water around us and reflected off the bodies of three or four dolphin fish cruising below the raft. The fish became ghostly torpedos of luminous green, and when they spread their forward fins, they balanced on wings of iridescent blue. It was eerily beautiful.

All of us were beginning to look forward to getting ashore in Taiwan. Geoffrey needed to go straight to the airport and catch the first plane back to Hong Kong and his office, and the rest of us anticipated a visit that would be a chance to stretch our legs on land as well as see Taiwan's cultural heritage. In particular, I wanted to take a look at the remains of the temple mounds which, according to Professor Needham, had been compared to the temple mounds of the Aztecs and Mayans in Central America and even as far afield as Peru. The theory was that there had been a cultural link between the mound-builders of the lands around the Pacific all the way from South-East Asia to South America because the high places they constructed for their worship were similar in layout and design. Most were pyramid-shaped with a special enclosed altar at the summit. Personally, I did not find this argument very convincing, as the shape seemed a commonplace way of building, and the comparisons were rather vague and generalised.

The strongest reason to get to port in Taiwan was a practical one: *Hsu Fu* was running out of spare parts. Every time we replaced a broken bamboo spar, or strengthened the cabin frame, or reinforced the lashings, or made some structural improvements to the raft, we ate into the small reserve stock of bamboo and rattan we carried on board. When we started from Hong Kong our spare bamboos had been lashed on each side of the main cabin as a crude fence which helped to break the force of the waves washing across the raft from the beam. Now that fence was nearly gone, its bamboos used in the various repairs. Similarly Loi's bundle of spare rattan was only half its original size. On Taiwan, I hoped we could replenish our vital materials for the raft.

But in the next twenty-four hours we found we were no longer in control of *Hsu Fu*. The Black Stream was taking command.

The problem was very simple. Initially we had made splendid progress up the Taiwanese coast. For two days the current and wind had been behind us as we headed for our target, Cape San-tiao on the northeast corner of the island. But when the wind swung round to the north, we were forced away from the land. The north wind was followed by calm, then again by a north wind, so that we were unable to get back to the coast but obliged to beat back and forth waiting for a change to a more favourable wind direction. Yet all the time the Black Stream was so potent that it was carrying us right past Taiwan. This was no sudden emergency, but a slow realisation that we were being swept in the wrong direction, and there was absolutely nothing we could do about it. By 6 June, two days after the visit from the pirate ship, I could see from the chart how the Black Stream was dictating our course. At noon we were thirty-five miles from Cape San-tiao and sailing towards the point under a light but favourable breeze. Six hours later we were forty miles distant. The Black Stream was more powerful than the effect of the wind.

I called a crew meeting in the cockpit.

'If we don't get a stronger wind in our favour soon,' I announced, 'it looks as if we won't be able to get ashore in Taiwan. I will give it another twenty-four hours, but I think we should begin to review the alternatives. The first is that we push the button on the distress beacon, and wait for someone to rescue us. But I really do not think that is an option as it is action to be taken only in case of grave and imminent danger. Second, we may be able to call up a passing ship and ask for a message to be relayed to Taiwan for someone to send out a towboat. But I think it is unlikely we will meet up with a ship as we are no longer in the main shipping track. Third, our friends in Taiwan may get worried and come looking for us. Fourth, we should begin looking for alternative landing sites. Our best chance would be to make for the Japanese Ryukyu Islands which lie down-current. Okinawa is the largest and three hundred miles away. We could reach there in about seven to ten days, but it means imposing strict rationing of food and water.'

A very thoughtful-looking crew heard me out. Then Joe spoke up. 'I don't think that pressing the panic button is an option at all. People have better things to do than come looking for us.'

'I am mostly concerned for Geoffrey,' I said. 'He has a business to run and expected to be away only a week or ten days. He has been remarkably patient so far, for which I commend him.'

'Well, there is not much that can be done about it,' said Geoffrey with a resigned shrug.

'Instead of whistling for a favourable wind in the traditional way,' said Mark with a grin, 'I'll play my bongo drums and see if that has the same effect.'

I felt relieved that I had such a resilient crew. The China Voyage was entering a new and uncharted phase.

Our predicament was a real-life example of what might have happened 2,000 years ago. Against our intention we were demonstrating how an early vessel could stray into unknown waters through chance. Scholars had written about 'accidental voyages' when the wind and current carried dismasted or damaged ships to new lands. But here we were aboard *Hsu Fu* showing that just a few days of head winds or calm could have a similar result. When a slow-moving vessel like a raft is gripped by a current as strong as the Kuroshio, the vessel is like a hot-air balloon which goes where the wind blows it. If at any time in the last 2,000 years, a sailing raft from China or Taiwan had ventured too far out on to the current and the wind had failed, then the crew would have been in the same predicament. The Black Stream could have swept the hapless vessel farther and farther away from land, first north, then east, towards Japan and then perhaps out into the Pacific and towards America.

That night I lay awake listening to the wind, and wondered just how good was our course towards Taiwan. Were we getting closer to land? Or was the steady creaking and groaning of the vessel which sounded as if she were moving through the water, nothing but delusion. Were we bobbing up and down, lifting and sinking in the swells, but in fact going nowhere, except where the Black Stream took us?

At first light on 7 June I checked the compass. *Hsu Fu's* blunt bow was still pointed towards Taiwan and on a good course. But I could see no land ahead. The wind was in just the right direction for her best point of sailing, but very light. *Hsu Fu* was advancing at just 1.5 knots. I plotted our position on the chart, and the picture became clear. In the night with a light fair wind we had again lost out to the Black Stream. Taiwan was fading into the distance. The wind seemed to be growing stronger so, to be sure of my calculations, I waited for another two hours, and once more checked our position. We had barely crept any closer to our target. It was time to make a major change of plan.

Once again I called the crew to the cockpit and showed them *Hsu Fu's* track crawling across the chart. I complimented Mark on his bongo drumming and explained that we had enjoyed a favourable wind for the past two hours and been sailing steadily. Yet at the end of that time we had advanced only a mile. At that rate it would require at least forty hours of favourable wind to make port – a virtually impossible prospect as the wind was bound to change. The logical alternative was for us to give up all hope of ever reaching Taiwan, and to take a new route across the current and head for the Ryukyus, the closest of which was about 130 miles away. But, I warned the crew, we would have to change our lifestyle. Gone was the free and easy time of three meals a day and as many hot drinks as we liked. At a stroke we were on firm discipline and short rations. By cutting back on our daily intake of food we could spin out our food and water for ten more days, and perhaps also gather rainwater and catch fish. The immediate worry was our supply of fuel for the cooker. We had two litres of paraffin left. It was only enough for one hot meal per day, plus two brew-ups for hot drinks at breakfast and at midday. From now on the regime was just one cooked meal in the evening. At lunchtime Joe looked glumly at the little heap of peanuts and raisins, two thin slices of salami, and the single water biscuit he had in his bowl.

'Do you think you could pass the chutney?,' he asked Geoffrey.

'Not if you are going to use it as a substitute for volume of food,' he replied. 'I can see I will have to put all the condiments under lock and key.'

'Well, you wanted to return to Hong Kong having lost weight and with a tan,' retorted Joe, 'and now you will do so.'

In fact, we had a glorious afternoon of sailing, once we turned round and began heading away from Taiwan. The sun came out, and *Hsu Fu* ploughed merrily across the Kuroshio which was rich with marine life. A small flock of gannets wheeled overhead, occasionally plummeting down to seize flying fish chased into the air by our escort of dorados which were hunting ahead of the raft. The flying fish would burst out of the water in their dozens, and go skimming away, glittering silver in the sunlight like handfuls of bright new coins flung across the water. The unlucky flying fish were the perpetual victims of the ocean, prey to all, whether fish or fowl. Sometimes they leapt into the air to escape the jaws of the hunting dorados and found our raft right in front of them. Then almost a look of panic could be seen in their timid round eyes as they saw the obstacle, and they seemed to hover horror-struck in mid-air, adapting their thin wings in flight, before banking steeply to avoid the raft, and flopping sideways inelegantly into the water and, as often as not, into the snapping jaws of a dorado.

It was remarkable, I thought to myself, how smoothly all of us had adapted to living on our semi-submerged vessel. Now we took it for granted that seawater came swirling up around our feet whenever we left the cabin or cockpit baskets. It seemed perfectly natural that the centre and bow areas of our raft were permanently awash. The waves which lapped over the stern of the raft were our waste-disposal system. Here we crouched, ankle-deep in the wavelets, to wash ourselves or to go to the lavatory. Everything was hygienically sluiced away by the ocean. Of course, our feet and legs were wet and clammy much of the time, and the skin became wrinkled and white. But when the sun came out, the circulation was restored, our feet soon dried off, and we could keep them dry by staying in the cockpit or on the cabin roofs. In fact, a good deal of daily life was spent perched on the bamboo matting on top of the cabins. Here we laid out clothes to dry, sat mending sails, wrote up our diaries, or Loi compiled his vocabulary lists, with Joe's help. Loi had a touching faith in these lists, carefully writing down parallel columns of Vietnamese and English words in a notebook like an old-fashioned ledger, with black covers and a red spine, which had been purchased for him in Hong Kong. The drawback was that, try as he might, he never could remember the words he wrote down. So even after three weeks at sea, his vocabulary was minimal. Still, that did not seem to matter. Loi was enthusiastic. Always up at first light even when it was not his turn to be on watch, always the first to volunteer for any job, always keeping his clothes scrupulously clean with daily washes in a bucket off the stern using hair shampoo for soap, Loi seemed to be thoroughly happy.

Our new food regime was not too arduous, or so I thought, though the ever-hungry Joe probably did not agree. Supper was our first 'ration' meal: rice and onions, mixed with a handful of what the Chinese call 'autumn blade fish' – tiny dried whitebait which had to be eaten up, as they were most of what we had left in the stores barrel. Nobody really liked the fish's taste but that was just as well. The insipid menu blunted our appetites so that the meal seemed sufficient. However, when it came to breakfast next day, and we received our helpings of bran and dried fruit – food which was popular – the miserable little serving of half a small bowl per man left everyone feeling rather hungry. Lunch was just as abstemious – a helping of last night's rice, served cold to save on our paraffin but quite appetising with a couple of wafer-thin slices of dried Chinese sausage, nuts, raisins and a single dried biscuit. All of us made the best of it, except Mark who held out his bowl and pointedly asked Geoffrey, 'Is that all?'

Mark seemed to be the only one of us finding it difficult to integrate fully into shipboard life. He tended to be slightly possessive, referring to 'my' tools or 'my' cabin when the rest of us shared fully and easily, and often he was rather blunt and tactless. It was, I supposed, because Mark had previously led such an independent and solitary life that he was unaware of the effect he had on others who were trying to be as easygoing as circumstances allowed. I hoped that with time Mark's slightly prickly manner would mellow as he came to trust his colleagues.

At least we no longer had the problem regarding fresh water, because a real monsoon deluge had fallen just before dusk the previous evening, then, after a short break, resumed after dark. Water cascaded everywhere, with a dense black sea and forked lightning sparking and fizzing in all directions and lighting up the horizon at every flash. We hastily dug out the advertising banners of our major sponsors, DHL and Hong Kong Telecom and the Mandarin Hotel, and stretched them flat to channel the rain into buckets. The water tasted a bit like the plastic of the banners, but we collected fifty litres in just half an hour, enough for at least three or four days with easy rationing.

Our target was now a chain of islands which stretch from a point sixty miles east of Taiwan all the way to the main islands of Japan. Scattered across an arc 650 miles long, the Ryukyus are so widely spaced that it was by no means certain just where the current and wind would take us, if it brought us to land at all and did not spit us through one of the wide gaps between the islands. After the lesson of failing to hit the very much larger island of Taiwan, I decided that the best bet was simply to steer *Hsu Fu* along the length of the Ryukyu arc, riding the Black Stream. Sooner or later, I hoped, we would find one of the Ryukyus directly in our path. I just hoped that this would happen before we ran entirely out of cooking fuel and were eating cold meals all day long. Also the islands themselves had to be approached with caution. Many of them were the tops of volcanoes poking out of the ocean, and most were surrounded by deadly coral reefs.

We were beginning to see ships again. Occasionally a big tanker or a bulk gas-carrier, like a bloated grain silo floating on its side, crossed our path. They must have been travelling from the Middle East to bring raw material to the hungry petro-chemical industries of Japan. On 9 June we managed to contact one of the tankers, the *Venus Victory*, on the walky-talky and her radio operator promised to report our position to Hong Kong. Three hours later, to our puzzlement, a small fishing boat scurried up in our wake, firing red distress rockets. I picked up the binoculars to take a closer look. There, on the deck of the fishing boat, jumping up and down, and waving frantically was the small but unmistakable figure of our Japanese artist, Nina.

We had last seen Nina in Hong Kong. She had come there from Tokyo to see us off and make sketches of our departure. From the very outset in Vietnam, Nina had always been determined to sail aboard *Hsu Fu* and at Halong Bay she and I had agreed that it would be more sensible if she waited until the raft reached Taiwan and she rejoined the crew there. As it turned out, the delay proved to be fortunate. Towards the end of her stay in Vietnam Nina had fallen ill with Hepatitis A, and on her return to Japan had spent a month in hospital. Even to come to see us leave Hong Kong she had discharged herself temporarily from hospital, and was so weak that she had been taken off the plane in a wheelchair when she arrived. She had hidden this fact from us, and stubbornly tried once again to join the crew. But I had been firm – meet us in Taiwan, I said, and then sail aboard *Hsu Fu* for the voyage up to Japan. So she had completed her treatment in hospital, gone to Taipei, and waited. Only *Hsu Fu* had sailed right past.

But Nina, as persistent and determined as ever, was not to be thwarted. When our friends in the Taiwanese Yachting Association had heard nothing from the raft, they decided to charter a fishing boat to search for us. Nina had insisted on accompanying the vessel when it set out. Theoretically the search was a wild-goose chase. With so much ocean and no real idea where to look for us, the chances of finding the raft were close to nil. Nevertheless, the Taiwanese yachtsmen, led by Robert Wu, had set sail, made an educated guess as to where *Hsu Fu* might be, and zigzagged back and forth checking on any targets they found on radar. For a day and night they had searched, and found nothing. The fishing boat skipper wanted to turn back because he was running low on fuel, but Nina and Robert Wu had insisted – try for just two more hours. Then they saw a blip on the radar screen, went to investigate, and found to their disappointment that it was an oil-tanker. Have you seen a sailing raft? they enquired by radio. And by an extraordinary stroke of luck, the oil-tanker was the *Venus Victory* and replied, 'Yes, we spoke to the raft *Hsu Fu* just one hour ago.' So here was Nina waving, yelling greetings, and trying to make quick sketches at the same time.

'Geoffrey, this is your chance to get a lift back to Taiwan and then to Hong Kong,' I said. 'The fishing boat will take you.'

He looked a little dejected. 'I feel bad about leaving you at such short notice,' he said. 'It's been a wonderful experience.'

'We'll miss you as quartermaster,' I said. 'But we still don't know where or when we will come to land. Better take the chance while you can.'

So Geoffrey scrambled up on the Taiwanese fishing boat, Nina came aboard *Hsu Fu* and after the Taiwanese yachtsmen had checked that all was well with us and left fresh fruit and bottles of drinking water, the fishing boat turned for home. We tidied up the bags of oranges and bananas, and then we all – Mark, Joe, Loi, Nina and myself, sat down in the cockpit to share a toast.

'Suddenly it feels quite different without Geoffrey here,' said Mark wistfully. 'It's just that he has left so suddenly, without either him or us mentally preparing for his departure.'

'It's always the same,' I observed. 'Without noticing it, a crew living and working together becomes a close-knit unit. Then whenever someone joins or leaves the group, it makes a profound change.'

'Well, he was a great quartermaster,' said Joe. And we raised a toast. 'To the voyage of *Hsu Fu,* to our allies in the Taiwanese Yachting Association . . . and to absent friends.'

Nina had arrived at just the right moment. The next afternoon at 4 p.m. on 10 June a twin-engined plane appeared from the north-west heading low and straight for us. As it turned and circled we could see the rising-sun emblem of Japan on the fuselage and the markings of the Japanese Coastguard. I showed Nina how to use the walky-talky, and she began to answer the questions which came from the sky: Who were we? Did we need help? Where were we bound from, and where were we headed? How much food and water did we have on board? Satisfied with our answers the plane flew off. Only later did it become apparent that the flight had also been on anti-piracy patrol. That same night *Hsu Fu* was approached by the green-and-white pirate vessel, and Nina and I nearly asked it for a tow.

The feeling that we had come under the protective umbrella of a rich and powerful nation became even more pronounced next morning,

Pirate Inspection

when another Coastguard aircraft – this time a large helicopter – appeared and hovered over us while a film crew took pictures. Once again Nina spoke on the little radio, and after a rather shy beginning was chattering away happily using all the radio jargon. She told the helicopter crew that we would try to head for the island of Miyako some eighty miles to the south-west, depending on the wind. If the Coastguard could inform the port authorities, perhaps they could arrange for a local fishing boat to help us into harbour?

Scarcely had the helicopter clattered away than the north wind we were hoping for began to blow, and *Hsu Fu* picked up speed to three knots, modest for any normal vessel but very acceptable for our half-submerged raft. We were thoroughly satisfied even though the rain was now pelting down. We had just arranged sails and leeboards to our satisfaction and were relaxing in the cockpit when there was a distinct, loud creaking sound and the foremast snapped. In an instant the top third of the mast disappeared over the side in a tangle of timber, sailcloth and rigging, leaving a splintered mast top pointing to the sky. The accident happened in a Force 3–4 wind and in broad daylight which, apart from the rain, was about as convenient a time to lose a mast as one could hope for. Indeed, for a potential crisis there was no drama at all – Mark was running forward at once to gather up the loose sail and splintered spar from the water. Loi arrived a moment later, closely followed by Joe. Together they wrestled the soggy mass of ropes and canvas and bamboo battens on the roof of the forecabin, and lashed everything down securely. There was no panic, no shouting, just well-directed, sensible work while I kept at the helm, maintaining course. Stays were unrigged, ropes coiled, damage-limitation completed. Then the salvage team came back to the cockpit, dripping wet from the rain and from the seawater which had been surging up to their knees across the exposed foredeck. They were in high good humour. There was nothing like a minor emergency to bring a team closer together in the shared satisfaction of having reacted properly and effectively. I could see that *Hsu Fu* was in good hands.

7

ALONG THE
RYUKYU CHAIN

Miyako, surrounded by its pale coral reefs, was a low, green, and pleasant island whose population took life at an unhurried pace because they knew very well that they had the best of both worlds. On the one hand, they were entitled to all the benefits of being Japanese citizens, and Tokyo sent them generous grants of government aid. On the other, they lived in a semi-tropical climate hundreds of miles away in terms of space and mentality from the high-pressure work style that made this economic aid possible. The islanders of Miyako raised a small amount of sugar cane, hoped for an increase in tourism, fished the blue waters of the Pacific for tuna and bonito, and waited for the next allocation of public funds from Tokyo. They already had a fine airport, excellent medical facilities and telecommunications, and a splendid, almost empty, harbour into which *Hsu Fu* arrived on 12 June.

Waiting for us on the dock stood an array of officials, fourteen of them. There were representatives from the Customs Service, Medical Service, Harbour Office, Marine Safety Department, Immigration Department, and Coastguard. They were all lined up at the edge of the quay, neatly dressed in uniforms, some wearing forage caps, most with document cases or briefcases, some even wearing white gloves. It was as impressive an assembly of officialdom as I had ever seen, and normally I would have been discouraged at the vista of form-filling and question-answering that any such congregation would expect. After all, Miyako was an unplanned stopover for *Hsu Fu*. The island was Japanese territory, a part of Okinawa Prefecture, and none of us had Japanese visas. In addition, there was sure to be all the customary paperwork for any foreign ship arriving in a new country. But I sensed there was something about the swarm of officials which was unusual, something out of character. Then I realised what it was. All these minor functionaries were standing there, trying to look very correct and formal. But most of them were also finding it difficult to stop smiling. They looked not so much like grave officials, but children eager to have a treat.

The invasion of officials scrambled down on to *Hsu Fu* as if on a holiday outing. They peeked and peered at everything, asked questions like schoolchildren on a visit to a museum, and noted down Nina's answers on their clipboards. Had we enough food and water when we arrived . . . and what exactly did we eat on board? Could we explain our route from Hong Kong to Miyako? Please would we list our safety equipment, the radio, the distress beacon, and so forth? The uniformed officers crawled happily on hands and knees through the low cabins, murmuring with interest and calling out cheerful comments to one another. Then they clambered back on the jetty, straightened their jackets and dusted off the knees of their uniform trousers, and tried to assume a grave and official pose. As they prepared to leave, I could see that they felt they had to justify their mass excursion to the raft. Luckily a customs man caught sight of the last of the oranges and bananas given to us by the Taiwanese fishing boat. Ah! he admonished us, this was foreign produce, and it was against quarantine regulations to import it into Japan. We could eat the oranges and bananas aboard *Hsu Fu* while in Miyako Harbour, but on no account could we have any picnics ashore. Thus the agricultural integrity of Japan protected to general satisfaction, everyone climbed into their official cars, and departed. Later I discovered that many of the officials who had greeted us on the dockside had come across specially from the neighbouring island of Ishigaki, because foreign ships so seldom visited Miyako that the island did not have a full complement of officials. These visitors had every intention of spending the rest of the weekend on Miyako before going back home.

Before he left, the Senior Immigration Officer asked if Nina and I would go to the Harbour Master's office after lunch, and bring all our ship's papers and passports.

Two hours later Nina and I presented ourselves at the harbour administration building and were shown into spacious and clearly under-used offices. By then the officials had taken off their uniform jackets, and were displaying spotless shirts and dark ties. Their desks were equally neat and tidy, and singularly bare of paperwork. Nina's presence as a crew member on *Hsu Fu* was much in our favour. If we had a Japanese crew member, then nearly everything about *Hsu Fu* was going to be satisfactory. Joe, Mark and I were quickly given permission to stay for three months in Japan and to sail in Japanese waters, and a stamp was pressed into our passports. Loi, however, was another matter. Here the Chief Immigration Officer became serious. Loi was Vietnamese, he had no visa, and Japan did not issue visitor visas to Vietnamese citizens except in exceptional circumstances. Careful checks had to be made into the background of any applicant from Vietnam in case they were economic refugees, and preference was given to highly educated or qualified applicants. After a lengthy investigation lasting three or four months, for example, a visa might be given to someone with a university doctorate. I explained that Loi was a simple fisherman, and had never been near a university in his life. The senior immigration man apologised deeply, but until Loi's official status was decided by higher authority he was not allowed to leave the raft. He must stay aboard *Hsu Fu*. He should not even step ashore. What about going to the lavatory? I asked. Would he have to use the harbour water? There was a hurried consultation, and the restriction was lifted. He could go ashore to go to the lavatory, but had to return immediately to the raft. Meanwhile Miyako Immigration would send a message about Loi to their headquarters on the main island of Honshu.

For the next twenty-four hours Nina and I shuttled back and forward between raft and harbour office while Miyako Immigration dealt with the Loi problem in their own special way. On our second visit we were told that Central Immigration Office in Tokyo had confirmed that Loi could not be given a visa. But, said the Miyako immigration officer, I could appeal this decision. I filled in the relevant appeal form and it was sent off by fax. On our third visit I was told the appeal had been turned down, Loi was still refused a visa. But another appeal could be made to a Japanese court if there was sufficiently good grounds for doing so. This time I filled in a document saying that Loi was essential for the safety of the raft, as he was the only man who knew how to tie rattan. The immigration officer read this through with satisfaction, then asked for Loi's passport. A moment later I heard the sound of a rubber stamp hitting paper, and glanced over and saw that the Chief Immigration Officer was stamping a visa into Loi's passport even before the formal appeal had gone through the fax machine. The entire rigmarole, I realised, was just a charade. Miyako Immigration was following all the official procedures, but they had every intention of letting Loi ashore.

The Chief of Immigration then locked his filing cabinet and announced that Nina and I were wanted upstairs in another office. I anticipated another round of form-filling. But when we walked in through the door marked 'Customs,' we found most of the officials who had greeted us at the dock the previous day. They were sitting around a table loaded with cans of beer and bottles of sake. It was a party they announced, and they wanted to introduce us to the Miyako custom of *omori*. This involved making a short speech, then going round the group with a bottle of sake, filling everyone else's glass, and drinking a toast with each person in turn. After that the toastmaster nominated another speaker-drinker, and the process was repeated until every member of the group had made the rounds. Then the circle was repeated. Little wonder, as I subsequently found, Miyako was notorious throughout the Ryukyus for its consumption of alcohol and was the only island in the archipelago where life expectancy was less than the Japanese norm. On the other hand, it was difficult not to warm to the Miyako way of dealing with official regulations, and realise that we had made a lucky landfall.

The islanders were proud of their reputation, particularly when it came to comparisons with their neighbours on Ishigaki. In the nineteenth century the Ryukyus had been an independent kingdom ruled by a king on Naha or Okinawa Island, and Ishigaki and Miyako had been the remoter islands where the government sent troublemakers and convicted criminals. But the type of criminal was quite different. Political prisoners and intellectuals were sent to Ishigaki, while common felons, murderers and thieves served their sentences on Miyako. 'People on Ishigaki still think with their heads and are cool and offhand,' I was told in Miyako. 'But we are proud to be the descendants of common criminals who respond with their hearts. Here as we say, we have big stomachs!' and my informant patted his own.

In fact, the people of Miyako felt themselves to be islanders first, and Japanese only recently. Their original dialect, though based on the Japanese language, was not understood on the main islands of Japan, and the people of the archipelago were a racial mix between the Japanese from the north and sea peoples from South East Asia. The Ryukyus had been controlled by the Chinese, by the Japanese, and most recently by the United States who occupied these strategic islands after the Second World War, before handing them back to Japan in 1972. Throughout these changes, the people of Miyako had continued their relaxed lifestyle and kept up a tradition of hospitality. Everywhere that *Hsu Fu*'s crew

Loi and his Miyako family on the quay

went on Miyako we were given small presents, invited in for meals, and offered help. An empty apartment within walking distance of the harbour was found for us where we could cook and sleep and wash. Every evening the local sub-aqua club invited us to their get-togethers where they barbecued the fish and shellfish they collected during the day, and then spent the rest of the evening practising *omori*.

Loi had announced that he much preferred sleeping on the raft even after he received his visa. He was more comfortable there, he said. So after supper with the Miyako divers I went with Nina to check that he was all right. As we came within sight of the jetty, I saw a little group sitting on the quayside. It was a Miyako family of mother, father and two small children gathered around a lantern on the ground. Loi himself was seated with the family, looking totally content as they conversed with sign language. Nina asked the visitors if she could translate. 'Oh no!' they laughed. 'We thought the Vietnamese sailor might be lonely so we came to keep him company. We've brought him food, and we will try to teach him some words of Japanese, and make sure he enjoys our island.' Every night after that, the same family and their friends could be seen chatting with Loi far into the night.

Miyako's town was a jumble of narrow streets, extending back from the harbour and lined with small well-stocked shops. Everything was on a small scale. Even the traffic was mostly mini-cars and mini-vans which purred up and down the streets, or went out to the well-tended suburbs

Traditional house, Miyako

of small bungalows and occasional modest shopping centres. Everyone seemed to have ample time on their hands. By day a succession of the little mini-vans would roll down to the jetty, park, and the drivers would simply sit there quietly for ten minutes gazing at the raft before driving off again.

Meanwhile we set about the serious business of replacing the broken foremast. Miyako had looked green from a distance, but the trees were not suitable for making masts. We were given permission to go wherever we wanted and cut down any tree that might suit us. But the trees would be too weak, we were told. Whenever a typhoon struck the island, the tops of the trees snapped off rather as Mr Ching's chestnut pole had snapped. So, with the help of Mr Sugama, the local shipping agent, we visited the backyard of the telephone company and scavenged two discarded wooden telegraph poles. We decided we needed two poles because Mark was worried by a weak spot in *Hsu Fu*'s mainmast and feared that it too would break. It would be better to replace the mainmast as well as the foremast while we had the chance. Mark then spent a week on the waterfront carefully planing down the telegraph poles to the right shape. All day long the local fishermen and building workers of Miyako would call by to bring him snacks, soft drinks, and small gifts. One day it was a new folding saw to cut timber, the next it was a replacement hammer handle made from the special tough wood of a kendo fighting stick.

Mark had originally volunteered to sail aboard *Hsu Fu* only as far as Taiwan. Now Taiwan was a couple of hundred miles behind us, so I asked him if he wanted to leave the crew and return to Hong Kong. No! he replied without hesitation. He was enjoying himself much too much, and would like to continue through to Tokyo if there was space for him aboard the raft. He was such a first-class workman that I had no hesitation in accepting his offer, though *Hsu Fu* would now be rather crowded as we would be a crew of six, because on Miyako we had at last been joined by our other original volunteer – Rex.

The first thing you noticed about Rex was his bushy red beard. It gave him a definite nautical air. The second feature you noticed was his thick spectacles which then made you think he might be an academic or doctor. This latter impression was then reinforced by his manner, which was quiet, polite, and very carefully considered. In fact, Rex was the most methodical and well-organised of men. Everything he did was planned in advance. He made lists, considered options, reviewed alternatives, and knew in advance exactly how he would spend his time for the next twelve months. Of medium height and medium build, there was nothing – except that red beard – to indicate that he was a passionate sailor. Rex was captivated by the sea in a way that others might be avid golf players or inveterate bird watchers. Rex read books about the sea, wrote magazine articles about the sea and sailing, mixed with friends who were interested in the sea, and even managed to scrape his living from the sea. He organised expeditions aboard his vintage sailing yacht, worked for nominal wages on the restoration of wooden sailing ships, and volunteered for any maritime expedition which was aboard a traditional sailing vessel. He did not possess Mark's craft skills, but Rex was competent to stitch canvas, splice ropes, handle sails, steer, and navigate. Rex was qualified to find a berth aboard a ship, preferably wooden and under square sail, where he could spend month after month on the ocean, and he did not care if he was wet, cold, and uncomfortable. In short, he was ideally suited for long-distance sailing on an increasingly waterlogged bamboo raft.

We stayed nine days at Miyako, and not only replaced the two masts but also succeeded in solving one element of the problem with the little satellite radio, which I took with me to Okinawa where American technicians working near the huge US airbase reinstalled a corrupted software programme. The lack of battery power, however, was to plague us until the main battery was replaced at our next port of call in Japan. Joe, meanwhile, had been put in charge of *Hsu Fu*'s food stores now that Geoffrey had gone. It was on the principle of turning the poacher into the gamekeeper. If ever-hungry Joe was put in charge of our food stocks, I reasoned, we would be sure to have a keen interest in the quality and amount of our food reserves. But shopping for food in Miyako brought a rude shock. The prices were breathtaking. Many items were three or four times more expensive than in Europe or Hong Kong, and our modest expedition budget could barely cope. Nina and Joe prowled the aisles of the supermarkets, while Nina translated the names on the packages, and Joe did his sums. Finally they collected together enough of the very cheapest food to supplement the remaining Hong Kong supplies and last us the three- or four-week voyage to the main islands of Japan, the next sector of our journey.

By 21 June we were ready to leave, and Mr Sugama was fussing on the quayside, beckoning to the little tug that would tow *Hsu Fu* out of harbour. Many of our new-found Miyako friends had come to see us off. There were the young scuba diving enthusiasts from the Miyako diving school. There were representatives from the Harbour Master's office and the Maritime Safety Agency who had checked our refurbished radio, and wanted to wish us good luck. And there was a shy little man who used to come on his motor-scooter every day after work just to sit on the quayside and gaze down at *Hsu Fu* until it was time for him to go home for his supper. He was a local government employee, I was told, and today had taken a day of his annual holiday in order to see us off. Loi's 'family' were there too, and they came loaded with gifts for him: a wristwatch, a clock, and a small portable radio. Paper ribbons were thrown between the raft and the bystanders as *Hsu Fu* was gently towed clear, and the yellow-and-green streamers stretched and stretched until they broke, and we lost our link with our happy island. All of us were sad to be leaving Miyako, but also we were glad to be on our way again, continuing with the voyage. We had made our first stopover, adapted and refitted *Hsu Fu* as best we could, and we knew that we had been lucky that the Black Stream and the wind had brought us to such a friendly and intimate landfall.

It is astonishing how quickly sailors return to their habitat. One moment they are ashore, feeling and behaving as landsmen, each with his individual interests and agenda, free to come and go as he pleases. The next moment they are back aboard ship and at sea, within constant sight and sound of one another, and smoothly re-establishing familiar habits and routines as if there had been no interruption. By common, unspoken agreement everyone is once again part of the team.

Those first twenty-four hours out of Miyako were special. The sky was a bright tropical blue, the ocean a deep azure, the Black Stream flowed in our favour, and a fine south-westerly monsoon breeze blew the puffy white clouds and the raft north-eastward. In a single day our raft covered ninety-nine miles. Loi caught a splendid dorado to provide juicy fresh fish cutlets. Only Nina was out of sorts. She confessed that after stopping at any port she was seasick for two or three days . . . and proceeded to prove it.

Naturally we kept a close eye on our two new masts to see if they would make any difference. They were fine and sturdy, but there was no doubt that they were much heavier than Mr Ching's chestnut masts. The extra weight acted as levers which made *Hsu Fu* twist and wrack even more. After a few days on shore I had forgotten just how flexible was our bamboo raft. Now the fifteen-foot swells built up by the monsoon wind made the boat bend and corkscrew alarmingly, and the foremast swayed from side to side, completely out of synchronisation with the mainmast so that at one time you saw the foremast leaning well out to the left of the mainmast, then a few seconds later it appeared swaying out to the right. I feared that the raft might literally twist itself into two halves under such colossal strain, and wondered at the workmanship of the raftbuilders of Sam Son and the miles of rattan that they had tied to hold the raft together. Also the stern of the raft was drooping noticeably lower. The bumpkin, the wooden pole extending aft to hold the ropes that controlled the mizzen-sail, was now underwater more of the time than above it. It plunged regularly in and out of the waves with the rocking motion of the boat, now and again scooping up the trailing safety line, Loi's fishing-line, or the cable for the log rotor that told us what speed we were doing. Where else I wondered did you find a vessel where sails were controlled by underwater ropes emerging from the sea? We had brought along our old masts as spares in case the former telegraph poles were flawed, and now there was no doubt that *Hsu Fu* was deeper in the water under the extra weight of our new spars and the extra stores. The breaking waves were washing clear across the midships space between the cabins. As they surged against the mainmast they broke and splashed in foam and spray which flicked into the cabins.

In the cockpit, too, I noticed how the larger swells coming up from astern, now rose right through the structure of the raft, collided with the aft face of the cockpit basket, and very often broke over the top rim, slopping water over our feet. These wave attacks were nothing dangerous yet; just a warning that a breaking sea might one day dump tons of water in the cockpit, swamp and drag down the stern. With every following wave came the regular whoosh of the crest surging up through the bamboos in the stern, swirling between the 'organ pipes', and then sweeping past each side of the cockpit basket, lapping at the edges in foam. Beneath one's feet the pressure of each passing wave pushed up against the flexible basketwork floor of the cockpit, which heaved up so that it felt like we were standing on jelly. I watched the passing waves and worried: would the cockpit or the cabin baskets one day be washed away completely by a massive breaking sea, and part company with the body of the raft? Or I watched the whole length of the raft heave and bend on the backs of the rollers, and I feared that *Hsu Fu* would snap, quite literally, in half. As she rode the crest of each wave, *Hsu Fu*'s body hung limply down each side in a reverse curve that must surely put a tremendous strain on the structure. I saw how the bow sagged weakly downward into the trough, only suddenly to reverse the bend as the wave travelled forward, pushing up the bow so that the raft took up the opposite bend. It was like taking a day-old, soggy stick of French bread and bending it back and forth. Surely at some stage, I thought, it would simply tear apart.

The second morning revealed that the constant flexing had snapped the two massive ropes, the hogging trusses, which we rigged like huge bowstrings along each side of the raft to hold it in a curved profile. The ropes were five inches in circumference and made of best manila, but they had snapped like cotton. The broken pieces had to be dismantled, carefully spliced together, and then rerigged. It was a job which took all morning, and before we had finished, another monsoon rain squall came hissing across the sea. I yelled at the crew to leave the work and lower the mainsail to just two panels. In the blinding haze of the rainstorm, it was impossible to see fifty yards, and surface of the sea seemed to be beaten flat, literally smoking with the force of the downpour, which came squirting in though every crack and rattan lashing hole in the cabin roofs as usual. Rex, unperturbed, quickly stripped off naked to wash himself and his clothes in the deluge of fresh water. An hour later when the squall had passed us by, we went round the raft to check the rig and found to our satisfaction that nothing had broken or failed during the onslaught. Instead we were left clean-smelling and well washed.

Now that the satellite radio was in working order, it turned out that we had a problem with the power supply to run it. In theory we had enough solar panels, eight in all, to generate sufficient electricity to store in the special twelve-volt battery, and the same battery could run *Hsu Fu*'s navigation lights and recharge the batteries of the hand torches we used on night watch. But the eight solar panels were not working to full capacity. They were lashed with string to the cabin tops, the only space available, and depending on the time of day, only half of them faced directly towards the sun. Also, the monsoon overcast tended to cut down the amount of solar energy available. We tried to be as frugal as possible, switching on the masthead light only when another vessel was coming close and needed to be alerted to our presence, and keeping use of hand torches to a minimum. But it was not enough. The radio could receive messages, but when I tried to send our daily reports, it ran out of power after fifteen seconds. Clearly it was time to set up our windmill to produce extra power, and there was much discussion as to where and how to rig it in the best place to catch the wind, but at the same time to erect it clear of all the normal working areas so that no crew member was injured by the whirling blades. Mark lashed the windmill to the inevitable bamboo pole, and we tried propping it near the stern. But by general agreement this arrangement was too unstable – the windmill was quite heavy – and it was too close to heads and arms for comfort. Should the windmill slip and fall, it would have come crashing down into the cockpit which was always occupied, and caused injury. Eventually Mark found a place for it far in the bows of the raft, like a miniature fourth mast. There the windmill spun away happily for the next four months, performing nobly, supplying all the power we needed, and well out of harm's way.

In fact, the windmill provided too much power. On 27 June we were all enjoying a leisurely breakfast in the cockpit on a bright sunny morning, when Mark said quietly and casually, 'Tim, there's a fire in the cabin.' I glanced up and saw smoke oozing out of the cabin door, and the glimmer of flames inside. I dropped my bowl of breakfast and dived head first into the cabin. On the cabin wall hung the waterproof briefcase which acted as the junction box for the wires to the windmill and the solar panels. Blue flames were running up and down the wires, and blobs of melted plastic insulation were dripping down. The cabin thatch would catch fire at any moment. I wrapped a rag around my hand, wrenched free the burning cable, and surveyed the mess. There had been a meltdown of plastic plugs and connectors, and charred cable. Thankfully, there was no secondary damage and I could mend the connections. When I checked the circuits I found that tiny threads of coconut fibre had got mixed in with the insulation and served as wicks, sucking seawater into the connections and causing a short circuit.

The calm way that everyone took this little drama in their stride emphasised how much our attitudes to raft sailing had changed since starting from Hong Kong. On that first sector much of our life had seemed damp and uncomfortable and disorganised as *Hsu Fu* plodded slowly along or simply drifted. Now when the wind dropped, we low-ered the useless sails, and everyone went about the maintenance and improvement of the raft according to the plans we had discussed over breakfast. Loi replaced worn rattan lashings. His work was endless among the constant wrenching and abrasion of the vessel. Mark designed and installed improvements to the masts and sails. Rex had established himself as the rope and rigging man, knotting, splicing, whipping ends, replacing worn sections. Joe lent a hand to all, and supplied much of the muscle. Nina, emerging from her bout of seasickness, would sketch and draw, and answer everyone else's questions about daily life in Japan. She was still a little unsure of herself on board, and one afternoon was sitting on the main cabin roof sketching, when the mainsail swung across acci-dentally, brushing her off. The rest of us heard a thin squeak, and started calling for her as she had vanished from sight. She crawled back up on the cabin roof looking dazed and bleeding from a cut behind the left ear where the boom had struck her. Joe examined the wound, and made her lie down in the cabin for a couple of hours, but she felt well enough to stand her watch that night.

The third dawn brought the most spectacular scene of the voyage so far. In the night the Black Stream had swept *Hsu Fu* close alongside a vol-canic island, and when the sun rose, it seemed that a painter of stage scenery had been at work. A mile away the mysterious bulk of the island climbed up to a volcanic cone in the centre, ending with the scoop of the caldera where a volcanic explosion had blown the peak away. Lower down and a little to the left rose the slimmer, more pointed cone of a second, subsidiary volcano. The slopes of both volcanoes were grey ash and black rock on the upper parts, pale green forest on the lower slopes. On the shore facing us shafts of sunrise picked out the dark emerald of cultivated land behind the beach, and the pale crescents of three sandy coves bright among the dark lava rock. To our right, at the southern end of the island, stood the spike of a lighthouse, and beyond it again reared up a pair of rocks shaped like the short horns of a snail. With the sun behind the peak, and clouds streaming from its volcanic summit, it looked to deserve its name – Takara Shima or 'Treasure Island'.

Past Takara Shima, I steered *Hsu Fu* east to cut through the Ryukyu chain, and head for the main islands of Japan. We were well pleased with ourselves, for this was the best sustained progress so far. Here occurred the only real flare-up among the crew when Mark started snapping and

Takara Shima - 'Treasure Island '

snarling at Loi, half in jest but half-seriously. They were sorting out a tangled fishing-line in the cockpit, and Mark had the fishing-line held in his mouth in order to free up his two hands as he untangled knots. Loi, not looking, jerked on the fishing-line which tugged painfully at Mark's mouth. Mark, as I had noticed earlier when he was struck on the leg by a piece of wood, reacted petulantly to pain, slapped at Loi and shouted at him. Then he repeated the abuse, and slapped him a second time. Loi, who had certainly not done anything intentionally to harm Mark, looked taken aback and hurt.

'Steady, Mark!' I had to interpose, as Mark continued to flare.

'It hurt!' he said peevishly. Then mimed the action of the line pulling at his mouth, and glared at Loi.

Handicapped by his lack of English, Loi looked uncomfortable and wounded. I felt sorry that Loi, with his lack of English, could neither retort, nor explain, nor apologise. He could only shut down and be unhappy, and for the next hour or so kept silent. Loi was such a straight-forward and friendly person that his linguistic isolation had to be very difficult for him. I knew that he longed to be able to talk with us, and on his morning watches he still studied his home-made word list diligently, as if staring at the list would make him learn the language. But he was making very little progress even though Joe and the others spent time trying to coach him. Fortunately the incident with Mark blew over, and the two men were fishing and joking together afterwards, Mark shame-faced and conscious that he had acted unreasonably. But I still worried that Loi's isolation would one day be too much for him.

Each day *Hsu Fu* seemed to settle a fraction deeper in the water. When we left Hong Kong I had noted that the waterline was across the middle of the central layer of bamboos on the stern. Now these bamboos were totally submerged, and there was seaweed growing halfway up the top layer of bamboos which had once been clean of any weed. As the raft's stern sank lower, seawater was beginning to ooze up through the floor of the cockpit so that the wickerwork and tar was always wet underfoot. The bases of the two cabins were still dry, but the impression was that *Hsu Fu* had sunk two or three inches in the seven weeks of the voyage so far. How long can this go on for? I wondered. Was the raft slowly foundering as sections of the bamboo split, the trapped air escaped and they lost their buoyancy and let in water? Or would the rate of sinking slow down and stop as the raft achieved equilibrium? The most positive sign was that the rattan lashings of the main hull seemed to be holding firm. There was no visible evidence of the three-layer main hull breaking up despite the alarming hogging and sagging that took place as the raft undulated over the swells. Nor were the terrible creaks and groans so alarming now they could be identified. There was the harsh squeal of the rudder post rubbing on the rear cockpit rail; the tenor groan of the bamboos running between the cabin roofs which we used as walkways, and the sudden thump when the wooden storage boxes shifted position. Everywhere was a constant rubbing, sawing, and abrad-ing as the raft flexed and twisted. It was a paradox that flexibility and resilience was needed to save *Hsu Fu* structurally, but at any moment a rope half-worn through by a rubbing bamboo might snap, or an electric cable be pinched and short out, destroying the equipment it served.

On 30 June I awoke to find that Joe and Loi, who had the dawn watch, were not in the cockpit but sitting up on the cabin roof. They had taken refuge there, they explained, because so many wave tops had been breaking over the stern of the cockpit basket and drenching them regu-larly. As usual, *Hsu Fu* did not need steering, but kept steadily to her course with the tillers fastened into position by a wooden pin rail. Wave tops breaking into the cockpit were not serious, but these were quite *small* waves, and later on in the open Pacific Ocean the waves could be much larger and swamp the raft entirely. One immediate solution was to try to lighten the ship, so I gave the order to dump overboard the old mainmast and the broken foremast. It went against the grain to jettison spare timber when *Hsu Fu* was already low on reserves and we had not been able to find any spare bamboo on Miyako. But if we got rid of the old masts, we would be losing at least a quarter-ton of dead weight. The crew clipped on their safety harnesses and lined up on the edge of the main hull, the waves surging over their legs, while they inched aft the old mainmast until they could shove it into the waves, and it floated away in our wake, our companion since the far-off days of sailing trials in Halong.

As *Hsu Fu* closed with the coast of Japan's main islands, we were once again among the big ships. The wind dropped, then turned to north, and it became cold, grey and miserable. Showers of rain, some of them very heavy, came sweeping off the land, and we experienced a peculiar visibility which played hide-and-seek with objects. One afternoon I saw the huge grey mass of a supertanker steering towards us, some three miles distant in the murk. Yet when I looked again, five minutes later, the great vessel had disappeared totally although it had to be much closer. Yet the murk looked no thicker. Once, briefly, I saw her outline again, safely on a parallel course. I knew the monster ship must be passing within a mile, yet I never saw her again. She was simply swallowed up like a phantom. The same thing happened an hour later when an enormous car-carrier ship – a giant shoe box of grey metal gliding across the sea and as big as a block of flats – appeared just a mile ahead, not out of fog but from what seemed to be a transparent grey horizon which played tricks on one's eyes.

Nina was now suffering from exhaustion, the combined effects of the blow on the head from the mainsail boom, and her premature departure from hospital. She looked so washed-out and wretched that I excused her from cooking or watchkeeping so that she could concentrate on her artwork when she felt strong enough or curl up in a sleeping bag and rest. Joe gave her rehydration salts to sip, and she lay there feeling very sorry for herself, bitterly disappointed that after all her tenacious efforts to join the crew she was not fit enough to participate fully. The grey clammy weather depressed her even more, and she wept a little. All of us were beginning to feel the strain, and when one night Nina complained, first to me, then to Joe, and then to me again at 5 a.m., waking me to do so, that there was a drip coming down on her from the cabin roof and she wished to discuss what should be done about it, she got curt answers. Joe told her brusquely that the drip was imaginary and that she should go back to sleep. I was just as cross when Nina then wanted to make us shift our sleeping bags, regardless of the fact that there was no place in the cabin to avoid the drips. It turned out that Nina had never been camping or even slept in a tent and was puzzled that water running down the side of the cabin wetted a towel that she had left pressed against it. Then I felt guilty that I had shown my anger and frustration. I felt sorry for her being unwell, and knew I was not being sufficiently grateful for her presence which had made such a huge difference in making all the arrangements in Miyako, and now on board the raft whenever we used the little VHF radio to contact the Japanese Coastguard and report our progress in Japanese. Yet at the same time, both Joe and I felt it was irresponsible of Nina to have pushed so hard to join the raft and stay on it when she knew she was not sufficiently recovered from her illness.

We did not realise it then but *Hsu Fu* was sailing through the worst summer on record in Japan for the previous forty years. There was so little sunshine and so much rain that the Japanese rice crop would fail to ripen, and the annual harvest would be a disaster. Aboard *Hsu Fu* it was difficult to believe that each day could continue to be so wet and unpleasant, and we kept on hoping that the next would bring a change, the sun would begin to shine, and that the summer would really begin.

July 2 and 3 brought perhaps the two most unpleasant days of the China Voyage so far. It all began well enough with the wind dying and then backing into the east – a head wind – as we approached Cape Muroto, a tall bluff-headed promontory on the south side of Shikoku. My intention was to stand off and on the cape until the head wind changed. But Muroto proved to be a sort of maritime crossroads with three lines of ships converging on it – from Tokyo and Yokohama in the north-east, from the south tip of Japan, and emerging from the Inland Sea. These lines of traffic met off the point, so that there were perhaps six to ten vessels in sight at any time. Of course they kept a sharp lookout in such congested waters for their own safety. But they were not looking out for a small, insignificant speck of a slow-moving bamboo raft. Ships churned past us, before us, alongside us, behind us, travelling across our bows or across the stern, travelling parallel, travelling diagonally, and all intent on going about their commercial business. It seemed that ships were moving in every direction and we were helpless in the middle of the traffic.

We had just got used to this sensation of being in the middle of a maritime motorway – or at least a little less nervous each time we saw a vessel heading straight down at us – when the wind died and the weather deteriorated sharply. By late afternoon the sky was completely opaque and a thick gloom hung over the ocean as if night had fallen prematurely. The sea was a dirty slate-green. Then the wind began to increase in strength, still from the east and blocking any progress. The new wind brought rain, and not just showers, but a constant soaking deluge flying sometimes straight at us. As the wind speed varied, so did the strength of the rain. At times it was a spitting hail, at others a complete deluge which shut down visibility to a circle around us of perhaps fifty yards. Inside that circle everything was grey – the sea, the air, the horizon. For hour after hour the rain kept up, all through the night, all the next day, and for most of the following night too. There was no respite. The dampness and wet penetrated everywhere. It mildewed towels, made sleeping bags clammy, soaked the pressed bamboo of the cockpit floor so it was unpleasantly slimy. Water penetrated the two cabins, ran down the sides, gathered in pools, speckled droplets on clothing and personal possessions. It was impossible to avoid being wet. To move outside the cabin meant putting on oilskins, wet outside and with wet linings. In short, the conditions were foul, and the cabins began to smell of damp clothing and unwashed bodies – it was too miserable to wash, and impossible to get dry again. Feet turned clammy and white, ropes swelled and became difficult to handle as the knots jammed; hair became damp, greasy and lank. And we could no longer see the ships churning towards us. We could hear them all right, particularly when lying in the cabin when we felt the characteristic vibration of ships' propellers through the bamboo hull or heard the thud and rumble of diesel engines. But to see them in the murk was impossible.

At night matters became even more fraught. One storage battery had failed so we did not have the power to run our masthead light all the time, and the fog meant that the solar panels were useless. So we peered into the distance trying to work out whether the lights of ships meant they were steaming straight at us or would pass us by. When we feared a collision we switched on our puny masthead light, and its bulb shone an insipid yellow, instead of bright white, from its tired battery. If there was no reaction from the advancing vessel, no change of course, then we sacrificed a few more milliwatts from the battery and turned on the flashing masthead light. And when *that* failed to have any effect, and the ship came thumping straight at us oblivious of our presence, then we prepared to strike a flare – one of our precious store of six – to warn the vessel that we were straight in her path. Except that the first time a flare was needed, I rubbed it briskly to ignite it, following the maker's instructions, only to produce a faint spark and no blaze of light at all. The striking mechanism was damp. I cursed the manufacturer who failed to make good quality equipment on which men's lives would depend. Our raft was no wetter than an inflatable rubber life-raft at sea, and castaways on a life-raft would have needed a reliable flare even more than we did. But the flare was useless and I tossed it overboard. A quick scrabble through the barrel of safety equipment kept by the helm in case we had to abandon the raft in a hurry, and a replacement flare was found, struck, and burst into a sputtering blaze of blinding white light. It worked! The advancing ship suddenly veered off collision course.

By late afternoon on the second day of continuous fog and misery I had grown tired and inattentive to my duties as skipper and navigator. I was helping out with shipwork, lashing down barrels of food and stores, and did not check our position when I should have done. Then to my dismay I suddenly caught sight of cliffs off to one side of the raft. The wind had pushed us right against the coast and into the Bay of Tosa where we would find it difficult to escape. 'Embayed' is the old-fashioned phrase to describe an unhandy vessel caught in such a place, unable to sail out the way she had entered, trapped by the wind and weather and land, and gradually being driven ashore. I explained our situation to the crew, and told them that we had no choice but to double back and forth like a trapped hare until hopefully the wind direction changed and allowed us to retreat. If that failed, our only other chance was to throw an anchor overboard and hope it caught before our raft was driven on to the inhospitable and dimly seen shore. The crew took it well, more concerned with hoping for a change in the wind. By now the strong east wind had built up long rollers which came surging up out of the darkness to our right, broke and went storming through and under *Hsu Fu*'s hull. She did surprisingly well – not flexing too much, staying relatively and no more wet than usual. Rex later commented on how smoothly she rode out the waves. Yet we were still being beaten on to the coast, and a lighthouse seemed to be looming over us, when, almost miraculously, the wind changed into the south-west. We wore ship and painfully crept out of the bay, counting the lights of the houses inching past us on the shore as we made two knots forward for every one knot sideways. We held our breath, hoping the wind would keep its strength and direction, and as daylight broke we found ourselves frighteningly close under Cape Muroto, waddling past the menacing teeth of rocks at the foot of the cliffs.

Muroto Misaki

8

H su Fu's
J apanese Shrine

We cleared Cape Muroto by less than a quarter of a mile, and lumbered gratefully out to sea, feeling rather shaken. The trouble was that *Hsu Fu* was so awkward to steer that you either aimed close to shore and risked a shipwreck, or you stayed a safe distance off the land and ran the equal danger of being swept past your destination as had happened at Taiwan. To navigate a bamboo sailing raft successfully you needed the right wind or the right current or both, at just the right time.

We had put a safe distance between ourselves and the cape when a small Japanese fishing boat appeared, roaring towards us over the swell. It was typical for the area, built like a speedboat with a long, narrow hull, flared deck, and bristling with radio aerials and electronic gadgetry. It was operated by one man. Short and well muscled, he was about forty-five years old, with a close-cropped head, very fair skin, and burly forearms. He handled his boat skilfully, spinning his craft so that it came to rest close alongside and he could shout his questions. Who were we? What nationality? Didn't we know there was a gale forecast with very heavy rain and high seas? He himself was heading for port and safety. Our vessel looked too flimsy to stay out in bad conditions. Were we sure we would be all right? He repeated this last question many times, to make certain that Nina understood. He looked very tough and competent and was clearly worried about our safety.

'It's all right,' Nina called back to him, 'we've been through plenty of bad weather before, and the raft is very safe.'

'Where have you come from?'

'We've sailed here from Hong Kong!'

The fisherman's mouth dropped open in astonishment. For a moment he looked as if he had been hit over the head with a plank. Then he went to a big plastic fish box, and hauled out a large red ocean fish. This he heaved across to us so that it fell with a heavy thump on *Hsu Fu*'s fore-deck. A present!

'Wait a minute,' Nina called out to him. 'Can you tell us about the Black Stream?'

The fisherman gestured towards the east. 'Go a little farther and out there it runs very strongly,' he shouted. His curiosity satisfied, he was in a hurry to get to port, and was reaching for the engine throttles.

'Ask him about the bamboo fishing floats,' I urged Nina. 'Quick! Try to find out how long they stay afloat.' Off Cape Muroto we had passed a line of fishing markers made of bamboo bundles.

Nina waved frantically to attract the fisherman's attention, and he reversed his boat so she could yell the question across to him. 'How long do your bamboo net markers stay afloat?' she called. The burly fisher-man looked puzzled, and Nina explained her question again. Then he understood, and thought for a long moment, before answering. Nina did not have to translate. The fisherman had held up five fingers to make sure we understood. 'He says the bamboo floats for five months,' said Nina. The rest of us had already burst out laughing. *Hsu Fu* had been launched nearly four months earlier, so in theory we had only one month to go before she sank. Yet we had barely covered a third of the distance between China and America, and had at least three months to go. Mark went forward to retrieve a piece of bamboo flotsam, a stick he had picked out of the ocean earlier that day. He struck it sharply against the edge of the cockpit and the bamboo crumpled in his hand. It was totally waterlogged and decomposed.

'Oh well,' he said with a grin, 'only a month left.'

The fisherman's gale warning proved to be entirely accurate. But this time the wind came from exactly the direction we wanted. *Hsu Fu* trundled off on an exhilarating downwind run, and I took the risk of steering directly for the headland of Shiono Misaki, the next turning point on our Japanese course. The risk paid off, and we came surging past the headland right on track for our destination, the little port of Shingu, which every year cele-brated their most famous visitor – the First Emperor's mariner, Hsu Fu.

Whether or not there was any truth in the story that Hsu Fu landed at Shingu 2,000 years earlier, the citizens of Shingu certainly honoured his memory. The town had a shrine to Hsu Fu, another site which was shown as the mariner's grave, a memorial to his band of disciples, and a flourishing branch of the Hsu Fu Association. The latter sent a motor-boat to greet our raft as we approached a magnificent coastline of imposing cliffs and headlands, with tier upon tier of forest-clad mountains rising up into the mists. The surroundings of Shingu were wild and rumpled, far more dramatic than anything I had expected. The sea around us had changed from the dark waters of the Black Stream, first to bright turquoise, then to a pale sandy green as the water shallowed in Shingu's bay. 'Welcome and congratulations!' called a man with a loud-hailer from the motor-boat.

A small reception committee was on hand to greet us, including the inevitable officials from the Coastguard and Maritime Safety Department, but no immigration men this time as our visas and ship's clearance papers from Miyako were still valid. Instead there was a line-up of children from the local school with bouquets of flowers, and an invitation to stay in Shingu as joint guests of the municipality and the Hsu Fu Association. Over the next five days we were given formal dinners of raw fish and sake, a reception and speeches by the city Fathers, and hospitality in karaoke bars where Joe revealed a talent for crooning tunes from the 1960s. There was even an invitation to visit the hot springs where Loi, who would happily strip naked to go swimming off *Hsu Fu* was too shy to do the same in a Japanese communal hot tub. At the dinner parties, however, he was a huge success. Every time he was offered a beer he drank it down in a single draught. Then he would rush around filling up everyone else's glasses. Our Japanese friends were delighted as Loi got more and more tipsy, speaking in sign language and broken English to say how happy he was. He was not quite clear about the difference between Japan, Miyako and Shingu, though I tried many times to explain on a map. Loi's finger would trace a line from island to island, and then grandly slide eastward into the Pacific as he crowed, 'Vietnam! . . . Hong Kong! . . . Japan! . . . Amelika!' and gave a great giggle and a sweeping wave of his arm.

There was a more studious side to our visit, too. Mr Okuno, a retired schoolteacher, was the leading authority in Shingu on Hsu Fu the navigator. According to local folklore, Hsu Fu had brought his small fleet of vessels – whether they were rafts or sailing rafts, the story did not say – into the mouth of the river, and anchored there. Close to their anchorage the Chinese established a small settlement on the riverbank beside a small knoll. Here Hsu Fu and his band of followers lived peacefully for three years, instructing the local people in the skills and technology they had brought from China. Before Hsu Fu's visit, the local Japanese people had lived very simple lives, hunting in the forests, gathering wild fruits and edible plants, catching fish in the rivers or collecting shells on the shore. Hsu Fu showed them new fishing techniques, how to hunt for whales, and – the most profound change of all – he introduced rice cultivation. Then, according to one version of the story, he and his men sailed away and went farther along the coast to repeat the process of instruction. According to a different version, Hsu Fu ended his days at Shingu and was buried there. He was laid to rest in a grave at his settlement on the riverbank and a shrine was raised in his honour. But his followers later transferred his bones to a site a couple of kilometres away. Hsu Fu, they believed, should be revered for his ideas and his contribution to civilisation, and not as a god. By shifting his body away from the original shrine they could separate the idea of the cultural missionary from any notion that Hsu Fu was perhaps a Buddhist saint.

This idea of Hsu Fu as a symbol of cultural diffusion was an agreeable surprise. It was much the same concept which had led me to name our bamboo raft in honour of the First Emperor's explorer. In Shingu, Hsu Fu was regarded as the man who had brought Chinese knowledge to that area of Japan. Several other towns and villages in Japan, Mr Okuno explained, made the same claim that Hsu Fu had stopped there too, and imparted his knowledge. But had Hsu Fu, or any of his fleet, gone any farther? Had any of them travelled on across the Pacific to bring some of the same knowledge to America? Could Hsu Fu be a symbol of cultural diffusion that reached right across the Pacific? That was something that our own *Hsu Fu* would put to the test.

Mr Okuno showed us the Hsu Fu sites. The great navigator's shrine was a small reliquary of white marble on a shaft and plinth beside the wooded hill where he and his men were said to have lived during their three-year stay at Shingu. The later grave was in the centre of Shingu town, on an open plot of land under a gnarled tree where ancient stones were carved with the announcement that this was the last resting-place of Hsu Fu and his leading disciples. The genial Mr Okuno explained that

Hsu Fu's shrine, Shingu

when they had raised enough money, the city authorities and the Hsu Fu Association proposed to enclose the plot of land within a wall, build a formal gate, and establish the place as a protected site. Only in the last ten or fifteen years, he said, had Hsu Fu's name become well known in Japan, though the story of his search for the Elixir of Immortality was familiar to many Japanese schoolchildren as part of their early education. It was said that the Happy Land where he sought the drug of longevity was Japan, perhaps on the slopes of Mount Fuji. And what about the drug itself? I asked. Had that been identified? Mr Okuno said that at least a dozen different plants have been suggested as the famous Plant of Longevity, but of course none of them really provided the famous elixir. The most likely candidate grew in the hills surrounding Shingu, and he pointed out a low, rather uninspiring bush with small olive-green leaves growing next to Hsu Fu's shrine. This plant, he explained, cured stomach pains and promoted circulation of the blood. Formerly the root of the plant had been dug up and used as medicine, but it grew so slowly that now the leaves were sold as a herbal tea.

Clearly Mr Okuno did not put too much faith in the medicinal properties of the little bush, but he did add to the historical background of

Hsu Fu's famous expeditions. Chinese historians had recently put forward the theory that Hsu Fu's expedition was a clever fraud on the First Emperor. Hsu Fu had manipulated the Emperor's obsession with finding the Drug of Immortality into a chance for Hsu Fu's own people to escape the tyranny of the newly expanded Empire. Hsu Fu's native province of Shantung had only recently been overrun by the armies of the Emperor, and the people were suffering under their new ruler. With his tale of searching for the Drug of Immortality, Hsu Fu had duped the Emperor into paying the costs of an emigrant fleet, loaded with people trying to escape to a new land. This, said Mr Okuno, was why Hsu Fu and his people had never returned to China. They had found a new country and settled elsewhere.

Our stay in Shingu brought unusual visitors to see the raft. I was on the jetty waiting beside *Hsu Fu* for the rest of the crew to arrive, when two vehicles came racing down the approach road to the harbour. They were being driven in a manner to attract the maximum attention, and the vehicles themselves were extremely ostentatious. The first was a long, gleaming Mercedes limousine with its bonnet star and wheel hubs in gold. The second vehicle was a large cross-country vehicle riding on grotesquely high tyres, a bank of spotlights mounted on a roof bar, and also polished until it sparkled. It was crammed with large Japanese men who seemed to be acting as an escort to the limousine. Both vehicles swirled to a halt, and out of the limousine jumped the chauffeur who scuttled back to whip open the rear door so that his passenger, a small man in a dark business suit, could alight and gaze around in a proprietorial manner. By now the cross-country vehicle had disgorged its complement of heavyweight occupants, also dressed in identical blue suits. They formed up around their leader and marched purposefully across to the edge of the jetty where they stopped and looked down at the raft. The few bystanders were studiously looking the other way, and I realised that this was a visitation from the local chapter of the yakuza, or Japanese gangster community. They must have heard of the raft and wanted to take a look themselves. And just as with the customs men of Miyako, the large, square heavyweights were like children on a holiday. One of the gangsters looked round, noted that I must be a foreigner from the raft, and detached himself from the group. He walked over and timidly asked if it was all right for them to go aboard. It was not a request I was likely to refuse, and the yakuza squad scrambled happily over the raft like youngsters in an adventure playground. Then they returned to their showy vehicles and went racing away with squealing tyres.

The following day, 10 July, once again saw dozens of paper ribbons stretch and snap between *Hsu Fu* and the jetty, as the raft left port to cries of 'Banzai! Banzai! A thousand years! A thousand years!' as the small crowd threw up their arms in a farewell salute.

We were now on the last part of our voyage in Asian waters. Only 200 miles ahead was the entrance to the great Bay of Tokyo where I intended we should make a final halt before tackling the main expanse of the Pacific. Here we would check over the rigging, make final adjustments to the raft, and load as much food and water as *Hsu Fu* could safely carry before we set out on the 4,500-mile attempt to sail to America. We had already come some 1,800 miles and shown how sailors from the mainland of Asia could have travelled by raft among the great and small islands like Taiwan, the Ryukyus, and Japan, whether they came to trade, to raid, or to settle. We had survived gales and monsoon winds, and *Hsu Fu* had ridden the Black Stream. It had taken us fifty-six days, and in one sense we had exceeded what we intended to show: we had come the long way. Hsu Fu and other mariners would have left from ports in north China and made shorter sea crossings, while we had set out from Hong Kong in the south, adding hundreds of miles to our route and travelling around the outer fringe of East Asia. It was likely, too, that early mariners had made longer stopovers on the islands, staying for months, seasons, or even years before continuing onward. Some probably settled permanently, as Hsu Fu was said to have done at Shingu. Others, having already found pleasant islands in the ocean, may have wondered if there were yet more lands to be discovered, and continued onward to the east. A few could have been carried forward by accident.

Once again the Black Stream could have been responsible, and for a reason only now becoming clear to me. The Admiralty Pilot Book warned that in some years the Kuroshio shifts its course. A meander develops in the run of water along the south coast of Japan, and instead of flowing parallel to the coast, the Black Stream abruptly swerves out into the Pacific Ocean . . . and would have carried sailors with it. The cause of this occasional meander or loop is a huge bubble of cold water which wells up between the warm water of the Black Stream and the coast of Japan. This bubble forces the Kuroshio to detour away from the coast, but quite when and why this bubble develops is not known. Some years it is there, but for most years it is absent and the current flows along the coast as normal. It is easy to imagine how early sailors had learned to take advantage of the current, just as we had done with *Hsu Fu* in order to travel along the Japanese coast. But then in a year when the cold water bubbled up, the Black Stream betrayed them and they were carried out to sea against their will.

The fickle behaviour of the Kuroshio was only one of my worries when *Hsu Fu* left Shingu. More immediate was the increasing danger of being run down by merchant ships. The closer we got to Tokyo and the great adjacent port of Yokohama, the more ships we encountered, and the more nerve-wracking was our progress. We left Shingu in a fog, and when it lifted we found ourselves stranded in a maritime traffic rush hour. Two lines of coasters were going in opposite directions on the inshore passage; while out on the horizon passed the giant shapes of supertankers and bulk cargo ships. *Hsu Fu* was right in the middle of the inner traffic zone, and we counted twenty small coasters within three miles of us. To confuse matters further, *Hsu Fu* was in the grip of a counter-current and was being carried backwards, so that any passing ship would have seen the raft heading one way, but in fact it was going the other. We attracted the interest of a tuna-fishing boat going back to port after a night's fishing with most of her crew asleep in their cabins. The vessel altered course to take a closer look, and fifteen or twenty men sleepily appeared on deck, all of them dressed in long grey woollen underwear as they lined the rail to gaze down at us and shout encouragement. Then they threw a line across with gifts tied to it – three frozen tuna fish and two large bottles of sake which for a moment hung between the two vessels like bizarre items on a washing-line.

Two days later we found the Black Stream once again, and there was no mistaking the moment. The boat suddenly began to lurch and sway. Looking round, we saw on our right the normal pattern of low waves, but directly ahead and around us were tumbling pyramids of water, white caps and a confused sea. In the space of twenty yards the sea changed from tranquillity to confusion. We were on the dividing line between the inshore waters and the Kuroshio. Going aft to use the 'lavatory,' the water washing over one's feet, was much warmer than before, proof that we were again riding the current.

Later that afternoon Joe came back to the cockpit, looking worried. He had been checking our reserve of fresh water. Most of it was stored in plastic jugs under the cabin floors, but about a third of the supply had been wedged in the space under the topmost bamboo layer of the raft. There, in theory, it would be safe and the weight would help stabilise the raft and prevent a capsize. Joe had discovered that at least twenty per cent of these water containers were gone, washed away by the sea. When he opened and tasted the water in the remainder, he found that a quarter of them had been contaminated and now contained salt water. His discovery was not too alarming because we needed only a few gallons of fresh water to reach the Tokyo area. But the implications for the long haul across the Pacific were ominous. We would need every drop of water we could stow aboard, and a similar loss would be disastrous. And we had to keep our water supply low down, or the risk of capsize would be unacceptable.

That same evening I called the crew together to tell them that I thought that the working atmosphere on Hsu Fu was getting too lax. Perhaps our pleasant time ashore in Shingu had something to do with it, but I sensed we were losing our edge of self-discipline and common purpose. Every member of the crew was still carrying out the shipboard duties adequately, but the feeling of an integrated crew was ebbing away. For instance, the night watch now headed off to their sleeping bags as soon as they were relieved, and did not appear again until mid-morning. I felt that the night watch should prepare breakfast for everyone else before they woke them, and then stay around until we had discussed the day's programme before they went off to rest. It was essential, I said, that we kept a team spirit alive. I spoke with some reluctance. It went against the grain to have to tell others how to behave. But to my relief I saw that the others took the advice very well. Rex was nodding his agreement, and Mark, who once might have objected to anyone telling him how to behave, spoke up to give his firm support when I finished.

One reason why everyone felt happier was that Nina had begun to perk up. The five days' break at Shingu had given her a much-needed rest, and even if – as usual – she felt seasick as soon as we set out again, she had much more energy, and she was joking and smiling. She even volunteered to wipe up the mould in the cabins, saying that scrubbing mould off the cabin floor would remind her of childhood. I guessed the background at once.

'Was it as a punishment that you were made to clean floors at school?'

'Yes, when I was ten and twelve years old, I was very, very naughty. Even through to fifteen years of age I was often in trouble and made to stay behind for extra duties.'

Now she took on a dreary job as there was a film of mildew everywhere. It clung to our clothes, speckled our towels, penetrated the airtight sandwich box where I kept the ship's papers so that the pilot books were growing fungus. Even the pages of my notebook were soggy to write on, and ballpoint pen sank into the softened surface. A sleeping bag put out to dry on the cabin roof on a sunny day felt dry and warm, but after half an hour in the dank cabin it was just as clammy as before. We could see how the cabins were letting in more and more rainwater and spray. Thin shafts of sunlight now shone in through pinholes in the thatch, and if you put your eye up close to a larger hole in the cabin side where the rattan lashings passed through, you could see the ocean waves only two feet away and just below eye-level.

On 14 July came another sign that the raft was settling deeper in the water. The washing-up bucket had gone when we came to clean up the dishes after breakfast. Since Hong Kong the bucket had hung in its place over the stern lip of the cockpit basket, safely clear of the waves. But a wave had plucked away the bucket, leaving only the handle attached to its rope. Previously no wave would have reached that high except in a gale, and that night the sea had been quite calm. Naturally this started everyone wondering about the amount the boat had sunk, and trying to remember the previous watermarks. Just how much water used to flow past the foremast step when we were in Hong Kong? Were the top level bamboos awash by the time we got to Miyako? We asked ourselves the same questions, and the answers were inconclusive. There was algae and seaweed growing on the top layer of bamboos, which was certainly not there before. But was this because the top layer was permanently underwater or because the waves washed over it so frequently that it grew seaweed like rocks on a tideline? We could not tell. The motion of the sea was always there, and there were no firmly drawn lines. The sea had become a part of our lives, flowing around us, washing through the structure, rippling, splashing or, most often, surging past.

The wind picked up that evening and big grey swells came charging in from the south-west. We had all gathered to eat a meal cooked by Rex.

It was noodles flavoured with flakes of dried tuna from Miyako. Suddenly three round-headed porpoises came bursting out of the nearly vertical wavefront immediately behind us. We had been overtaken by hurrying schools of dolphin off Taiwan, watched three cruising sperm whales close to Shingu, and even seen a black marlin jump clear out of the water near Miyako. But all these creatures had paid no attention to *Hsu Fu* and were going about their own business. The porpoises were different. They came because *Hsu Fu* was there. They wanted to get a closer look at us and timed their aerial inspections like circus performers shooting from a wall of water. They were not the acrobatic, slick dolphins you see cavorting in an aquarium, but plump, rounded creatures – the impression of lumpiness enhanced by one that was mottled, and by their round heads rather than the streamlined beaked noses of the normal dolphin. They were, in a word, ungainly. But this was no matter. They burst out of the water, flinging themselves clear of the grey sea, and plopped back with a thunderous series of splashes, more explosive than the bursting wave crests. Each time they did this – and they performed four times – it drew gasps of approval from us, particularly when the mottled dolphin corkscrewed ponderously through the air. After a few wonderful minutes they were gone, and their finale was either deliberately excessive or a mistimed flop. In its last jump the mottled porpoise tumbled in the air and came down flat on its back in a massive splash like a novice diver overbalancing into a swimming-pool.

As so often seemed to be the case, the cavorting sea creatures heralded bad weather. A squall line ambushed us in the night. Luckily the raft was running only under mainsail, already reduced by two panels. Rex and Joe detected a darker line of blackness behind them, and had just lowered two more panels when the squall smashed out of the darkness with a crisp clatter of hard, cold raindrops. The crackling cascade on the roll-up canvas door of the cabin alerted me to scramble out of my sleeping bag, pull on oilskins, and emerge like a bear from a cave. I found no one at the tillers, and the usual blinding, all-enveloping cascade of a rainstorm. *Hsu Fu* was driving forward over an angry sea; the gale gusts had pinned the sail against the mast and rigging, and Joe was on the cabin roof struggling to get the sail farther down and reduce pressure before the mast snapped. Rex must have gone forward to deal with the foresail. I scrambled up to join Joe and together we clawed the tan cloth downward, tugging first at the cotton, and then when we could reach up to grasp a bamboo batten, pulling down on that as well. The final panel proved impossible to dislodge, its length was jammed tight against the mast. 'Up you go!' I yelled at Joe above the roar of the rain, and without hesitation he leaped upwards to cling to the top spar. I boosted him with a shove in the backside and in a moment he was aloft and using his weight to bring down the spar. It slid to the base of the mast so we could lash down the flapping canvas with extra sail ties. The job was done. All this was accomplished in the dark and rain by Joe who, until he volunteered for the expedition, had never sailed in his life. Yet it was a normal night's sailing activity on *Hsu Fu*.

Dawn revealed that the rough seas had once again snapped the hogging trusses which sagged pitifully on each side of the raft. Luckily the swell and waves had abated, so *Hsu Fu*'s untensioned length rippled and flopped without too much risk of falling to bits. Mark and Loi could begin the task of knotting and splicing, but for the moment there was something more interesting to catch our attention – there to the northeast was the unmistakable cone of Mount Fuji.

The Japanese Coastguard had asked us to check with them by VHF radio every six hours as we approached the maritime crossroads off the tip of the Izu Peninsula. Here, they said, was the busiest choke point for shipping in the country with numerous vessels heading in and out of Tokyo and Yokohama. The Coastguard also added that several passing ships had reported a raftload of Vietnamese boat people trying to land illegally. Would we please hang up our sponsor banners so that we were not mistaken for refugees? But when we reached the peninsula we had more pressing problems. The wind died away completely, and we were left motionless as the fog rolled in. It was a peculiar sort of fog which lay on the sea in dense banks striped with narrow, clear channels. When *Hsu Fu* was in one of these open channels, the prospect was terrifying. The fog sat like a heavy grey wool blanket about twenty metres thick. Inside the wool moved ships, and we could see the tips of their masts travelling above the fog like disembodied spikes. But the ships could not see us, for the fog obscured their bridges, and they were running on radar, and sometimes we could see the scanners spinning above the fog level. We hoisted *Hsu Fu*'s radar reflector to the top of the foremast and hoped fervently that it gave a reflection that made us look like a big ship at anchor. Eventually, to our relief, another small tuna-fishing boat suddenly appeared out of the fog wall, and glided alongside. I seized the chance to

ask for a tow, anything to get us clear of that suicidal place. The fisherman was equally nervous of the passing ships, and in a trice a heavy line
was hauled aboard and he was pulling us out of the traffic and into the
outer harbour of the nearby port of Shimoda, clear of danger, leaving the
treacherous game of blindman's-bluff behind us.

The unknown fisherman – we gave him our last bottle of whisky in
thanks – had been very decent and helpful, so it was all the more puzzling and shocking that there now occurred an incident which nearly
wrecked *Hsu Fu* due to the indifference and callousness of local fishermen.

We left Shimoda as soon as the fog lifted, and attempted to sail on to
Tokyo Bay. But once again the strange summer weather thwarted us. The
normal southerly or westerly wind of that season did not materialise.
Instead *Hsu Fu* met a cold blustery north-east wind which within two
hours forced us to drop anchor off the long sandy length of Shirahama
Beach. I was worried. *Hsu Fu* was trapped off an exposed coast, our
home-made anchors were unreliable, and if the wind grew stronger
there was every chance that the raft might be driven ashore and
wrecked. So I paddled ashore in the rubber dinghy with Nina. Through
binoculars I had noted the breakwaters of what appeared to be a small
artificial harbour just a mile along the coast. It looked like perfect shelter, and when we got there, we found it was a tiny place, protected by a

Mount Fuji

Shirahoma Beach

big sea wall and occupied by five fishing boats anchored tied to the quay. The harbour was very crowded, but there was just room for our raft in one corner. A fisherman was painting a small dinghy drawn up on the slipway, and Nina walked over to ask him if it would be possible to bring *Hsu Fu* into shelter. But the fisherman was either drunk or incredibly rude. He swore at Nina and told her to clear off. Very taken aback, she walked on to a nearby house where we found another fisherman sitting in a shed making up fishing-lines. This time we got a more civilised reception, and were told that the little harbour of Itado was operated by the fishermen's union and only the union could decide whether we could bring the raft there. However, the fisherman would be happy to drive us to the office of the fishermen's union where we could put our case.

By now I was thinking that our simple request for shelter was turning into a rather cumbersome affair. But I had heard that the fishermen's union was all-powerful in the management of any Japanese fishing harbour, and according to Japanese custom such a request would normally be dealt with by formal channels. So we were taken to the union office where we were greeted politely by the local union official and explained to him that *Hsu Fu* was exposed to danger. Could we have temporary shelter in Itado in case the weather grew worse? The response was that the matter would require consultation with the main union office in the next town. Once again, this was the normal Japanese pattern I had been led to expect – cross-reference and group discussion before reaching a decision. Several telephone calls were made, while Nina and I waited patiently. It was now four hours since we had come ashore. Then the local union official delivered the shattering reply: no, our raft could not be brought into the little port.

I was thunderstruck. In twenty years of sailing I had never come across any mariners who would refuse to offer safe harbour to a visiting vessel at risk from bad weather, least of all such an unusual vessel as *Hsu Fu* whose crew would obviously be having an uncomfortable time.

'Please ask him why not,' I asked Nina.

'Because it would be inconvenient,' came the reply.

The union had judged that if our raft was tied up inside the harbour the local fishing boats would have difficulty manoeuvring. This was not true, there was adequate space. But I was too disgusted to want to protest. Instead, trying to salvage a little help from the bad situation, I asked if it would be possible to anchor the raft closer to the harbour mouth where the shelter from the north wind was slightly better. Even this trifling request – really only a polite formality – was the subject of several more telephone calls, and only when a local fisherman personally offered to tow *Hsu Fu* to the new location, was there a begrudging agreement. I returned to the raft quietly seething with anger at such boorish behaviour.

So *Hsu Fu* was towed to the new spot. We dropped anchor there, and the fishermen disappeared back into harbour, leaving us to our fate. Sure enough, to confirm our worst fears, the wind grew stronger in the evening. Wet and cold, we put out all three of our anchors, working from the dinghy and cursing the local Japanese fishermen when we could have been safe inside the little harbour barely fifty metres away. It was lucky that we took the precaution of setting extra anchors. In the night one of the anchors did not hold, and the raft was driven backward for twenty yards before the other two anchors took the strain, and we were indeed nearly wrecked on the entrance to the tiny harbour. Our danger was all too evident next morning, but still no one appeared to offer us a helping hand or tow us into harbour. Quite the opposite, all that day and the next and the one after that, not a single fisherman showed up. The weather was too rough for their fishing, and they stayed in their homes or workshops and left us to our fate. And, of course, since they were not able to go out fishing, there was no question that we would have been in their way if the raft had been allowed into the harbour. For three days we lived in wet, dangerous conditions, keeping anchor watch at night, repositioning anchors, serving watch and watch about, and wondering if we would lose the raft. Finally on the fourth day one of the anchor ropes sheered through and we lost that anchor to the gale.

That afternoon we saw that two of the fishing boats were preparing to leave port. Thinking that their departure would free the extra space for *Hsu Fu*, I immediately returned ashore in the dinghy with Nina to ask if now we could come into shelter. It was pointless, we were told. All five

Squid fishing Boat

fishing boats were abandoning Itado Harbour because a typhoon was on its way and Itado Harbour was unsafe in a typhoon. This was shocking news. If Itado was unsafe for powerful modern fishing boats then it was certainly not the place for *Hsu Fu* to stay. But no one had bothered to tell us about the approaching typhoon. The fishermen were simply making arrangements to save their own skins. Yet their attitude was to get even worse. The nearest typhoon shelter was Shimoda Harbour back down the coast, and to get to Shimoda from our anchorage in the rising gale, the raft needed to be towed out to sea to a point where we could safely hoist sail. Via Nina I asked if a fishing boat could spare a few moments, as it passed *Hsu Fu*, to give the raft a tow, a mere half a mile would be sufficient. We would have the tow rope ready when the fishing boat went past us.

To my astonishment, the answer was that the fishermen would have to discuss whether to give us a tow or not. For the second time the selfishness of the fishermen's organisation took my breath away. But I held my temper, and asked if they could perhaps meet to discuss the possibility. At dusk Nina and I found ourselves sitting on the floor of one of the fishermen's houses while the local committee of six or seven fishermen debated whether or not they would assist *Hsu Fu* to avoid a typhoon. The situation ran so counter to all the traditions of mariners helping one another against the sea, that I felt I had strayed into another, totally alien world. I could not believe what I was observing. I was not alone in finding the discussion intolerable. Early in the discussion one young fisherman spoke up to volunteer to tow *Hsu Fu* the necessary mile offshore, but the others gave him such a concerted glare of disapproval that he fell silent. As the evening dragged on and the discussion continued – all over a one-mile tow – and more telephone calls were made to ask the opinion of other fishermen, my incredulity grew and grew. Here were half a dozen seamen unwilling to help a raft that needed to be pulled to safety. Nina kept up a running translation for me. The elder fishermen were arguing whether they had any responsibility for the raft, who would pay for any extra diesel fuel used, whether to ask the Coastguard to do the job, and so forth. Finally, after three hours of uninterrupted discussion, I could stand it no longer, and interrupted. Throwing diplomacy to the winds, I asked Nina to translate exactly what I was saying, without mincing words. Then I stated slowly and clearly that I had sailed the Atlantic, the Mediterranean, the Black Sea, the Arabian Sea, the

Indian Ocean, the Sea of China in my time, and never, never, in any place had I encountered seamen who were not prepared to help out another ship in danger. There was a long silence when Nina finished translating.

'We'll make one or two more telephone calls,' said the group spokesman, looking slightly shamefaced. Twenty minutes later Nina was telling me that the fishermen as 'an unusual favour' had agreed to tow the raft a little distance out to sea. It was a grudging, mean-spirited offer of help, and though Nina, who was intensely proud of being Japanese, kept telling me that the fishermen were really doing something unusual to help us at all, I could not help feeling that as a group the fishermen of Itado did not deserve the title of mariners. As we were towed the half-mile the next morning by the friendly young fisherman, I looked back and imagined a huge sign painted on the harbour entrance, which read 'DO NOT DISTURB'.

Shimoda Harbour was close-packed with scores of fishing boats, gunnel to gunnel, taking refuge from the forecast typhoon. In fact, after three days the typhoon veered in a different direction and never materialised, but by then I had given up the idea of proceeding to Tokyo Bay. Too much time would be wasted struggling north, and we could do our final fit-out and revictualling just as easily in Shimoda before setting out on the main Pacific crossing. In contrast to the rudeness at Itado, the local boat service company in Shimoda had found us a convenient and safe berth close to the beach where we could unload all our barrels and ropes and sails, and tidy up *Hsu Fu*. The local Customs Office and Coastguard went out of their way to be helpful; and the townsfolk were hospitable. In eleven days of hard work we had *Hsu Fu* in as good shape as we could expect of a fragile bamboo raft after two and a half months wear and tear. Mark fitted a set of replacement sails sent by Mr Ching in Vietnam, new manila ropes were purchased in Shimoda to back up our rattan rigging, and Joe managed to find space for 1250 litres of fresh water under the cabin floors and in the stern cockpit. Joe also did his best to restock the larder, though food prices were even higher than in Miyako. To go with our staples of rice, spaghetti, and noodles, we could only afford to purchase small quantities of dried bonito, tinned tuna and dried salami. On the North Pacific the same menu would have to be repeated every three meals, so there was no doubt that our diet was going to be deadly monotonous. To add flavour we bought beancurd paste and dried seaweed, and for luxuries a quantity of chocolate and some packets of boiled sweets, which would be doled out at the miserly ration of two squares of chocolate or three sweets per person per day.

Then it was time to say goodbye. First to Mark, who had generously stayed on to help with the final chores. He would remain in Japan for a few weeks and then return to Hong Kong. Originally he had anticipated that he would spend only a week on the raft, but in the end he had chosen to extend his stay to nearly three months. Indeed, when he came to wish us well in the next stage of our voyage, there was a catch in his throat, and it was clear that he found the parting difficult. Mark had discovered a sense of comradeship aboard *Hsu Fu* and knew he had been really valued for his skills. The second farewell was to Nina. She had come to accept that the Pacific crossing would tax her beyond her physical strength, and she, too, knew that her role had been held in high regard, not only because she had worked so hard on our behalf as intermediary between the crew of *Hsu Fu* and our contacts in Japan, but also as an artist sketching and drawing the daily scenes from Vietnam to Shingu. She would return to Tokyo to work up her brush-pen drawings,

Shimoda

aware that by her tenacity and courage she had earned the lasting respect and affection of her shipmates.

To replace Nina as ship's artist and Mark as seaman-craftsman there was just one new recruit – my old friend Trondur Patursson. He arrived looking very much the same as on the last three occasions he had joined one of my maritime expeditions. Now his luxuriant beard had just a touch of grey, but he was still the same compact, quiet, self-composed man of the sea that I remembered. He was the most ingenious fisherman, the most resourceful craftsman, and the most competent sailor whom I had ever met. Without him I would not have wished to tackle the immense Pacific Ocean that now lay before us. Typically, his first reaction was to inspect *Hsu Fu* long and silently before making the terse announcement that it was one of the most beautiful vessels he had ever seen. His second remark came with a quiet smile of confident anticipation: to him the next months on the ocean would be an ideal holiday.

PART TWO

OCEAN

Drawings by
Trondur Patursson

9

INTO THE WIDEST OCEAN

The Pacific is so vast that a jigsaw of all the world's great continents, plus Antarctica, would fit on its surface, and there would still be space to add Africa a second time. Then, too, the ocean is so deep that its volume is six times greater than all land above sea level. When compared to the Atlantic Ocean the Pacific contains twice the amount of water, and is much wider so that the distance from Tokyo to San Francisco is half again as far as from New York to Southampton in England. Thus, if you add the distance that *Hsu Fu* had already travelled to get to Tokyo from Hong Kong, then a successful Pacific crossing would be roughly the equivalent of sailing across the Atlantic from Europe to America *and back again*. Why then try to attempt such an enormous trajectory in a wash-through bamboo raft, particularly when there had already been several successful voyages on the Pacific by traditional vessels? A number of Chinese junks have crossed from Asia to America in this century, usually in the hands of Western yachtsmen, and the pioneering voyage of the balsa log raft Kon-Tiki from Peru to Polynesia in 1947 encouraged half a dozen similar raft journeys. Two years before our own venture a solo oarsman from France succeeded in rowing his way from Japan to the American coast along the route which *Hsu Fu* was now about to attempt.

The short answer was that *Hsu Fu*'s voyage set out to test particular and rather different conditions. First, it was a raft voyage in the northern and cooler part of the ocean. The previous raft voyages had, for the most part, stayed in warm tropical waters where living conditions were usually much more agreeable and the winds blew steadily from astern. In a sense these were downhill voyages, while *Hsu Fu* was faced with travelling, if not uphill, then at least against winds which would vary, sometimes in our favour, sometimes not. And, of course, the weather in the North Pacific was likely to be more stormy. Second, the earlier raft voyages were not usually intercontinental endeavours. *Kon-Tiki*, for example, had finished up on the Tuamoto group of islands about two-thirds of the way across the ocean after 4,300 miles. Third, *Hsu Fu* was a very different sort of raft. She was made of flexible bamboo, while the majority of the other rafts had been more massive, sturdy timber structures. So *Hsu Fu* was both more fragile and at the same time attempting to travel farther than most rafts. The successful voyages by modern Chinese junks had not been archaeological experiments as far as I was aware, but well-managed cruises in traditional Chinese vessels which were not deliberate replicas of ancient ships. But the main reason for *Hsu Fu*'s voyage was that it was an experiment to be made for its own sake. Crossing the Pacific successfully on a bamboo raft would not prove conclusively that there had been cultural contact between Asia and pre-Columbian America. It would only test whether the bamboo raft could have been a vehicle for such contact. Just as important was what we would learn during the voyage itself. Already we had discovered a great deal about the construction and sea-handling of bamboo rafts – subjects on which virtually nothing had previously been known. Now we would see how long a raft would endure, and what it was actually like to live on the North Pacific in a wash-through structure. So the day-by-day experience of living on the world's greatest ocean lay at the heart of the project. We would find out what it was like to be surrounded by the great ocean, isolated by the ocean, and because our raft was virtually absorbed within the water, what it felt to become a part of the ocean.

As a crew we kept our thoughts to ourselves as we sailed from Shimoda on 5 August. All five of us – Joe, Loi, Rex, Trondur, and myself – knew we would be living together in cramped conditions for ninety days, probably more. But none of us were novices. With the exception of Trondur we had already lived aboard the raft for nearly three months. So four of us knew how to sail the vessel, cook, eat, sleep in the dog-kennel huts, live shoulder to shoulder. As for Trondur, he may have never been on the raft before, but he knew more about the sea and ships than any of us, and to him the start of a voyage was a welcome return to his favourite environment. Even as *Hsu Fu* was gently towed out of the mouth of Shimoda Harbour, Trondur was comfortably seated on the bow of the raft with his sketch book and pencil, ignoring the regular surge of the waves rising up through the bamboos and washing across his sea boots as he drew pictures of the Japanese coastline beginning to recede in the distance. He looked as relaxed as if he had been at home in his studio.

Our departure was as muted and low-key as could be imagined. We left at first light, towed out behind a small fishing boat in response to a request from the Japanese Coastguard that for safety we should get as quickly as possible across the busy shipping lane. There was no one on the pier-head to see us leave, except for the lone figure of the local cable television cameraman stooped over his camera on its tripod. It was still so dark that I could see the red light glowing beside the lens to show that his camera was switched on. The cameraman, Mr Hasegawa, was a quiet, gentle person who had been the first to greet us on arrival at Shimoda, and was now the last to see us leave. He had been kindness itself, visiting the raft almost daily to ask if there was anything he could do to help, running small errands in his car, bringing little gifts. On the last day he had shyly held out a sailor's knife and – in carefully rehearsed, soft-spoken English – asked if I would take it with me on the voyage as a memento. Now he straightened up from his camera, and quietly raised a hand in farewell.

Hsu Fu was ridiculously low in the water. A ton and a quarter of drinking water and a third of a ton of food had been loaded, and the extra weight was pressing the raft down into the sea so that the entire hull was buried, except for the upturned bow, a few feet of the stern, and the topmost outer bamboo around the edge. Every little wave sent back by the fishing boat ran down the full length of the raft, washing up over bamboos, lapping around the cabin and cockpit bases and then filtering away through the chinks between the bamboos on the stern. I watched a small ripple travel along the side deck of the raft, where on a normal vessel there would be a channel or scupper to carry water off the planked deck and send it overboard. But on *Hsu Fu* there was no watertight surface, and no difference between deck height and sea level. Indeed amidships the bamboos were submerged by as much as five inches below the sea even in a flat calm, so that anything stowed there – food barrels, spare timber and rope – was standing in water.

OCEAN

Loi was on the bow, keeping watch on the tow rope. His previously gaunt frame had put on weight since Hong Kong and he was looking a little more solid. He had learned not to rush about so fast or fling himself headlong into any job. Now he paced himself and took matters more steadily. He glanced back, caught my eye, and gave a great wide grin, all straight teeth. 'America,' he mouthed, too far away to be heard. Rex, who shared the forward cabin with Loi, was out of sight, probably sorting out his notebooks and observation sheets which he would use for making a maritime survey of all the animals, birds and fish, and the pollution we would encounter. Joe was busy making up nets in which to hang up our stock of 200 oranges, 50 lemons, and enough onions to allow 2 per day for the crossing. The nets would give the fruit the best chance of survival, and we had learned our lesson in restocking perishable food from Hong Kong and Miyako. This time we had not even bothered to buy bread or cabbages. We would go directly to our shipboard diet of dried bonito, salami, or tinned tuna fish, and hope that the fishing was better. Trondur had already set out fishing-lines – a thick heavy one for large fish, a lighter one with a spinner for smaller fish. To him it was inconceivable to be at sea without trailing a hook in the water. Earlier he had picked up an old umbrella that Joe had been given while shopping in the rain in Shimoda, and tossed it overboard. 'It's bad luck,' he had announced.

The moment we were across the shipping lane, we dropped the tow. Just ahead lay the outlying volcanic islands of To Shima and Nii Shima, and the wind carried us slantwise between them. There was no way of selecting the correct channel because I had left all Japanese coastal charts behind. They would be useless on a voyage on the wide ocean, and anyhow the coastal charts would soon grow mildewed. So we steered by eye, judging the water by the surface ripples and the colour of the tide race, and passing very close under the cliffs of Nii Shima.

'You can see the power locked in there,' commented Trondur, gazing up at the contorted rock layers in the cliffs where they had twisted and folded in flows of molten rock aeons ago. It was his first time on the raft under sail, and he nodded approvingly. 'She got through the passage all right. I did not think she would,' meaning that the raft's sailing ability had surprised him. 'Looks like two different ships,' he observed, gesturing at the way the mainmast and foremast leaned and swayed in opposite directions and to their own individual rhythms on the flexible body of the raft.

158

To Shima

Ian Lloyd, the photographer commissioned by the *National Geographic* magazine to take pictures of our departure, had said that from his vantage point in a helicopter *Hsu Fu* appeared like a 'snake wriggling over the sea, bending with each wave'. Now Ian caught up with us aboard a well-equipped deep-sea game-fishing boat hired from Shimoda to take his farewell pictures. The fishing boat circled and circled, all chrome and stainless steel deck gear, powerful engines throttled back, radio aerials whipping in the wind, glimpses of a well-appointed stateroom, the helmsman dimly seen behind glistening glass, warm and comfortable at his controls. Aboard *Hsu Fu* we felt grubby, slug-like, and basic.

But as the dusk gathered and the wind rapidly increased up to gale force from the north-east, it was the splendid game-fishing boat, rolling and pitching abominably in the waves, which had to turn back. Unable to keep at sea comfortably, a quarter of a million dollars' worth of modern high-speed boat ran for shelter, leaving our battered, low-slung, crazy-looking raft, half-submerged and held together with knots and rattan, to plod forward across the crashing waves like a 2,000-year-old bird's nest.

So deep-laden, the sensation was nothing like before. Now there was no dry spot on the raft – the water oozed up through the cockpit floor, the cabin floors were wet, and through the open midships section at the foot of the mainmast the waves swirled through unhindered from one side of the vessel to the other, and raced away into the darkness. The bow deck, which had been mostly above water on the way to Japan, was now regularly submerged within the waves. And the edge bamboo on the lee side was underwater for nearly all its length. Yet we still used the outer bamboo as our narrow, slippery walkway to move along the length of the raft, stepping out of the cockpit basket, grabbing on to a fore-and-aft rope as a handrail, and then shuffling along ankle-deep in the sea to move forward to work the ship.

It was as he was moving forward at the end of his watch to return to the forward cabin that Rex noticed the potential catastrophe. In Shimoda I had purchased four stout tubs from the fishermen's cooperative to store our vital supplies of extra food. These four tubs had been stowed in the open midships section by the base of the foremast. But the waves surging across the raft had ripped the lids off three of the four tubs. One tub was already full to the brim with seawater, the other two were half-full, and, of course, all the food they contained was rapidly getting soggy. Some of the food had been washed overboard, and the rest would follow or soon be ruined. Rex raised the alarm, and the entire crew rushed forward in the rain and darkness to try to limit the damage. Working by the light of torches, with rain and spray flickering through the torch beams, and up to our knees in the sea, we struggled to do the salvage work. Joe dabbled into each barrel which was becoming more and more like a goldfish pond, and pulled out the dripping lucky dip – tins of coffee, packets of dried soup turning to mush, milk powder. He handed each item to Rex who was perched on the bamboo roof of the main cabin. Rex wiped off the worst of the seawater with a cloth which was itself wringing wet because it was impossible to keep anything dry, then handed the item on to Loi to stack in the forecabin. Meanwhile Trondur calmly knelt in the waves, wearing sodden heavy army trousers, undoing the ropes which held the tubs in place, ignoring the waves which surged up to his thighs, and lashing down the tubs more securely.

Tomato paste, mayonnaise, and most of the tins of coffee were saved – items which had been so expensive in the supermarket at Shimoda and on which we had planned to live for the next hundred days. But the milk powder was ruined, and so, too, were many of the packets of dried soup and flavourings. The three barrels contained about twenty per cent of our carefully calculated food stock. By daylight we could try to dry out whatever we had managed to salvage. But we all knew that we could never save everything. Many items when we later opened them to eat would be mouldy from that first, sad night – but by then we probably would not notice. We would be so hungry that food, any food, would suffice.

Ever since leaving Shimoda, Joe and I had been noticing loud swishing noises from under the bamboo-slat floor of the main cabin which we shared with Trondur as living quarters. At first we paid no attention because it was much the same sound that we had been hearing since we left Hong Kong – the swish of wave tops brushing the bottom of the cabin basket as they washed their way through the body of the raft from one side to the other. Now, of course, the raft was floating much deeper in the water, and we supposed that the louder noise was simply because the waves were swirling across the bottom of the cabin basket much more often and more boldly. But should it be quite that loud? And from time to time there was a puzzling new gurgling sound which we had not noted previously. I tried peeking down through a gap between the bamboo slats. Underneath was a space, about four inches deep, to the woven basketwork of the cockpit unit. In that space we had stowed drinking water. To my surprise there seemed to be rather a lot of water swirling about between the drinking water cans, inside the cabin. That did not seem to be right. Had the cans begun to leak? If so, that was serious as we would be losing our precious reserve of fresh water calculated to last us all the way across the Pacific. There was nothing for it but to shift away all the waterproof kit-bags which contained our clothing and kit, the watertight boxes of camera and medical gear, our sleeping bags and all our paraphernalia so that we could get at the bamboo-slat floor and roll it back.

When we did so, it was obvious that something was wrong. Three inches of water sloshed back and forth inside the basket, and it was not fresh water but salt. When we left Hong Kong, I had been quite proud of the way that the cabin units had kept out the sea. But now the ocean was getting into what was supposed to be a watertight unit. We quickly traced a distinct surge and splashing sound to one corner. Indeed, there were little fountains of seawater spurting up between the water containers at that spot. We levered up a couple of water cans to have a look . . . and I found myself staring straight down into the blue depth of the Pacific Ocean through a four-inch-square hole in the bottom of the cabin basket. It was remarkable. There was nothing whatsoever between me and the bottom of the Pacific. I could even see a couple of small pilot fish swimming across the hole, just eighteen inches away. Each time a wave rolled under the raft, a solid column of water came gushing up through the hole and into the cabin, then most of it drained out again as the wave rolled onward. The surge and splash we had been hearing was not the ocean caressing the underneath of the cabin basket, but the sound of the wave top rushing in and out of our sleeping accommodation. In fact, we had been blissfully ignorant, sleeping just two inches above wave-top-level over a large open hole in the cabin, and thinking that the water noise was the sound of the ocean being kept out.

'The swirling of water will never sound so comforting again,' commented Joe, gazing down at the solid spurt of water jetting into the cabin, 'nor the cabin ever feel quite as snug as before.'

'If we had been in a normal closed hull boat,' I pointed out, 'we would have sunk by now.'

The problem was obvious. Back in Vietnam I had sewn and fitted four sock valves into each corner of the cabin floor to drain out any storm water which might come bursting into the cabin through the door when a really big wave hit us. The sock valves were ingenious but very simple devices – tubes of canvas stitched into holes in the cabin floor so that they hung down loosely into the ocean like short elephant trunks. In theory they allowed any water trapped inside the cabin to drain out through them, but when the outside waves surged up, the pressure of the water squeezed the dangling sock valves shut, flattening the canvas tubes so that no water could flow up them. In operation the sock valves were extraordinarily reliable and effective. Only a very small amount of water got up them before they closed off in response to the action of the waves. But in Vietnam I had made a mistake: I had sewn the sock valves from best quality cotton duck usually used for making heavyweight tents and awnings. But cotton canvas, as Trondur told me, never lasted very well in the sea. I should have used a flax- or hemp-based cloth. After four months immersion in water, often very polluted, the cotton canvas had simply rotted right away. Now in the floor of the cabin we had four neat square holes, four inches by four inches, fringed by a few rotten scraps of green canvas that were as easy to rip as a thin pancake. Beyond that was the pale blue-green of the Pacific Ocean. We really were at sea in a sieve.

All that day, and the next, and the next we sewed and fitted replacement sock valves as a matter of urgency. Every valve in the raft, four in the main cabin, four more in the forecabin, and another four in the

cockpit was either in the same shredded condition or about to disintegrate when you gave it a gentle tug. As a replacement we had a few yards
of grey-green canvas which I had bought in Hanoi market, recognising it
as being the material used for the rain canopies of Russian jeeps. Luckily
it was made of flax. Sewing them in place was a tedious and wet job. It
was impossible to stitch the new sock valve into place while working
from outside the cabin, because the cabin was resting on the bamboo
deck of the raft and there was no access. So you had to crouch down
inside the cabins, wearing the sock valve like a sleeve on your arm which
was thrust out through the hole in the cabin floor and down into the sea.
From there you had to reach back and upward to the floor of the cabin
to poke the heavy sewing needle through the basketwork and make the
stitch. With each wave a gush of water spurted up into your armpit and
slopped into the cabin. And because it was impossible to see what you
were doing with your arm sticking down into the sea, everything had to
be done by touch, groping for the sharp point of the needle when it was
coming downward, or poking and prodding blindly to try to find the
hole in the basketwork where it could be pushed back into the cabin.
After an hour or so the hand that was outside in the ocean was dead
white and clammy, the fingers bloated and soft with prolonged immersion. It was cramped, backbreaking work, squatting doubled up or
kneeling, your face and cheek sometimes pressed to the soggy floor to
get the reach out into the ocean, and it took one man a full day to stitch
one sock valve into place.

Rex and I were crouched in the main cabin, sewing away, when a
large white onion suddenly popped up into the cabin, bursting up
through the hole on the head of one of the columns of water gushing into
the cabin. It was like a conjuring trick. Rex and I looked at one another
in amazement. An onion, bobbing up from the ocean? How very strange.
We rescued the onion from the three-inch bath it was taking in the
cabin, and handed it out of the cabin door to Joe who was sitting in the
cockpit stitching up the next replacement sock valve.

He looked at it startled. 'Oh Hell!' he exclaimed. 'One of the onion
nets must have burst.' He went off to inspect the larder of nets of
oranges, lemons and onions hung in every spare corner of the raft. Five
minutes later he came back looking puzzled. 'I have no idea where it
could have come from,' he confessed. 'All the onion nets seem OK.' Ten
minutes later Trondur who had been lashing down barrels in the midship

came back, also carrying a battered-looking onion which had been bobbing around his feet. Joe made a second search, and this time came back looking crestfallen.

'It's the onion net by the cockpit,' he announced. 'It's burst open. I don't know how many we have lost. But I'm afraid we will have to cut back on onion eating. One onion per meal divided among the five of us is all we can allow until I take stock of what is left.'

Loi gave his usual grin, laughed, and pointed at Joe. 'Onion bye-bye!' he crowed.

Loi was levelling the score with our ship's doctor. With his usual disregard for physical risks, Loi had incautiously put his arm behind one of the heavy leeboards to do some task or other. The leeboard had shifted with the roll of the raft, trapping the upper arm, and squeezing it severely. Joe had checked the arm and found no broken bone, but the muscles had been crushed, and the arm was badly bruised. So for two days Loi had been sitting like a bird with a broken wing, miserable and moping and obviously sorry to be left out of the teamwork and activity of running the raft. Joe had given him painkilling tablets to ease his discomfort, but this only made matters worse. Loi had probably received very little drug medication in Vietnam, and now reacted badly to the drugs. He complained to Joe that whatever he was giving him caused dizziness and vomiting. This put Joe into some difficulty. As a medical principle he disliked issuing drugs except in real need; on the other he wanted to ease Loi's pain and show that he was concerned with Loi's health. Now to see Loi perk up and begin to tease him was as much a tonic to Joe, and definitely a good sign for the rest of us.

Joe, Loi and Rex were also getting their first chance to judge Trondur for themselves, and they must have been wondering if he was as at home on the sea as I had told them he would be. The weather continued wet and miserable. A north wind, fresh to gale force, was sending grey seas washing through the raft, occasionally splashing over the cockpit and wetting the crew. Joe spotted one big greybeard roller about to strike the vessel, and yelled a warning 'Incoming!' He and Rex ducked for cover, and sure enough the wave burst over the cockpit showering its occupants. Joe and Rex looked up in amazement. Trondur had ignored their warning, and just sat there. The wave had deluged him, and he was sitting there calmly, his oilskins glistening and the water dripping generously from his enormous beard.

'He didn't move a muscle, as if to say "What's all the fuss about?" ' Joe later told me in amazement.

Joe's opinion of Trondur was reinforced next day after we had passed a difficult night, battling with heavy seas and rain showers, and caught a glimpse of shore lights reflecting in the western sky. It was our last sight of land. By dawn the wind was easier, and the sea a broad expanse of grey waves marching steadily to the horizon under a thick overcast.

'Now it has the feeling of deep ocean,' commented Trondur quietly and contentedly, as he watched a few shearwaters skimming the waves and a pair of fulmar, characteristic birds of the deep seas. There was a single bird of another species, but it was difficult to identify.

'What kind of bird is that?' Joe asked Rex, who was beginning to keep his nature log of all the birds and fish we would see.

Rex hesitated. 'A gannet, I think,' he said. Then he paused. 'Quite a young one, this season's.'

'Two to three months old,' observed Trondur softly and authoritatively.

'He probably knows its registration number too,' muttered Joe in awe.

For the next four days the weather smiled on us. The sky was a sharp blue, the air bright, and the wind in our favour. White caps and a glittering swell extended to a clear horizon, and the Pacific had a quick, lively motion which was a tonic. We were sailing north-east, roughly parallel to the Japanese coast and well out beyond the coastal shipping lane so we saw just one small freighter on the horizon. Rex finished up the work on the replacement sock valves. Joe spread the soggy salvaged food on the cabin roofs to dry out as best it could. Loi's bruised muscles mended so that he could take up his carpentry again, finally breaking the original woodsaw he had brought with him from Sam Son, its blade already so well used that it was wafer-thin. Trondur sketched and painted in watercolours, or rearranged his fishing-lines, the larger one as thick as my little finger, with a huge, ferocious hook 'for something big', as he put it. One sunny morning he and Loi spent two hours cavorting like seals in the water off the stern replacing the end loop of one of the hogging trusses which had been worn through by the constant flexing of the raft. The two of them were tied on with safety harnesses, as it was tricky work, fighting the surge and backwash of the waves which swept them on to the bamboos so they emerged scratched and bleeding from dozens of barnacle cuts, but happy with the result of their labours.

Hsu Fu was advancing at a sedate one to two knots, though the swish of the sea through the bamboos and the fact that we were so close to the sea level rushing against our basketwork shelters gave the impression of much greater speed. Already we were establishing a far closer community with the sea than any normal vessel, and the impression of the ocean's wonders was heightened by our first sight of an albatross with at least a six-foot wingspan, swooping and curling close around us for most of the day. It was probably a young Black-Footed Albatross, said Rex consulting his reference guide to seabirds, and probably a young one. For me it was a special moment. Despite sailing the North Atlantic, Indian Ocean, and the China Sea, it was the first time that my sailing vessel had been consciously escorted by one of the greatest of all ocean travellers.

Perhaps it was only psychological, but knowing that we had fully embarked on the main ocean seemed to give a greater sense of scale and

Dorado

power to the sea around us. The sunshine brought out our predatory escort of dorados, and they seemed larger and fiercer than any we had encountered before. Often their electric-blue fins and yellow tails could be seen in the ocean beside and below the raft. I had just pointed out a large specimen to Trondur when there was a great flurry in the water as the animal shot forward to pounce on a flying fish. In the clear water we could follow the twisting, turning acceleration of the prey, the powerful lunge of the hunter, and then the flying fish leapt from the water in desperation, skimming away in the air only to be followed by the streamlined dash of the dorado in pursuit – it must have exceptional eyesight to follow the flight path of the fleeing flying fish – driving itself through the water as fast as the prey could glide, looking upward and hurling itself forward like a deadly killing machine so that when the flying fish did splash into the water it was into the very jaws of its hunter. There was a white foaming swirl, and that was the end of the chase. Without a word, Trondur went forward and began shaving down an oar handle to make the shaft of a light fish-spear. With 4,500 miles of the Pacific ahead, we would not be needing the oar for rowing, and the thought of dorado cutlets was mouthwatering.

As always the task of repair and maintenance was endless, and gruelling. On the same evening we finally finished sewing the new sock valves into the main cabin floor and were rearranging the cabin contents, Joe pointed out a gaping hole that had appeared in the forward end of the basketwork. The maststep had worn right through the wickerwork, due to the constant flexing and stretching, and twisting of the vessel. Indeed, it seemed that the entire main cabin unit had crept forward on its lashings and was now slightly nearer the bow than when built. The new hole was a gash about twenty inches long and looked impossible to repair. Every time a wave washed through the midships section, a substantial tongue of water came slopping into the main cabin, and drained out towards the nearest sock valve. It would be much worse when we were in a heavy sea, when the entire cabin could flood. I was too tired to think of a solution right away, and decided to postpone a proper inspection until next morning, only to discover that there was yet more water sloshing around the main cabin floor because the slit at the mast step had widened in the night. I could not see how such a large and awkwardly placed hole could be mended, but Trondur was unperturbed. He spent all day with chisel, knife, needle and thread, cutting away the damaged area and then trimming back the maststep before stitching on a patch cut from an empty water container – a mixture of materials from the Bronze and Plastic Ages, but at least recycling the plastic. We had already debated what we should do with *Hsu Fu*'s inevitable accumulation of empty tins and plastic bottles on the Pacific sector in the light of our experience from Hong Kong to Japan. Then we had thrown overboard everything that was biodegradable and kept the rest in a special rubbish barrel. But the barrel had been a horrible shipboard companion with all its smell, slime and flies. So now we decided that it would be more realistic to weight and sink all the rubbish we did not need. As matters turned out, it was more theory than practice. As the voyage progressed we found ourselves salvaging and reusing every tin, every jar and every bottle, so desperate became our shortage of materials.

August 13 was almost windless and sunny, and the raft lay becalmed when we saw our first large school of great whale come to the surface about half a mile astern. Trondur was up the foremast in a flash, gazing at them. The Faeroese Islanders still hunt the large schools of pilot whale which pass their islands, and the whale hunt is still a deeply engrained part of their sea culture.

Sperm whale breaching

'Sperm whale,' Trondur informed us as he returned to the cockpit. 'About twenty. The big sperm whale, he doesn't like to stay with the group. These are only women and children.'

The big animals lay there, placidly wallowing, occasionally giving the characteristic forward spray of the sperm whale's spout. Their blunt heads were clearly visible as they loitered, grey-black like bow-headed submarines. Occasionally one animal rolled over to expose its belly to the sun, or made a shallow dive, and the dorsal fin cut gently through the water. Towards the end of their visit, which must have lasted about ninety minutes, one animal of about forty feet in length, hurled itself clear of the water and fell back with a mighty splash.

'Much beef,' I heard Trondur mutter to himself into his bushy beard, ever the sea hunter!

'You should buy meat from Ireland, instead of eating whale,' I said.

'Don't like to eat pig too much,' he said with a smile.

'No, I mean good Irish beef.'

'Not so bad then,' he answered. 'But in Faeroes half of all the meat we eat is whale.'

'Is it expensive?'

'You can't buy it,' he replied. 'We divide among the families.' Like the Eskimo, he explained, the Faeroese hoped that they would be allowed a special quota to catch whale, as it was a traditional, non-commercial operation.

'If you were allowed to catch whale only in boats that were rowed or sailed, and had no engine, then that might be fair.'

Trondur agreed. 'Maybe. Now when we see whale, we lose one in five. If we had no engine in the boat maybe we lose two of every three. Anyhow, when we have the whales in the bay we already use only rowing boat to follow them.'

Hsu Fu was obviously floating on a rich feeding ground, the border between warm and cold waters where plankton, krill and all the lower food chain were available. A large flock of shearwaters was wheeling excitedly over a spot about halfway between the whales and *Hsu Fu*. There must have been a hundred or more birds intently studying what was happening below them in the water. Suddenly, directly underneath the circling flock, a patch of water a hundred feet across boiled in white foam, as if hit by an intense hail storm. 'Squid,' commented Trondur tersely. There must have been thousands upon thousands of small fish driven upward to the surface by hordes of squid feeding from below. The fry made the water seethe. Above them the shearwaters shrieked and screamed in ecstasy and swooped and fed and gorged themselves while the squid continued to harass their meal, seizing their prey in their sucker arms. Again and again the scene was repeated and the patch of foaming water vanished, then reappeared elsewhere in a white lather of thrashing small fish as if a fire hose were being directed at the surface of the sea. Each time the ravening shearwaters feasted.

In the next twenty-four hours the water temperature rose from 24 to 27 degrees, and then fell back to 24 degrees, indicating that *Hsu Fu* must have passed across a branch of the Black Stream flowing like a river in the ocean. Rex was taking the water temperature three times a day, but it did not need his thermometer to detect the difference. Whenever you stood on the stern to wash or to use the lavatory and the waves splashed over your bare feet, the change in temperature was immediately noticeable, and this led me to wonder if the early Asian navigators could have used the Black Stream to help them in their ocean navigation. According to Professor Needham the Chinese already knew by the first century AD that the world was a sphere, and compared it to the yolk of an egg or the round bullet of a crossbow. And as early as the third century BC they also seem to have had some notion of the Black Stream which must have fitted into their general oceanographic concept that the waters of the Pacific or the Eastern Ocean flowed eastward until they were swallowed up in a great vortex. Thus, if the Chinese knew vaguely about the eastward-flowing currents of the North Pacific, and the Black Stream was already so important for coastal navigation, then perhaps the early explorers would have been bold enough to try using it to continue east, checking their position relative to the current simply by dipping their toe in the water. If they did so, then they would have chosen by accident the most logical and convenient route from Asia to America, because the Black Stream after leaving the coast of Japan becomes the North Pacific Current and travels on across the North Pacific in a broad arc which is also the optimum trans-Pacific track for a sailing vessel.

The ancient Chinese would have had no difficulty in confirming their general direction of travel by the sun and stars, because they were highly experienced astronomers. Since remotest antiquity the movement of the stars and planets had been used to determine the times of religious festivals in China, and Chinese texts dating back close to Hsu Fu's era mention the use of stars for navigation purposes. While there is no reason to suppose that the Chinese used the magnetic compass at sea until much later, they did have the 'lodestone spoon' available. This was a device used on land in necromancy and fortune-telling, shaped like a spoon and placed on a flat smooth surface such as glass or a metal mirror so that it pivoted on the spoon's bowl. The handle pointed south. However, in the humdrum business of day-to-day sailing, their ocean navigation would have been much as we practised it on *Hsu Fu* 2,000 years later: we simply sailed eastward as best we could, depending on the way that wind, waves and current took us.

10

FLOATING BIRDNEST

'I think Rex has gone mad,' said Joe with a grin. 'Look, he's trying to drink seawater!' I turned and saw Rex in shorts and T-shirt kneeling on the outside edge of the raft, with his bottom high in the air, and his face pressed against the surface of the sea, just as if he were drinking from the ocean.

'Definitely mad,' added Joe a moment later. 'Now he's talking to a plastic bag.'

Rex's beaming face with its fringe of red beard had emerged from the sea, and sure enough he was speaking solemnly to a plastic bag in his hand. He was also wearing a bright yellow face mask which set off his gingery fringe of beard and hair and bright pink sunburned skin. 'I'm doing a hull growth survey,' he called back to us. And bowed down to resume his strange rump-in-the-air and face-in-the-sea posture. Some minutes later he was again hanging over the side of the raft, this time level with the cockpit, and peering down into the water. In his hand was a small tape recorder sealed in a plastic bag. 'Station Five,' he intoned into it. 'Upper bamboo layer – light cellophane weed, three goose barnacles. Middle bamboo layer – medium to heavy weed, light coating of barnacles. Lower bamboo layer – heavy grass weed, no barnacles.' He broke off his note-taking. 'I'm checking all marine growth on the hull at various points around the raft. In future every time the water is calm enough I will take another series of measurements to see what changes are taking place as we sail across the ocean. I've already found quite a number of goose barnacles and bright pink acorn barnacles, as well as what look like worm casts. But there is surprisingly little weed. If this was a normal wooden ship we would expect perhaps six inches of weed growth, but *Hsu Fu*'s bamboos don't seem to offer a good home for weed. Most of the seaweed is barely ten centimetres long. And all the longer streamers of thirty-centimetre weed we had a month ago have disappeared.'

'Maybe it's fallen off because of the change of water temperature, or perhaps it's been eaten by fish,' I said.

'I don't know, but I tried eating the short crisp seaweed myself, and it doesn't taste too bad, a bit crinkly and thin. That's the one I'm calling cellophane weed. The other weed isn't much use – short and grey and a bit slimy.'

It was a bright sunny day, with very little wind and a slight choppy sea. The sun was sending shimmering beams of light five metres down into the blue water, and shoals of the little yellow-and-black-banded pilot fish swam through the sunbeams. Trondur reached under the edge of the raft, and broke off a small cluster of barnacles. He showed me how they had formed a curve around the shell of the bamboo.

'Easy to take off,' he said. 'They can't stick on the bamboo.'

Trondur had spent the last hour, poised on the cabin roof, watching the sea, fish-spear in hand like Neptune with his trident. He was waiting for big dorados, three of which Rex reported from his hull survey. The dorados were swimming in the shadow of the raft, avoiding the direct rays of the sun. Occasionally they ventured out to see if there were any flying fish about. But each time it was a sudden sortie and took Trondur by surprise so he was not ready to spear them. Joe tried luring the dorados out by dangling a silver fishing lure over the edge of the raft. But still no luck. The dorados stayed where they were until, for some unknown reason, they would abruptly charge forward from the shelter of the raft and go ploughing out ahead of the boat to see if they could catch any flying fish unawares. There they would stay, scouting ahead of the raft, just out of spearing range, their vivid blue-and-yellow shapes tantalisingly visible – and mouthwatering too, for we were becoming a little tired of our monotonous round of dried bonito, salami and tinned tuna, and would have relished some fresh fish.

Later that same day, 15 August, we saw another whale, a single animal which Trondur, who again swarmed up the mainsail using the battens like a step ladder, identified as a sei whale or rorqual which fed on small

Rorqual

fish and plankton. Early the following morning a pair of large adult sperm whale wallowed to the surface about a hundred metres away from the raft, perhaps a breeding pair. Our engineless vessel, slow-moving and quiet, was a superb observation platform for marine life. We were not able to go to search for animals, but they came to us, or they were simply living there in the ocean, going about their normal lives and ignoring the raft. Indeed for the fish who lurked beneath *Hsu Fu* whether the hungry dorados or the half-dozen unidentified plump, pale-grey fish who were so sluggish they must have been plankton feeders, the raft was a benefit. It provided them with shade on bright days, and a fixed point in the ocean. We ourselves had only a passive role. We waited there on our bundle of bamboos, hoping for a favourable wind and content to be positioned almost exactly on the wriggly arrow printed on the chart which marked the east-going current.

The weather was typical for that time of year: a series of low pressure systems passing over us as they headed out into the Pacific. They usually brought a spell of favourable south-westerly wind with some sunshine, then the wind turned to the north and brought rain, before easing to a damp calm followed by a south-westerly wind, and the cycle began again. The repeated showers, some of them heavy, meant that the surface of the raft and its crew and contents never dried out. The bamboo-mat covering of the cockpit floor was always sodden, and occasionally covered by a thin film of a puddle spreading right across it – partly from the sea washing in through cracks in the corners of the basket, partly from the ocean coming right up through the fabric of the cockpit, bubbling and oozing between the weave of the bamboo basket where the coating of tar had been worn away by the constant flexing and shifting of the raft. I had begun wearing deck shoes because the soles of my feet had turned dead white as a result of going barefoot. By day and on night watch we were usually standing in a puddle for sixteen to eighteen hours so that shoes or boots were only a partial solution as they rapidly got soggy too, and our feet were encased in wet chambers. Joe recommended that everyone thoroughly dried and massaged their feet before climbing into a sleeping bag or they risked skin rot. The floors of all three baskets – cockpit, main and forecabins – also seemed to be softer, flexing up and down more easily as the waves passed underneath them and pushed them upward. Trondur had compared the movement to the heartbeat of a great animal.

August 17 was a red-letter day because at last the dorado-catching campaign succeeded. For hour after hour our two fishermen – Trondur and Loi – had experimented with every possible device and technique in their attempts to catch the escorting dorados. They had tried spinning with silver lures, trailing imitation squid, putting scraps of food on hooks, spearing and harpooning. All failed until finally Trondur decided that the dorados were too wary to come close enough to be speared, and too canny to be duped by imitation spinners and lures.

'They eat flying fish,' he announced, 'and they know very well what flying fish look like.' So he sat down to use his craftsman's skills to make an imitation flying fish. Taking a ready-made blue-and-silver plastic minnow for spinning as the 'flying fish' body, he carefully cut out two pairs of gossamer wings from a scrap of wrapping material. These wings he carefully stitched to the plastic minnow, and with no more than an old bamboo pole and twenty feet of line tied to the end, he flicked his creation into the water. As usual a hungry dorado prowled out from under the shade of the raft to see what was floating in the water. Normally the fish would take one look at the lure, and turn back in disgust. But not this time. First one, then another dorado lunged at the fake flying fish but failed to take the hook.

Trondur carefully hauled in the lure. He had been watching closely.

'Wings too long,' he said. 'The fish mouth do not close on the hook.' Taking his knife he trimmed half an inch off the gossamer wings. Back into the water went the lure and thump! within five seconds a predatory dorado had bitten on the hook. After three days of total frustration trying to catch the elusive fish, Trondur did not give the dorado a chance. Whoosh! and a fine ten-pound dorado was plucked out of the ocean and came flying through the air to land with a splattering, thrashing thump in the cockpit.

Trondur had a smile of pure triumph on his face. 'Beautiful fish,' he declared, staring at its brilliant, jewel-like iridescence. 'Before we eat it, I paint it.'

Imitation flying fish lure

While he was painting, Loi borrowed the rod and new lure. With his fifth cast he, too, had a dorado firmly hooked, and flapping on the fore-deck. Our fishermen had cracked the problem. Until the dorados learned to be wary of the new-style 'flying fish', we had a ready-made swimming larder escorting the raft, out of which we could pluck our supper, just so long as the fish we caught and ate were replaced by new-comers. If that was so, *Hsu Fu* might have the makings of an entire self-sustaining biosphere. We could not eat both of the dorados at one sitting, so Trondur cut the throat of the second fish to drain the blood, removed the guts to stop it spoiling, and hung it up overnight. In the morning he opened the fish and rubbed it lightly with salt. That way, he said, it would keep for at least ten days, and when we came to eat it, all we would have to do was to soak it in seawater for three or four hours to get rid of the curing salt.

The other outstanding success of the voyage so far was the perfor-mance of our little satellite radio. It was working flawlessly. Every day I would switch on, connect up with the satellite, and send a message to be delivered to the Mariners' Museum a quarter of the globe away at Newport News in the State of Virginia, or to our friends in the DHL office in Hong Kong. To Hong Kong I reported our daily position, and for the museum there was an update on daily life aboard *Hsu Fu*, which the museum distributed over the educational computer links to participating schools and colleges in Virginia. Schoolchildren, college students, and visitors to the museum learned what was going on aboard *Hsu Fu* within hours of the event. It was strange to sit there in the middle of the Pacific on a half-awash raft, with the ocean gurgling and splashing all around, totally remote from the outside world, almost stationary in that immense ocean, and write out short reports for people who would be travelling to work or to school in cars and buses, eating normal meals, washing in hot water that came from a tap, wearing dry clothes, and sleeping in beds without the constant routine of waking up to go on night watches. And then there were the responses, the questions sent in by schoolchildren ranging in age from seven years old to teenagers. What did we eat? How difficult was it living so close together in such a small area? Were we afraid of sharks? and where did we go to the bathroom? That last question was the one we had been expecting, because Rex had already met it in Japan. Two days before we sailed from Shimoda he had been invited to give a talk at a local primary school. When he finished speaking, the teacher asked if there were any questions. Immediately one small Japanese arm shot up at the back of the classroom. Where did we go to the bathroom? came the question which was at the front of every child's mind whether in Japan or Virginia.

At midnight on 17 August a bright blaze of light flared up on the horizon to the east of us, from the open ocean.

'Californian lighthouse!' joked Joe. 'We must be there already,' though we knew there were 4,000 miles of open ocean between us and America. The lights must have been from a squid-fishing boat using arc-lights to attract the squid shoals to the surface, and early in the following dawn we had a brief glimpse of a distant hull disappearing over the horizon. It was only the second vessel we had seen since leaving Shimoda, which was surprising since our raft was close to the Great Circle route, the shortest track between Japan and the United States, and we had expected to see more shipping. Our only previous sighting had been a small tanker which steamed past *Hsu Fu* at a distance of only three miles and in broad daylight, but probably never even noticed the bamboo raft so low in the water. In the next few days, if progress was good, our chances of seeing other ships would reduce even farther because by then I hoped we would have reached the latitude of forty degrees north where we would turn directly east and leave the Great Circle shipping route.

The new course would add several hundred miles to our crossing, but would have been the most likely way the early Chinese mariners would have sailed, using the technique called latitude sailing when they made east-west passages. In its simplest version latitude sailing means keeping the Pole Star at the same distance above the horizon as you sail, and this ensures that you are travelling directly east or west. Possibly the Chinese would have had much more sophisticated ways of measuring the angles of other stars, using templates which they held up to the sky, or they would have recorded the angle of the sun at noon in various seasons of the year. Such skills would have been helpful, but not essential. Merely by sailing directly east or west on the Pacific the early navigator could have directed his path with enough accuracy to make scouting voyages, whether looking for islands in the sea or distant lands to colonise. For *Hsu Fu* the choice of the 40th parallel was a matter of common sense. If we strayed too far north of the line, we would enter an area where there was a much higher risk of severe storms. If we wandered too far south we would lose the advantage of the North Pacific Current and probably meet more head winds. But nothing was certain. A great deal would depend upon our weather luck: whether the depressions passed north or south of us; whether we were hit by really ship-killer storms; whether we were becalmed. Our raft travelled so slowly that we could not run away from bad weather. We had to accept whatever came at us, and we could not even guarantee to be able to stay close to the 40th parallel. Prolonged head winds or winds from the beam could drive us well off our desired route. We would just have to wait and see what happened.

In fact, we now entered a fog belt. For the next three days the raft lay in a dense, clammy shroud. There was no wind, and the sea swell gradually eased until at times we seemed suspended in a grey miasma with no horizon and no way of gauging distance, almost making you feel disoriented. Ropes became fringed with a rime of dew. The motionless sails stiffened and grew dark with the water soaking into the cloth. Inside the cabins all our clothes, the bamboo-slat floor, the bamboo framework were wet to the touch. Droplets of water condensed on every surface. The only consolation was that it was still warm enough, twenty-two degrees, not to be uncomfortable, just clammy. Discomfort came when strange, unexpected sprinkles of rain dropped through the fog shroud, falling silently and vertically through the still air.

Through this grey mist came fluttering a small shore bird. Perhaps it was exhausted, perhaps it had lost its bearings in the thick fog. But it suddenly appeared out of the grey surroundings, and settled on the cabin roof with a thin scratching sound of its claws which could be heard over the absolute silence of the fog bank. We were accustomed to birds settling on the raft to rest. It had happened on the way to Taiwan, a couple of times off Japan, and a similar migratory bird had briefly stopped on the raft two days earlier. Hitch-hiking birds are a cliché of ocean sailing. So we paid little attention. Normally such temporary visitors stay a few hours, a day at the most, and then fly on their way, or perhaps are found dead next morning, from exhaustion or hunger. This little creature seemed no different. It was a shore feeder, a young turnstone, with soft brown plumage overlaid with elegant diamond netmarks of olive, yellow, and buff. It had a straight, sturdy beak, and spindly, long legs, deep coral-red, with wide, thin feet so that it walked with a high-stepping, almost mincing gait. Naturally we put out a small saucer of fresh water in case it was thirsty, and some biscuit crumbs, and then thought no more about it. The bird stayed on the main cabin roof, watching us nervously. Every time anyone moved forward, walking along the cabin roof, the little hitch-hiker would leap nervously into the air, fly out a few yards over the sea, then curve back to land again safely out of reach on the forecabin, or on the little woven shelter by the helm which we called the 'Number 9 Bus Shelter'.

That night a gentle breeze sprang up from the west, and at dawn, although the fog was still there, *Hsu Fu* was gliding forward at walking pace over a calm sea. As the sun rose higher, it became powerful enough to break through the fog layer directly above us and shine down on us to create a strange, enclosed, isolated sunlit world – our own private patch of sunlight and warmth, while twenty-five metres away a solid-seeming wall of grey vapour enveloped us through 360 degrees and was the limit of our existence and senses. There was no vision beyond that wall, no sound except the nearby murmur of the sea rippling between the bamboos of the hull.

We opened a tin of porridge oats, one of the tins we had bought in Hong Kong, and kept back as a luxury to vary our breakfast diet. But after so long at sea, with random baths in seawater when the ocean had invaded our storage barrels, the tin had leaked. The oats looked firm and fresh, but were rancid. Trondur and I liked porridge so did not mind, and we ate our serving. Loi and Rex looked dubious, but Joe was delighted. He hated porridge and as the person in charge of ship's stores was happy to condemn the tin as unfit to eat, and open another pack of muesli. He was about to dump the contents of the porridge tin overboard when we remembered our hitch-hiking friend. To our surprise the little bird was still with us. He had not flown on his way, and after twenty-four hours on board was strutting around, even looking mildly miffed when anyone disturbed him. He seemed to regard the roof of the main cabin as his own territory, and not a place for humans. In offhand style we had named him Fred, but had failed to persuade him to eat anything. Fred obviously preferred fresh meat, and had marched up and down the lattice-work of the cabin roof, poking and prying with his narrow pointed beak into every crevice, winkling out any of the remaining ants and lice which might still be lurking there. But after three and a half months at sea there could have been scarcely a single insect left, and Fred must have been very hungry. Joe tried scattering a few flakes of rancid oats on the cabin roof, and rather to our surprise Fred pecked at one, and seemed to find it to his liking. The previous day he had rejected an offering of hard yellow lentil seeds which we had found unpalatable and difficult to cook. Now Fred picked up another flake, and then another, stalking from one offering to the next. We noticed that he

'Fred'

walked around the oat flakes lying in the open, and preferred to dig out those flakes which the wind blew into the cracks between the bamboo strips. The concealed flakes must have reminded him of hunting for food on a shingle beach. In any event, we carefully put the entire tin of porridge oats aside for Fred's meals for as long as he cared to stay as a hitch-hiker, and *Hsu Fu*'s cabin top acquired what seemed to be a light scattering of dandruff as we regularly sprinkled Fred's daily rations for him to hunt and peck out of the nooks and crannies.

All this time Trondur had been trailing a mess of disgusting-looking shark bait in the water beside the raft. On the end of a heavy fishing-line as thick as a pencil he had tied various lumps of offal, most recently the head, guts and backbone of the dorado he had caught, and these pieces of offal were gradually disintegrating and growing white and ragged. Trondur had not bothered to attach a hook because, he said, he did not know what sort of sharks and big fish might swim in that part of the ocean, and he wanted to find out before he set about trying to catch them. Always alert to animals in the sea around the raft, Trondur had already seen three different sharks, at various times, come swimming up to inspect the trailing lure, reject it, and sink back into the depths. Just before noon he caught sight of another large torpedo-shaped fish, about four feet long, approaching the revolting bundle of bone and guts. Once again the marauder rejected the offering, but instead of veering away or diving, the questing fish cruised forward about two metres away from the side of *Hsu Fu*, swimming along the length of the raft to see if there was anything else to eat. Reacting quickly, Trondur had already scrambled forward to the foredeck, unlashed his harpoon which was kept tied to the forecabin roof, and was waiting for him. Thunk! With a beautiful clean throw Trondur made a direct hit. He threw the heavier of his two harpoons, the one normally used for small whales, and the head of the weapon smashed clean through the big fish, killing it instantly. Trondur hauled his catch on board, and found he had an eighteen-kilo kingfish, a fish like a giant mackerel, and we would have a fish bonanza, fish steaks for the next three days and a welcome break from our dreary rota of bonito, salami and tinned tuna.

But Trondur was not yet done. Now that he had an idea of the size of the local sharks, he reset the shark line, fitted this time with the correct hook and wire trace. At two in the morning I was awakened by tremendous thumps and crashes which were shaking the cabin. Scrambling out,

Kingfish

I found Trondur on the foredeck in the darkness, wrestling with a very lively five-foot shark which had taken the bait during Trondur's night watch. Typically, Trondur had not considered it necessary to get help. Rex, his watch companion, was still in the cockpit attending to the helm. Apparently Trondur had noticed that the shark bait had been attacked, gone to the foredeck, and hauled in the brute single-handed. Heaving the enraged shark on to the foredeck, he was calmly dodging the snapping jaws amid flying spray as the shark thrashed back and forth on the semi-submerged foredeck, and Trondur steadily shortened the fishing-line until he had literally tethered the animal like a dangerous dog to the foot of the foremast, tying its head tightly to the timber. Only then did he call back to Rex to bring him the big kitchen knife, and he cut the shark's throat.

'You said you wanted to try shark steak,' I said to Joe who had appeared, rubbing the sleep from his eyes.

He groaned. 'I've not yet digested last night's massive serving of kingfish we had for supper, and there are at least three more meals from that catch.'

Dawn was a flat calm and as the fog lifted we could see the specks of two deep-sea fishing boats in the distance. They were inquisitive and came over to see who we were. They proved to be two medium-sized Japanese vessels, one of them a fishery research ship, the other an escorting trawler. As usual they were lavishly equipped, bristling with the latest electronic gear, and kept in immaculate condition. Each vessel must have cost a huge sum, and carried at least a score of men on board. Every crew member had a pair of binoculars, and the bridges of the two ships looked like the display windows of binocular shops as curious eyes scanned us, and the two boats circled what must have looked to them like a floating vegetable disaster. From the flying bridge of the nearest boat the skipper called out something in Japanese over his loudhailer system, and we waved cheerfully to show that everything was all right. A few moments later we saw a short, burly Japanese crew member wearing sea boots run forward on the deck of the vessel. He opened up the lid of what must have been a fish tank holding their live catch. Dipping in his hand, he pulled out a small, rather meagre-looking silvery fish, and a moment later it was thrown flying through the air to land on the raft. Then there were gestures from the fishing boat which obviously meant 'did we want any fish?' Trondur could not resist the opportunity. He too clumped forward in his big sea boots, reached down on the foredeck and pulled up the blue-grey length of a five-foot shark. Lifting it up so the Japanese could see our catch, he held the shark in one hand and the little Japanese fish in the other, and shook his head solemnly – no, we have our own size of fish, thank you! The Japanese sailors applauded.

The captain of the research ship was waving a piece of paper at us and then pointing to it. I looked through my own binoculars. He was holding up a weather map, and then making exaggerated wave motions with one hand. 'Hurricane!' boomed the skipper's voice over the fishing boat's loudhailer. A storm was coming! I gave the thumbs-up sign to say we were all right and had understood. Finally the research vessel began to sidle sideways towards us, using its bow thrusters to close the gap with *Hsu Fu*. What looked to be the youngest and most junior crew member was leaning over the ship's rail holding out a big black parcel to hand to us, obviously a gift. When he was close enough, Loi reached out and accepted the package. It was heavy, carefully wrapped in plastic sheeting, and sealed with tape. '*Origato! Origato!* Thank you! Thank you!' we called out, and waved our thanks. The skipper of the research ship was still pantomiming the action of big waves, and making gestures that he would now be heading for shelter. '*Origato!*' we called again and the two fishing vessels began to move off, picking up speed so quickly that they were soon small dots in the distance.

'I wonder what it contains,' I said to the others, weighing the heavy

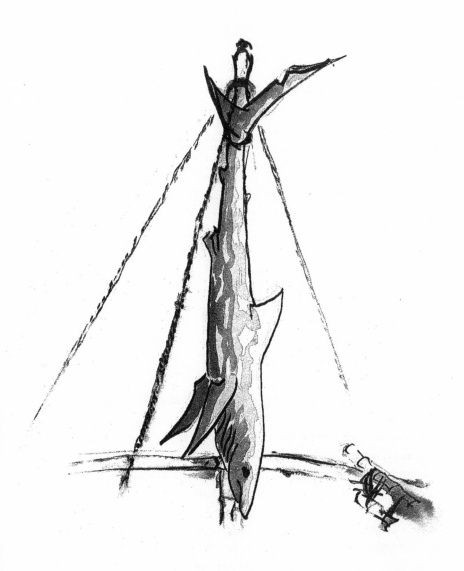

package speculatively. The parcel was oblong and quite heavy. Two bottles of sake, someone guessed. A cake? Some tins of food? It was too heavy to be cartons of cigarettes, a traditional present between ships meeting at sea. All of us were wondering, and all of us were hoping that it contained some sort of food to vary our monotonous diet. No more guessing games. I put an end to the delicious speculation by slitting the plastic wrapping with my knife and peeling back the cover. There, neatly tied up in a bundle were two dozen Japanese comic books and five or six soft-porn girlie magazines! All of us were convulsed with laughter.

Twenty-four hours later we had emerged from the fog zone, and *Hsu Fu* looked like a busy laundry. Every spare surface was covered with items put out to dry. Clothes, sleeping bags, spare canvas, all were hung up or spread out to catch a few rays of sunshine. Only the solar panels were kept clear so they could continue to generate electricity. Fred the migrant bird was very irked that his foraging and strutting area was so restricted, and that he should be disturbed every few moments by someone rearranging a shirt or a damp set of oilskins. He showed his disgust by defecating on a clean shirt – Joe's inevitably. Fred was enjoying the good life, now that he had his regular issue of Quaker Porridge Oats, but he still liked to keep up an appearance of being a migrating bird. At dawn and dusk he would launch himself upward determinedly from the cabin roof as if to fly to the far side of the world, climb up to about one hundred feet, circle and look around presumably to see land or to stretch his wings. But after one or two quick circuits he would change his mind, turn back, and come in on his favourite patch of cabin roof making a quick scratchy landing. There he would shake out his feathers and hunch down comfortably, looking as if he had owned the spot all his life. He was adapting so well to living on the raft that our only fear was that he would fall off the cabin while sleeping. His thin claws found no grip on the slick surface of the solar panels, and when he lost his balance he would slide down the panels like a novice skier before reaching safer footing on the bamboo weave. Nor did he like being disturbed at night, giving a short sharp peep of protest whenever the night watch had to clamber across the cabin roof to handle sails. He was still shy enough not to let anyone touch him, and he scuttled away if you got too close. But if you stayed still, Fred would come stilt-walking over to within six inches and examine you with his beady eyes. And if you lay down on his patch of cabin roof to relax, you would feel the featherlight touch of his matchstick feet as Fred strutted right over you.

To preserve our surplus fish meat Trondur built a drying chimney on the foredeck. Using side panels of woven bamboo, he contrived a system of racks and strings on which he spread or hung the chunks of shark meat and kingfish to dry in the air. Unfortunately, the drying chimney had a marked resemblance to an outside privy, which looked very odd perched on the bows of a raft, while the display of fishing mementoes was truly gruesome. There was the rotting head of the kingfish with its beak-mouth

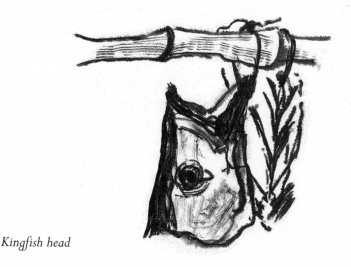

Kingfish head

gaping and glazed sunken eyes, shark jaws, strips of rancid shark meat, and the backbone of the kingfish clearly showing the hole in the spine where the harpoon smashed through the skeleton. With this assembly dangling off ropes and stays, and swaying and smelling in the wind, I could not decide whether *Hsu Fu* looked more like the backyard of a peasant's hut in the Dark Ages or the offerings in a Red Indian burial-ground.

Now that the sun had come out the ocean itself turned the most remarkable shade of blue. It was something which Trondur noticed with the eye of an artist. Under those conditions the blue of the Pacific was very different from any other sea. It was not the pale green-grey turning to blue of the North Atlantic, nor the azure of the Caribbean or Arabian Sea, nor the dull brownish-blue of the China Sea, but a deep indigo-blue. What is more, the special Pacific blue seemed to transfer to everything in the sea: the electric luminescence of the plankton was a more powerful luminous blue, the blue of fish more vivid, the shadow under the raft deep blue, even the shark we had caught was such a startling blue in the first few hours after it came out of the water that I thought it must be some rare new species. Only later did the skin of the shark turn back to its more usual blue-and-white shading. As for the water itself, it was such an intense colour it seemed that blue was the only colour in the spectrum, and the special signature of the Pacific.

Loi and I were watching the ghostly blue shapes of dorados swimming under the raft on the night of 25 August. It was three in the morning, and our dorado escort had now increased to an astonishing total of thirty or forty predatory fish, ranging in size from two feet in length to monsters which must have weighed thirty kilos. They loitered under the raft, or split up into smaller packs and went hunting, swimming out thirty or forty metres from the raft where we could still see their luminous trails fizzing through the surface like meteors as they attacked their prey. Loi was hoping that a dorado would come close enough to the raft to be speared, and was balancing on the edge of the raft, holding Trondur's lightweight harpoon. Occasionally he would jab futilely at a passing luminous trail. I shone a torch into the water hoping to attract a curious dorado to the light. Suddenly I sensed a flashing movement out of the darkness, felt a slight blow on the hand holding the torch, and there was a furious flapping and splashing on the outermost bamboo by my feet. Loi's reactions were incredibly quick. He leaned down and grabbed something before it could slip back in the water, then held it up for me to see. At first I thought it was a snake, but then saw that he was holding an extraordinarily thin fish – a snake fish. It was about two feet long, a bright silver ribbon with a mouthful of needle teeth and a ferocious expression. It must have been attracted to the light and tried to attack it, flinging itself out of the water only to land on the raft where Loi promptly slit its throat to use its flesh for bait the next day. Soon afterwards Loi gave up his fruitless fish-stabbing, and we watched the first light in the eastern sky, when whoosh!, close to the boat and just visible on the black water, was the blacker slick shape of a thirty-foot whale which had surfaced no more than twenty metres away. Twice more the great animal rose to breathe, the appearances about a minute apart, and then it was gone.

Dawn came, bringing in a hot sunny day without wind, and Joe made the sad discovery that Fred was missing. He had last been seen at dusk the previous evening, foraging for his usual supper of porridge oats on the main cabin roof. Joe noticed his absence in the night, shining a torch to avoid stepping on him but finding no sign of Fred. Now there were only the uneaten remains of his porridge flakes, and no sign whatsoever of our elegant little companion with his olive-green-and-yellow netmarks. He was, it is true, never a very satisfactory mascot. He never lost his fear of human motion, but we had grown accustomed to him being around, living his own hunt-and-peck spindly-legged existence and sharing the raft with us. We could only hope that he had not fallen off the cabin roof at night, but had deliberately chosen to resume his migration flight, well rested and well fed on plenty of porridge.

The morning calm was Rex's chance to carry out his second survey of hull growth. Joe walked around the raft keeping pace with him and making notes, while Rex swam down the length of *Hsu Fu*, a ruler in hand, visiting the various observation points and calling out the new measurements of weed length and barnacles. He had almost completed the circuit when I shouted to Loi and Trondur who had been seated on the bow fitting a new heavier handle to a fish-spear: 'Look! The dorado pack is hunting!'

It was like a pack of hungry wolves which had seen the deer. A single dorado sighted a school of small fish and sped towards it. His sudden movement, perhaps the vibration of his rush, alerted the other dorados in the group, and they, too, took to the chase. Suddenly the sea split open in a dozen places, as dorados leaped gracefully, almost, joyfully into the air, curving down in elegant arcs and leaping again as they raced towards their prey. When they reached their target, the water churned with energy as the dorados circled a shoal of terrified fish, circling and circling until they were tightly packed, then rushing in for the slaughter. The dorados were in a feeding frenzy, oblivious to all else. The small fish broke into smaller shoals, desperately seeking escape. The dorados, and about forty of them by then had drawn to the killing ground, also divided into groups of eight or ten and continued to harass and slaughter, charging into their prey and feeding. The whirlpools of activity became three or four, each marked by the flashing blue shapes and yellow dorsal fins and tails of the dorados which often showed above the surface of the sea like the fins of goldfish in a pond. A circling, whirling commotion of killing approached the raft, and Loi and Trondur standing on the stern tensed in anticipation, fish-spear and harpoon in hand.

Soon the hunting dorados were themselves the hunted as they came within striking distance. Time and again Trondur and Loi jabbed down into the clear sea with their weapons, but the dorados were moving so quickly, flickering and charging here and there that it was difficult to strike the target, and the refraction made it difficult to judge the angle. But even with the tips of harpoon and spear flashing down among them the ravening dorados paid no heed until finally Loi gave a great whoop of triumph as he thrust downward with his newly hafted fish-spear. He had struck a splendid ten-kilo dorado clean from the top, a shrewd hit as the hatchet-shaped fish presented a narrow target from above. Before the fish could twist away, Loi followed up with a second quick downward push and this time pierced the fish clean through. Like a veteran Loi twisted the shaft so the barbed head would not pull back, and heaved the wounded dorado on board where it lay thrashing on the bamboos. Still the other dorados paid no attention whatsoever, so intent were they on their slaughter, not fleeing even when Trondur's heavier harpoon knocked a deep gash out of the side of the largest dorado in the pack, a great fifteen-kilo brute.

Five minutes later and the hunting pack had moved out of range, when Loi excitedly drew back his fish-spear to stab at another, larger shadow that came gliding up out of the blue depths.

'Loi! No!' I said and caught his arm before he could strike. 'It won't taste so good. It's shark!'

'They have good nose,' said Trondur. 'They come when they smell blood.'

'Want to get back into the water to complete your notes on the last observation point ?' I asked Rex, who had hauled himself on board to watch the fun.

'No, I think I will wait for that last set of figures,' he replied.

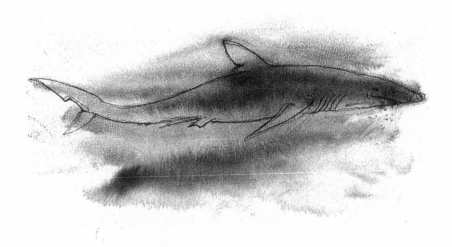

1 1

S UNFISH AND D OLPHINS

It began as a bubble in the great warm mass of tropical air which lay in a belt extending north of the Equator by some fifteen degrees, a bubble of unstable energy which unsettled the ordered pattern of pleasant summer weather. Within hours the bubble had begun to expand and rise, sucking in the surrounding air. As it rose, the rotation of the earth gave the bubble a twist so that it began to gyrate, adding strength and speed to the inrush of air. Very soon the bubble had a life of its own, growing destructive energy, and a name – Keoni.

'Steve', 'Tasha', 'Vernon', 'Winona'. Formerly the names given to typhoons were all feminine but now the meteorologists gave out boys' as well as girls' names when they were born, like all typhoons before them, over warm water. The south-western part of the North Pacific is the world's major breeding ground for typhoons, and the season when they are most likely to form is between July and October. The more notorious storms work up their maximum power over the ocean, track towards the coasts of China or Japan, then strike the land with terrific force, causing enormous devastation. But the moment they leave the sea and move over land, the typhoons began to lose their virulence. So the worst effects are felt on the immediate coastal areas, or on islands like the Philippines and Ryukyus . . . or by seafarers.

The entire schedule of *Hsu Fu*'s voyage had been shaped to minimise the typhoon risk. By leaving Hong Kong in May, and travelling as quickly as possible to Japan, I had hoped to clear the main typhoon region by the onset of the worst typhoon months. Even with *Hsu Fu* sailing so slowly, the plan had worked reasonably well. Behind us there had been typhoons over the Philippines and Taiwan, and we had escaped the first major storms to hit Japan. But we knew there was no reason to be complacent. Each day there were warnings and advisories about the movements of typhoons or near-typhoons – 'Severe Tropical Storms' as the meteorologists called them – which were tersely printed on the screen of my little laptop computer as it collected the ocean weather forecasts broadcast via satellite radio from the national meteorological agencies in Japan and the United States. Most of the typhoons and their near cousins were far away, and no cause for worry. But occasionally a storm sent a shiver down the spine, particularly the day when a typhoon was reported as smashing into Miyako, bringing eighty-mile-an-hour winds and huge waves. We wondered how our friends in the little harbour had fared, and how many of their green trees had been snapped.

Now came Keoni. As a typhoon Keoni probably did not even rate a mention in the newspapers or on news bulletins because she stayed out to sea and caused no land-based damage. But because Keoni never left the water, the typhoon's lifespan was longer, and the accumulated force was all that much more extended. Keoni was born south-east of us, in the open ocean not far from Midway Island. Pressure at Keoni's centre was already dangerously low at 960 millibars, when the storm system was first reported. She had already begun to gyrate and deepen, before expanding like some mammoth top. By 24 August Keoni was a full-blown typhoon, spinning viciously and like a giant child's top when it touches the ground, had started to move along a curving path of her own, away from the Tropic and into the North Pacific. From the very earliest moments of her life, radio warnings began to be transmitted to all ships and aircraft potentially in her path – winds of over 70 miles an hour in her centre, 50 miles an hour within a circle up to 100 miles from the core, and gale force winds on a radius of as much as 200 miles. There were also predictions about Keoni's course. Weather satellites kept their electronic eyes on her. Hourly they sent back pictures of her erratic and destructive progress. At first the meteorologists thought that she would travel almost due north. Then they sent out another warning. Keoni had changed direction.

Keoni began to head north-west, in the general direction of *Hsu Fu*. On board the very thought of Keoni was enough to have me lying awake worrying at night. It was an unhappy coincidence that she had appeared from the direction of Midway. I remembered all too well that it was here that the American writer-adventurer Richard Halliburton, very well known in the United States for his recreation of historic travels and with a long series of successful journeys to his credit, had vanished when his Chinese junk *Sea Dragon* went down with all hands in a typhoon. At seventy-five feet *Sea Dragon* had been larger than *Hsu Fu* and a much more substantial vessel than a flimsy bamboo raft. For three days I checked Keoni's position, transferring the weather data to my chart. At first Keoni had seemed very remote, too distant to be a real worry. Then as she began to move towards us, her predicted track appeared to carry her well clear of our position, and again my worries eased. They eased still further when it began to be reported that Keoni was weakening, the core pressure was rising and the winds sucked into her maw had begun to ease. But on 24 August Keoni unexpectedly began to intensify and deepened again. Core pressure fell back. The wind speeds rose to storm force and, worse, Keoni changed direction and began curving on a collision course with us.

We knew that Keoni was out there somewhere. The raft lay on a windless sea, rising and falling to a huge swell from the south-east, a sure sign of heavy weather in that direction. Unconcerned, a small flock of five albatrosses, sat in a cluster on the ocean, watching us, until they took to the air. Then they pattered along on the oily swell, their wings slowly beating, slapping their feet on the water like swans taking off, until the enormous wingspan gave enough lift to carry them soaring over the face of the ocean, turning them from ungainly duck-like creatures, with the beaks and heads of dodos, into the most elegant airborne wanderers. Trondur had offered to catch the albatrosses for our larder, a regular habit of Faeroese fishermen who devise little floating rafts baited with fish offal and armed with tangle hooks to catch the seabirds. Nineteenth-century British and American sailors thought nothing of killing and eating albatrosses, but out of superstition I forbade it. With a major typhoon hovering over the horizon, it would have been tempting fate unnecessarily.

The night of 25 August was particularly fraught. The meteorologists now located Keoni about 350 miles south-east of us, and were uncertain of the direction the typhoon would take. Keoni was moving erratically, travelling at fifteen knots, then slowing, then accelerating again, covering 200 miles per day, perhaps half that distance the next. The weather service could not predict her position twenty-four hours in advance with any accuracy better than a hundred miles. At that rate we were within one or two days of potential disaster, and on the morning of 26 August there was no question about the direction from which trouble might come. At dawn the south-east horizon had a sickly look. There were lowering banks of heavy cloud, shading from pale grey through to an intimidating black, and through them a blood-red sun appeared fitfully.

There were uneasy puffs of wind associated with the clouds, and though it was no more than a gesture, I directed that *Hsu Fu* should turn about, and sail north to put a few more miles between us and the typhoon. More reassuring was the noon report from the Japan Meteorological Agency that Keoni had moved another fifty miles closer but then halted, and was spinning on the same spot. The vortex was gradually filling. Keoni, they reported, was blowing itself out, and would shortly be downgraded from full-typhoon status to being a Severe Tropical Storm. I checked the pilot book. A Severe Tropical Storm contained fifty-five-knot winds at the centre. *Hsu Fu*, I judged, could withstand fifty-five-knot winds provided they did not last very long, and the sea state was not too severe.

All that day and the next we crept away from the northern perimeter of the storm. Thankfully Keoni stayed where she was, radiating the same steep, fast-moving warning swells which now encountered short, ugly waves arriving from the east. The surface of the sea became troubled and confused. The night was particularly bumpy with the waves thumping into the side of the raft, crashing against the sides of the wickerwork trays, and occasionally breaking high enough to deluge the thatch-and-bamboo plait cabin roof. When that happened, the slap and shudder of the wave was immediately followed by the loud trickling sound of seawater pouring down through holes in the cabin roof where the rattan lashings passed. We had rigged an inner lining of tent material to shield ourselves and our belongings, so the next sound was the drumming splatter of water hitting the fabric, before being diverted away to the side of the cabin and down to the floor where eventually the water would drain out through the sock valves. I lay listening to the creaks and groans and thumps of waves and bamboo, counting the number of times *Hsu Fu* was pummelled every minute, wondering if the waves were getting heavier or more frequent, and trying to calculate from the angle of heel and the rocking arc of the cabin whether the swell and waves were getting dangerous, reassuring myself with the memory of the very satisfactory capsize trials made with the test raft so long ago in Sam Son. But then I would recall that the capsize tests were made without masts, and that in Miyako we had fitted *Hsu Fu* with a pair of very strong, but very solid masts which surely would have made her more top-heavy.

But there was little we could do to improve the situation. We tried to make the raft more stable by sliding the eight leeboards deep down into their slots, as far as possible into the water, so that their weight would lower the raft's centre of gravity. But the force of the wave tops hitting the body of the raft and pushing it sideways made the lee boards act like great knife blades stuck between the bamboos, and twist so they began to prise apart the bamboos and risked splitting the vessel asunder. We dared leave the leeboards no more than halfway down, with ropes and guys rigged to relieve the sideways pressure. For the rest of the time it was a question of patience under uncomfortable conditions, particularly on the night watch. One man would stay on lookout duty, and his watch partner tried to relax, stretched out on the slats of the cockpit bench, fully dressed in oilskins and sea boots and with an old scrap of tarpaulin pulled over him to deflect the occasional wave which broke into the cockpit. It was like a tramp spending the night sleeping on a park bench while an occasional passerby threw a bucket of water over him.

For thirty-six hours *Hsu Fu*, deep-reefed, rode the periphery of the storm, while Keoni slowly expired. On the night of 27 August she was at her closest to us, only 130 miles away, but had changed course again, taking the characteristic swerving track of a fading typhoon which would move her clear of our position. By then Keoni was a spent force, no longer meriting the status of a Severe Tropical Storm, but now described as an extra-tropical depression. And at dawn we could see the pearly grey clouds of the outer edge of the storm system and realise how close she had come.

Of all the crew Rex appeared to have been the least perturbed by the typhoon's proximity. His ultra-methodical approach seemed to block off any doubts he may have had about our danger. It was as if he held a plan of his day's or week's activities in his head, and was carrying that plan whatever the circumstances. As a result he gave the impression of being totally without fear, steadily conducting his daily observations of wind

direction and speed, sea life and pollution even under the worst conditions. He also had a high threshold of discomfort. Unlike the rest of us,
his sailing clothing was inadequate. Joe and I both wore modern ocean
racing suits, and I had supplied a set for Loi. Trondur favoured enormous, traditional thigh-length sea boots and a long yellow oilskin cape
with a matching yellow sou'wester hat, which made him and his splendid beard look like a well-known advertisement for Fisherman's cough
lozenges or – if he briefly discarded the boots and wore his heavy sandals
instead – like a seagoing Russian Orthodox monk. But Rex had brought
along a second-hand Arctic sledging suit for his sea clothing. A red cov-
erall, it looked like a child's playsuit, and was designed to combat snow,
not spray and solid water, so was permanently wet inside. Unconcerned,
Rex put up with the dampness and ill fit, even when the suit rubbed
angry boils on his feet and wrists. And he appeared so promptly on
night watch when the changeover time came that Trondur and I could
only suppose he slept in it, too.

Trondur himself was more mellow and relaxed than I had ever known
him. He was quicker to smile and, where I had remembered him on former voyages as being taciturn, he now told jokes and chatted to the
crew. What he had said about the voyage being a holiday for him was
obviously turning out to be true, and he was so evidently the best seaman among all of us that I, as skipper, was often embarrassed to direct
him to any task. Yet he would respond instantly, because he was a sailor
to his fingertips and had inherited a long tradition of how a vessel should
be run. His ingenuity and artistry never ceased to intrigue the others.
Wedging himself in the cabin, he would paint with watercolours or
sketch in pen and ink, undeterred by the cramped and difficult environment. Or he would spend hours adapting, improving, and inventing
new fishing devices, whether melting down lead to recast it around a
fish-hook to make it sink to the correct depth, or devising a swivelling
reel from a discarded Japanese line-holder so that he could cast farther
using a home-made bamboo fishing-pole.

Loi was as much of a fishing fanatic as Trondur. He would go on casting and retrieving, casting and retrieving, a fishing lure with no thought
for time. And if a fish actually bit the hook, then Loi abruptly changed
from his normal self, quiet, friendly, and polite, into quite a different
person, intense and frantic. Loi and I shared watches, and one morning
I had seen him throw out and haul in the fishing-line at least a hundred

times since the first grey glimmer of dawn, the hour when he solemnly vowed – again like all fishermen – that the fishing was best. Suddenly a fish took the lure. With a shout of triumph Loi struck, saw he had a fine dorado on the line, and began hauling in. But the hook failed to catch firmly, and before the fish was safely aboard, the dorado shook itself free with a spectacular leap, twisting frantically through the air in a burst of green, silver and gold. When Loi lost a second fish in the same way half an hour later, he scrambled back into the cockpit, grumbling noisily in Vietnamese and shaking the lure in disgust. With vehement gestures he indicated that he thought the hook was wrong, and, without asking the owner's permission, burrowed furiously into Trondur's bag of spare fishing-tackle. He then selected a large double hook, snipped off the old hook with wirecutters, and using hands and teeth to pull the knots tight, fastened on the new hook, his hands shaking with haste. Moments later he was gone, hurrying back to the bow to start fishing again and leaving the cockpit strewn with fishing gear. It was a Jekyll-and-Hyde transformation. Normally so courteous and tidy, if Loi was fishing, he became brusque and rude, oblivious to his surroundings. Nor did he take account of the fact that we were barely a quarter of the way across the Pacific, and ahead lay week after week surrounded by the ocean and presumably all that time to fish. Loi's only priority was to get the fishing-line back in the water and a fish on the end of it.

The catch was welcome, but more to vary our diet than stave off hunger. The rations we had stowed aboard in Japan were monotonous but sufficient, and we were getting used to them. Dried bonito was rapidly becoming our favourite despite the fact that the hard chunks of fish had the shape and consistency of bits of well-seasoned teak. To prepare a meal of bonito, the cook first had to break up the fish into little pieces using a hammer and chisel, then soak the morsels in water for a day. The result was still very chewy, but generally considered delicious. Our chief regret was that the meagre supply of fresh fruit and vegetables – oranges and onions – was disappearing faster than planned. It was a race between rot and rationing. In Shimoda we had stocked up, or so we imagined, with enough oranges for each man to have one orange per day for the first forty days, and for Joe, the quartermaster, to issue three onions each day for the cooking throughout the ninety days I anticipated the complete Pacific crossing would take. But the oranges were going bad more quickly than expected, and so we were perpetually condemned to eating up the rank, soft oranges to prevent wastage. The onions were not much better. Some, of course, we had lost in our first bout of heavy weather when leaving Shimoda. Many of the others had gone damp and mouldy, and by the time the brown and putrid outer layers had been pared away, there was very little left to go into the frying pan. So any small triumph by the cook-of-the-day was appreciated by the rest of us. Joe earned murmurs of approval by discovering how to improve the tiny, hard lentil seeds which we had bought in Shimoda because they were cheap. The lentils had proved to be so hard, gritty and tasteless that it was like munching on a spoonful of coarse sand. Even Fred the hitch-hiking bird had rejected them. Now Joe discovered that if you spent half an hour patiently grinding the little seeds to fine powder, using an old bottle as a rolling pin, they could be mixed into a reasonably appetising paste. With dried bean curd and dried radishes, the lentils had been written into our menu rota as a vegetarian change from the standard sequence of dried bonito, salami and tinned tuna, so it was a great relief to be spared the prospect of thirty meals of yellow grit. However, no one was going to get fat. A standard lunch of rice or noodles was accompanied by one hundred grams of dried fish or meat, and those hundred grams were divided between five hungry men.

So hopes of a fish feast rose sharply on 30 August when Loi, who was standing stark-naked on the stern doing his wash, suddenly called out, 'Trondur! Trondur! Big fish! Big fish!' and pointed excitedly. There, barely five metres off the stern of the raft, a grey fin was sticking about a foot above the water. The animal, whatever it was, seemed to be lazily inspecting the raft. 'Shark!' said Rex. 'No, dolphin!' was Joe's opinion. The creature wavered now to one side of the raft and then to the other, the fin seeming to flop slightly with each change of direction. It was a very odd fin, and why was the creature swimming so slowly? Was it a questing shark? The animal's unconcerned behaviour seemed to indicate that, unlike a dolphin, it did not rise to the surface to breathe.

'Fish! Fish!' Loi was hopping up and down with excitement. He had grabbed his fish-spear, and was waving it menacingly at the strange fin. He could have been an Amazonian Indian on the edge of a dugout canoe in the midst of Brazil with his lanky black hair and yellow-brown skin, and not a stitch of clothing on him. Trondur had hurried forward to fetch his biggest harpoon which he kept strapped across the bows. He scrambled back, clutching it and the mysterious fin was still there, now no more than three metres off the stern and closing the gap in leisurely fashion. It was a foggy, chilly day, without sunshine so the sea was murky and opaque. In the grey-green water we could dimly see a large, pale body beneath the grey fin. Trondur took up his throwing position, crouched in the stern. Loi was literally quivering with excitement. The animal was just out of range. Like a lion tamer in a circus coaxing forward a reluctant lion or tiger with his whip, Trondur leaned out and gently splashed the tip of his harpoon on the water, enticing the animal forward. The fin moved a little closer, and hung there wavering. Thunk! Trondur hurled his heavy harpoon, and a split second later Loi's fish-spear went whizzing after it. Both weapons scored direct hits. Trondur hauled in mightily on the harpoon line.

No wonder we had been puzzled. The fish – for it was definitely a fish and not a mammal – was drawn closer to the boat and then heaved up with great difficulty on the bamboo stern, and it looked like no fish that we had seen before. It seemed to have forgotten its tail. It was big, at least four feet across, and almost circular, and swam on its edge like a great grey disc. At the leading edge was a soft, thick-lipped mouth, ridiculously small for such a large body, and a broad cowlike forehead. Indeed, the impression of a seagoing cow was heightened by the large, staring, rather stupid eyes, and a grey brindled skin. The fish had no real tail where one would expect. Instead there were two big fins, one on the upper edge which we had seen poking out of the water; the other fin projecting downwards from the lower side of the disc. It weighed almost forty kilos.

'A sunfish,' I announced, finally recalling that I had seen these curious-looking animals in a large aquarium. 'Let's hope it's good to eat.'

The fish was much too big and heavy to carry up the raft, so Trondur tied a rope to the carcass, levered the body back in the water, and towed it to the foredeck, the only space big enough to cut up the animal. Rex took measurements and found that the disc-shaped body was actually broader between the upper and lower fins, 1.33 metres from top to bottom, than from mouth to tail, 1.15 metres from front to back. Between the cowlike eyes it measured 20 centimetres. As Trondur cut up the catch, we waited hungrily.

But we were to be very disappointed. After sawing through the thick, rough skin, Trondur found that all the flesh was blubbery and glutinous. What looked like firm bone was white cartilage which his knife could cut through. The bits of flesh simply slithered and flopped and oozed and looked revolting.

'Like basking shark,' Trondur pronounced in disgust. 'No good to eat. Only liver is fine.' The liver looked hardly more appetising. It was massive. A spongy yellow blob thirty centimetres long and fifteen centimetres thick, and appeared more as if it came from a full-sized ox than a fish. It had an unappealing oily sheen. Trondur put the massive organ in a bucket and carried it back to the cockpit. 'Don't eat too much,' he said. 'Liver very heavy for stomach.'

His warning was unnecessary. We all looked at the mess of yellow matter with some foreboding. Warnings of blowfish, which contain deadly poisons in their livers, came to mind. What if this strange creature also stored toxins in its liver? The fish looked odd enough to provide all sorts of surprises.

'Have you eaten sunfish liver before?' Joe asked.

'No,' answered Trondur with his usual brevity. He cut up the liver into slices, boiled five of them with a dash of vinegar, then fried them with garlic and pepper. The portions were served up. I tasted mine cautiously. At first it tasted of almost nothing, just an incredible soft, almost insubstantial texture with a faint tinge of liver taste. It was like eating very soft, uncooked marshmallow or egg pudding. Then the flavour came through – it was rather good, slightly fishy like delicate cod's roe.

'Not bad, like duck or cod's liver,' I said.

Sunfish

Joe looked at me in disbelief, nibbled a small portion, then refused a second helping. No one, not even Trondur, was very enthusiastic.

'We'll boil up the rest of the liver to extract the oil,' I announced. 'Use it for greasing the ropes and blocks.'

The others, except Trondur, looked somewhat relieved.

In fact, the morale of the crew was very high, if morale was the right word. Everyone seemed to get on with their work and with one another, and not give a second thought to our overall situation. There had been no quarrels, no disagreements, and no tensions. Maybe this matter-of-fact approach was due to the maturity of the team. At twenty-eight Joe, our doctor, was the youngest, and the next in age, Rex, had experienced a long sea voyage to South Africa when his yacht was dismasted and brought to port on the Skeleton Coast of Namibia under jury rig in a voyage that had been planned to last two months, but lasted 104 days, the majority of them crawling along at less than a knot. Trondur, of course was imperturbable by nature, and Loi was as happy – if not happier – on sea as on land. With his village background and -straightforward fisherman's philosophy, Loi gave the impression that it was enough to think about the present, and to look forward to seeing America when he finally got there. Exactly when we might end our voyage was largely a matter of idle speculation. The past week had brought little or no progress towards America. The effects of Typhoon Keoni, head winds, and calms meant that the raft was almost stationary. Unless we got a month or more of favourable winds, the hoped-for landfall in late October was already looking very optimistic, though of course we made theoretical calculations. As navigator I constantly updated a 'most likely' window of arrival, but that window varied from sixty to eighty days ahead, and was so vague that it was barely good enough for simple practical purposes such as allowing Joe to keep an eye on how much food and water we had in reserve. We hardly ever discussed the conclusion of the journey because it seemed so remote and irrelevant. We all knew that many things could go wrong – storm, capsize, the loss of buoyancy and slow sinking – and each one of us had undertaken the voyage not for the moment of stepping ashore, but to experience what happened to us on a bamboo raft on the world's broadest ocean.

The evening after he harpooned the sunfish, Trondur turned his attention to the dozen or so smaller fish which we had noticed hovering around the stern of the raft for the past week. They were quite shy and nervous, usually swimming a metre below the surface, and about two metres away from the raft. But occasionally they would move out to one side of Hsu Fu, where they kept pace with the raft, riding the waves so that we could see by their profile that they were about fifty centimetres long, quick and agile. Selecting a smaller hook and lure, Trondur targeted the largest member of the little shoal, a handsome-looking fish, the shape of a small tuna. His choice of hook and lure was perfect. It took him just twenty minutes to pull in five of the fish – all of them bright silver with yellow fins and a dashing yellow horizontal line down each side of the streamlined body. It took him another ten minutes to fillet them for our supper. As he sliced open the second fish he grunted, 'You want more sunfish?' He held up the contents of the stomach – a piece of sunfish which had been thrown overboard and snapped up by our escorting yellowfins, as we called them for want of a more precise identification. The yellowfins were Hsu Fu's garbage collectors.

The efficiency with which Trondur caught the yellowfins taught me something about the way that ancient raft sailors could have survived at sea. On four previous voyages on replica ancient vessels, I had noted how few fish we managed to catch on a long voyage once we got out on the deep ocean, even with an expert fisherman like Trondur on board. On those trips it would have been possible, but only just, to have survived on the number of fish we caught. Now, adding up the number and size of the fish we had caught since Trondur had joined us at Shimoda, it was clear that if we had been, say, the crew of a raft on the Pacific 2,000 years earlier, we were catching easily enough fish to sustain us without any extra rations. So why the difference between the Pacific voyage and my previous sea journeys? The obvious reason, the more I thought about it, was that we were on a raft and not a normal hulled vessel. Hsu Fu's broad, shallow platform was a floating island where sea life chose to congregate. Each time it was calm enough for Rex to plunge his head underwater on a marine survey, he found himself staring into a huge fish tank the inhabitants of which ranged from tiny fish hiding in the fronds of cellophane weed, through shoals of fingerlings the size of cigarettes, to the yellowfin garbage collectors off the stern, four or five large dorados, half a dozen lazy plankton-eating brown fish, and occasionally a trio of tuna swimming in line ahead, about three metres down. A raft acquired a marine world of its own, and if the crew in early times had included expert fishermen with line and hook or with fish-spear, they should have been able to feed themselves.

A similar lesson could be drawn from our rainfall records. *Hsu Fu* was sailing through an uncommonly bad summer so presumably there was more rainfall than usual, but by our calculations we would have been able to catch enough rainwater to survive if we rationed it carefully and rigged efficient rain-collectors.

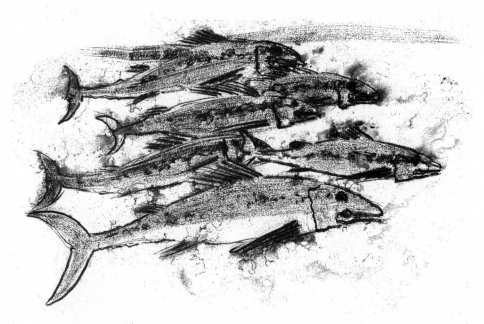

Yellowfin escort

Hsu Fu's experience was not the only evidence that sailors could survive aboard slow-moving vessels on the Pacific. In October 1832 a small Japanese trading vessel, *Hyojun Maru*, was crippled by a storm while sailing along the Japanese coast on a short-haul voyage. The little ship lost its mast and rudder, and was swept out into the Pacific. For more than a year the vessel drifted, prey to the winds and currents while her fourteen crew members tried to survive. Luckily their cargo included rice which they supplemented by catching fish and collecting rainwater. One by one, as the castaways died, their colleagues stacked the corpses in barrels. Three men were still alive when after fourteen months at sea, the *Hyojun Maru* went aground on the American coast south of Cape Flattery in what is now Washington State. Their ordeal was not yet over. In the depths of winter they were promptly enslaved by the local Indians, and held captive until word of their plight reached the Hudson Bay Company in Canada, and a trading ship rescued them. One of the group, a man named Otokichi, learned to speak English, but when the British authorities tried to return him to Japan, the Japanese refused him permission to land on the grounds that he had left Japan illegally. So Otokichi lived out his life in Singapore. Several other drift voyages across the Pacific by disabled Japanese vessels have been reported, all with the theme that their crews survived the experience by fishing and collecting rainwater. But the *Hyojun Maru*'s tale is the only one to have been thoroughly researched and documented, establishing the possibility of survival all the way across the Pacific.

The first day of September brought visitors. We were making good progress over a disturbed sea, the raft twisting and bucking, when Rex called out 'dolphins!' and a very large school of common dolphin – 300 animals we calculated – came rushing past us. For twenty minutes they sped by. They came in small squads, streaking past the raft a dozen dolphins at a time, curvetting and sometimes leaping clear of the water, curious about the raft and eager to get a closer look at us, yet still intent on their headlong rush south-eastward. In the bows Trondur and Loi poised with fish-spear and harpoon in hand, and half a dozen times each of them threw. But the dolphins were moving so fast, and the heaving tossing foredeck of the raft was slippery underfoot, the waves bursting up through the bamboos and foaming up to the knees of the hunters, so their aim was distracted. The entire school of dolphins raced past unscathed, to my private satisfaction.

The new month also brought a distinct drop in air temperature, and for the first time the crew began to appear in warm clothing. Joe and Rex still wore shorts in the daytime but now they put on warm jackets; Trondur donned a large baggy pair of ex-army khaki trousers, and Loi dug out a much-patched pair of trousers that had been his winter wear in Vietnam. I felt the cold much more than the others and was already wearing warm underwear, and hoping that I still had enough spare clothing in reserve for when the weather really became cold. Life on *Hsu Fu* was becoming a little more raw, a little more demanding.

Dolphin

Lunch that day was made from the two remaining pieces of dorado, slightly rotten. One piece had been hanging in the bows, successfully drying in the wind. But the other had fallen from the drying rack during the night, and been swirling about on the foredeck regularly washed by the sea, without being swept overboard, and was disintegrating. When I went to retrieve it for the cook, I noticed how a small black fish about the size and shape of a goldfish was picked up on a passing wave crest and tossed into the maststep. Stunned, the little fish dropped into a space between two crossbeams, and began swimming about in confusion, washed by the sea waves but unable to find a way clear. *Hsu Fu*, I thought, had to be one of the only ocean-going vessels to have fish swimming under it, clean through it, and even over it. When I returned to the cockpit, Joe was preparing our ration of dried bonito for the next day, cutting it up before the essential twenty-four hours of soaking.

'Now there are maggots on the bonito,' he announced, and held up a slice to show. Sure enough, it was sprinkled with several dozen small white specks. The specks were moving. 'I've wiped most of them off already,' added Joe. 'Do you think it will be all right to eat?'

'I've read that in the early nineteenth century the ship's biscuit was so riddled with weevils that you tapped your biscuit on the table to shake out the vermin,' I said. 'It's something you can tell your grandchildren, that you had to eat maggot-infested dried fish which was so tough you had to cut it with hammer and chisel.'

'It's true,' said Joe. 'But what they won't believe is that it is delicious.' And he prised off a morsel of bonito to nibble.

To an outsider, our raft would have appeared already to be on the verge of extinction. A strong north-westerly wind built up a fifteen-foot swell which came rolling down on us, crests breaking. An observer would have seen only the tip of *Hsu Fu*'s mainmast and its tattered yellow scrap of a wind burgee poking up above the crest of the wave, the whole body of the raft hidden in the trough, as if the vessel had been swamped. On board, even after twenty-four hours spent facing the advancing walls of water, I could still wonder if the next big wave would break awkwardly and come tumbling down like an avalanche, destroying everything in its path. But no, as the toppling water wall seemed about to engulf the semi-submerged raft, the bamboo platform rose smoothly and sedately up the watery cliff. The wave surged under us, its ridge actually passing through the body of the raft so you could follow the crest moving across the midships or, if you turned and looked over the stern, you saw the wave top lapping briefly against the rim of the cockpit basket. That was the instant when the basketwork floor of the cockpit suddenly bulged upward under the soles of your feet, sometimes welling up so powerfully that you were thrown off balance, or if you were sitting on a barrel, the whole barrel was tossed up into the air and your legs went flying outward. Then, just as quickly, the raft was slithering down the harmless back of the wave, surrounded by foam as the big wave hurried downwind, leaving a seething white froth behind it. Now, if you glanced upwind, there was the next water wall already bearing down on you, already threatening, and beyond it another wave, another crest, and another and another to the ragged line where the grey sea met a gloomy, overcast grey sky filled with heavy, menacing clouds, everything streaming towards you as inexorably as the advancing swells beneath it.

To stand on the creaking cabin roof, looking forward past the bow, brought an even more intimate sensation of the rythm of the ocean. As each large wave crest approached the raft, the wave was clearly defined by its own individual shape and its own pattern of foam. Then it struck the raft amidships and disappeared from view for a moment. A shudder of the vessel, followed by the distinctive rush and swirl of water around the base of the mainmast, told you that the wave was just then travelling through the open waist of the vessel. Spray came up where the wave collided with the heel of the mast and surged round the food barrels lashed there. Then, suddenly, the wave reappeared on the opposite side of the raft to where you last saw it. It was the same crest, the same foam, and a second or so later you appreciated how the raft and wave had intersected, the water surging unseen beneath you between the gaps in the bamboos, squirting through the crevices, breaking and reforming through the open structure so that, almost unhindered, the wave could go on its way across the face of the ocean, having intermingled with *Hsu Fu*.

The temperature continued to drop, as for the next four days the strong winds from the northern quadrant brought cold air down from the Aleutian Islands where a major low-pressure system was affecting the sea across a radius of 600 miles to the south of it. The Japan Meteorological Agency continued to broadcast gale warnings of thirty- to forty-five-knot winds, and *Hsu Fu* jogged along under deep-reefed sails, driven one mile south for every three miles we advanced. Daily our clothing became heavier – Trondur now in a thick knitted Faeroes wool sweater, Joe, Loi and me in warm oversuits, Rex still in his strange red sledging suit. It was too rough to fish, and our only companions were the albatrosses. All the other species of seabird seemed to have been driven away by the bad weather. The albatrosses, however, remained. Up to four of them were in sight at any one time, soaring and gliding among the large waves, sometimes like scraps of chaff, at other times like droop-winged aircraft from the jet age when they came towards us head-on, skimming over the waves to the raft, dipping in and out of the crests, the tips of their six-foot wingspan only inches above the surface of the ocean.

Finally the gales ended and left us becalmed on a moderate swell. The raft shifted uneasily on the sea, the bamboo stiffeners in the sails clattering on the masts. For the first time Loi was not his usual cheerful self. He sat huddled, looking pathetic and sorry for himself, and he would not smile. Wishing I spoke Vietnamese or he spoke better English, I struggled to find out what was the matter. We worked with an English-Vietnamese phrase book, Loi turning the pages and pointing out the words he wanted me to understand. In advance he had prepared a message and written a list of page numbers inside the front cover. But

it was still an agonisingly slow process as the words came out . . .
Pain . . . evening . . . need to see doctor . . . emergency . . . please help
me. Then Loi pointed at his abdomen and grimaced with pain to make
sure I understood. At first Joe and I thought that he had a stomach problem, but then as the phrase book was brought into action again, it turned
out that the pain was in his chest. Joe gave him a thorough medical
checkout in the main cabin, blood pressure, stethoscope, thermometer,
etc., and with the help of the phrase book Joe explained to Loi that he
was suffering from an infection in the lower right lung. But Loi refused
to accept a diagnosis from Joe. It had to come from me. Once again the
pages of the phrase book set out his thoughts. 'Hong Kong. Truc say you
help me.' I explained to Joe that it was not as if Loi mistrusted his medical skill, but that Loi had known me for more than a year, and when he
left Vietnam Truc had told him that if there was any problem, he should
turn to me. In a sense Loi was the child and I was the father. Loi
promised to keep warm, and Joe started him on a course of antibiotics
to try to clear the lung infection.

It was not our lucky week for weather. The next low-pressure system
passed south of us, bringing a gale from the east, and once again we had
to reef the sails deeply. While setting the reef, Joe was heaving on a
mainsail rope when it snapped, and Joe fell spectacularly backwards on
the cabin roof. Fortunately he was dressed in full ocean racing gear and
sufficiently padded not to be hurt. He was also clipped on with a safety
harness so, though he slid to the edge of the curved cabin roof, he did
not fall overboard, though it was a sharp reminder to wear a safety harness at all times. As Joe scrambled to his feet, Rex shouted and pointed
upward. One of the main shrouds, the ropes which supported the mainmast, was about to break. The shroud was made of three heavy strands
of rattan twisted together in a spiral and two of the strands had already
parted. The loose ends were untwirling crazily in the gale. Hastily we
dropped the mainsail to take the pressure off the mast before it toppled
overboard, and lashed everything down. Now we were being driven
backwards but there was nothing to do but ride out the gale and wait for
calmer weather to make repairs. Yet there was an awkward question left
in our minds – why had the heavy rattan cable snapped. It should have
lasted for at least a year. And if the rattan stay was breaking, what was
happening with the thousands of rattan lashings which held the raft
together? Were they breaking too? We examined the broken ends of the

rattan stay and found black spots of mould growing inside the strands. The rattan smelled sour and rotten. Perhaps the rain was the culprit. Fresh water rotted natural fibre, while seawater preserved it. We certainly hoped so, because the thought of the hull fastenings disintegrating was a fearsome prospect.

12

A CROSS THE DATE LINE

By 11 September, the thirty-ninth day since leaving Shimoda, *Hsu Fu* had covered a third of the distance between the two continents. Our noon position was exactly 3,000 miles from Cape Mendocino in northern California, our notional landfall along the Great Circle route. The day was, at last, calm and sunny, ideal for getting some of the damp out of our clothes which were spread on the cabin tops. I was experimenting with a rope tied to prevent the mainsail from flapping irritatingly from side to side as a gentle swell rocked the raft. Clambering up on to the cabin roof, I walked forward to adjust the rope. As usual I kept an eye on the mainsail in case it suddenly swung across the ship and swept me off. It was the classic accident aboard a sailing vessel, and had happened to Nina off Miyako, concussing her. Sure enough, as I walked forward the mainsail began to swing, gathering speed, and I took a quick pace forward to dodge. Clumsily I missed my footing on the sloping cabin roof, tripped, half-turned and was teetering off-balance when the mainsail slapped into me. I was knocked backwards, twisting and falling, and landed heavily on my back, square across the heavy bamboo pole which extended from one side of the raft to the other just aft of the mainmast. As I struck the bamboo, I heard an ominous cracking sound and wondered if I or the bamboo had made the noise, or both. In a cry of pain the breath was knocked out of me, and as I tried to move I knew that even if the bamboo was undamaged, I was not. For a few moments I lay spread-eagled on my back, unable to change position. My cry had alerted the others, and Rex and Joe scrambled forward to help. The mainsail was still swinging back and forth, sweeping the cabin top, so it was lowered and tied down. Then Rex and Joe rolled me off the bamboo crossbeam, and very slowly I pulled myself crab-like across the cabin roof, down into the cockpit, and gingerly levered myself through the narrow cabin entry and to my sleeping space. The pain of the short trip brought tears to my eyes. Joe gave me painkilling tablets. An hour later, when the shock was over, he confirmed my fears: I had broken two ribs.

My first thought was, what a trite accident! To be knocked down by the boom of a sailing vessel was so banal as to be embarrassing. Perhaps I was getting too old and not nimble enough, and too brittle in the bone. My second thought was, what a stupid place to be laid up: 1,500 miles out into the Pacific on a damp bamboo raft. My injury would mean extra work for the rest of the crew. Joe had warned me that for the next few days I would have to lie as quietly as possible until the ribs began to knit together, then it could take four or five weeks before I was fully fit. But the situation could have been worse. Joe was fairly confident that the broken ribs had not punctured the lungs, and if I did have to lie flat on my back and mend, I was less likely to be twisted and knocked about on a stable raft than a normal, more lively boat. For a moment I considered, but immediately rejected, the notion of leaving *Hsu Fu* or calling off the expedition. On board was a qualified doctor, and if I left the raft by transferring on a passing vessel, there was no likelihood that I would be able to rejoin *Hsu Fu*.

I could hear the broken ends of a rib clicking together as I breathed. The pain was so bad that I sincerely hoped that in the next two or three days we did not encounter a storm before the ribs began to knit together. I was deeply thankful that the accident had occurred on a sunny day and with a calm sea. To be knocked down by the mainsail under such stable conditions might be an embarrassment, but it was far better than to have suffered the accident in heavy weather and finished up like a partially squashed insect curled up in a cold, drenching, howling gale. Of course it was Trondur who inadvertently cheered me up. At the time of the accident he had left the other crew members to help me reach the cabin, and calmly continued with his work. That evening as he crawled into the cabin, and began to put on his foul-weather gear for the night watch, he said calmly, 'Extra watches, no trouble for the crew.'

'You'll have to take over running the ship,' I told him.

213

'Oh no, you are the skipper. We wait.' Then he paused. 'Nature is good. On the farm sometime sheep breaks a leg. We tie up with an old stick and some rope, and no problem. Week later. Sheep OK.'

I remembered that back on the Faeroes Trondur had broken his own leg some years previously. 'How did that happen?' I asked him.

'Hunting pilot whale,' he answered. 'We had driven them to the beach, and my leg was caught between two whales. Not much trouble.'

There were very few people in the twentieth century, I reflected, who got their legs crushed between whales.

In fact, the weather was against us. Next day started with heavy rain, followed by a gale from the south. Once again the bigger waves began to break into the cockpit, and Loi always seemed to catch the worst of the onslaught. One rogue wave drenched him from head to foot, and left four or five inches of water swirling about the cockpit floor. Several times the wave tops extinguished the cookers in their wooden cook box beside the entrance to the main cabin. Luckily the little rusty cookers themselves stood up to the punishment. We picked them up, mopped

Cookbox

Using the computer to send a daily report to the Mariners' Museum, USA, via satellite radio. (*Joe Beynon*)

Loi and Trondur re-fastening the rudders after the holding ropes had worn through. (*Joe Beynon*)

Hsu Fu was semi-submerged throughout the journey – view aft along the port side. (*Rex Warner*)

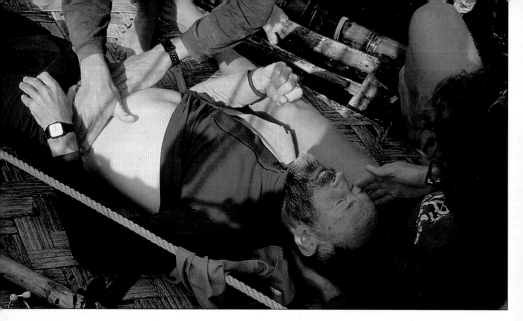

Breaking two ribs in the middle of the Pacific. 'I could hear the broken ends of a rib clicking together as I breathed.' (*Loi*)

Hoisting Trondur aloft to replace the rotting mast stays. (*Joe Beynon*)

Rex surveying hull weed growth. (*Joe Beynon*)

Trondur and Loi at harpoon stations. (*Joe Beynon*)

Trondur hauling in a harpooned sunfish.
(*Joe Beynon*)

Cutting up kingfish for air drying.
(*Joe Beynon*)

Trondur with his fishbow. (*Rex Warner*)

Trondur and Joe examining the fish arrow made from a bucket handle. (*Rex Warner*)

A visit from US Coastguard cutter *Jarvis*. (*Rex Warner*)

The boarding party from *Jarvis*. (*Joe Beynon*)

Heavy weather in the middle of the Pacific. (*Rex Warner*)

Rex and Trondur lashing down the sails in gale force winds. (*Joe Beynon*)

Waves constantly washed through the bamboos of the hull. (*Rex Warner*)

Trondur and Joe look on as Tim uses a handheld navigation instrument, protected in a plastic sandwich box, to read satellite signals giving the raft's latitude and longitude. (*Rex Warner*)

Above left: Trondur tying in loose bamboos as the raft begins to disintegrate. (*Joe Beynon*)

Above right: Tim checks the rotten fastenings as *Hsu Fu* continues to shed bamboos. (*Joe Beynon*) *Inset:* Damaged rattan fastenings. (*Joe Beynon*)

Below: The arrival of the container ship *California Galaxy*. (*Joe Beynon*)

off the seawater, shook them to get the paraffin to saturate the wicks again, and with patient application of a cigarette-lighter flame, managed to get them to light again. They could be coaxed back into life even when the waves were so persistent that seawater invaded the paraffin reservoir itself, trickling down through the wicks. Then we merely skimmed off the paraffin floating on the surface, poured out the seawater, put back the paraffin, and lit up. Unfortunately, lying flat on my back in the cabin during the gale, I found that I had become a human wave gauge. I could detect every shift and change in the bad weather and sea state. The cabin floor rippled underneath me with each wave, and it was impossible to lie rigid. So the rib that was broken in my back gave a stab of pain when a roller pushed up the basketwork floor in one direction, and the break in my side made a small clunking sound when *Hsu Fu* twisted in the other plane.

Waiting for the ribs to mend, I had plenty of time to work out *Hsu Fu*'s schedule. My original estimate had been that *Hsu Fu* would advance at an average rate of fifty miles a day, so the crossing from Japan to America would take about ninety days. But, in fact, *Hsu Fu* was averaging only forty miles each twenty-four hours, and this meant we would need about 120 days to reach northern California. Of course, the actual distance the raft was travelling over the ground or through the water varied. Some days we went backwards because of head winds; other days we might be stationary in a calm; on a good day we could go sixty or seventy miles, though not always on a direct course for Cape Mendocino. The Kuroshio, now the North Pacific Current, was still in our favour, but nothing like as strongly as off the coast of Asia, nor was it consistent. Sometimes we could detect a helpful current of half a knot in our favour, at other times there was no current, or even a counter-current that swept us sideways or blocked us.

The extra thirty days for a successful crossing raised some awkward questions. Water, the most obvious and important resource, was not an immediate problem. At our normal consumption rate of ten to twelve litres per day we carried enough water to see us through the longer voyage, even without gathering rainwater. Nor was food going to be a major worry. Joe calculated that we had enough rice and noodles, as well as our staples of dried bonito and tuna, if we rationed carefully. Our stock of onions, however, would soon be gone. We had enough onions, our only vegetable, to last for another fifty days at the rate of one onion per day.

Similarly our stock of garlic would soon be finished, and then our diet would be very drab. But the real concern was fuel for the cookers. We had bought only eighty litres of paraffin in Shimoda, and we were finding that this would barely last the original ninety days. If we ran out of paraffin during the extra thirty days, then we would be hard-pressed to cook our food, most of which — like the rice and noodles — would be unpalatable to eat raw. We could of course burn our few remaining scraps of spare bamboo, and perhaps we could salvage and dry out the occasional item of floating driftwood, but in the end we would probably be reduced to chewing on cold, dried, and maggoty bonito. It was not an appetising prospect, particularly with the colder autumn weather coming on. Joe and I made a shopping list in case we met a passing vessel which could resupply us. We composed the list by order of priority and it read: paraffin (or diesel fuel as a substitute), onions, coffee, tinned meats, any vegetables. It gave an accurate insight into what the crew valued.

The prospect of sailing into the late autumn was itself the major worry. Shortage of food or other supplies might be inconvenient, but probably not life-threatening. Sailing a bamboo raft through the late autumn and early winter storms was definitely perilous. *Hsu Fu* was suited for travel in the normal sailing season, but was not intended as a vessel to survive prolonged heavy weather. One thing that I had learned about early mariners, whether Greeks, Arabs, Norsemen or whatever seagoing tradition, was that they took good care to get off the sea when the sailing season was over. To be struggling on across the Pacific, closing with the coast of California, in deteriorating weather in mid-November or into December would be very rash indeed. And that begged another question — if our voyage was to last another eighty days, just how long would *Hsu Fu* herself be able to carry us? First there was the question of the raft's buoyancy. The bamboos were now approaching the five-month limit of buoyancy that the Japanese fisherman had projected, and obviously they would not stay afloat for ever. Quite how long would it be before they sank? And that was not the only problem. The integrity of the raft's structure had to be considered. To stay at sea an extra month would put a tremendous strain on the thousands of rattan lashings which held together the 220 bamboos of *Hsu Fu*'s hull. Every hour these lashings had to withstand repeated stresses as the raft flexed and twisted in the waves. Eventually the lashings would weaken and

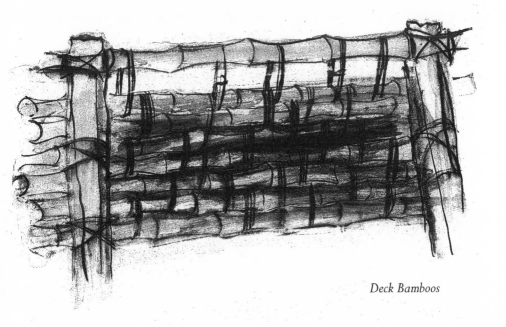

Deck Bamboos

break. When leaving Hong Kong I had made a rough calculation that the raft would flex or twist two million times on the way from the China coast to America. If the last sector, from Japan to America, added an extra month at sea then the rattan lashings would be subjected to another four hundred thousand movements. It seemed a very heavy burden to put on thin cords of water-soaked jungle vine.

On board there was now a widespread and unspoken understanding of the need to husband our resources. To save paraffin we stopped having a mid-morning coffee break. We boiled water only at breakfast, lunch, and in the evening when it was stored in a flask ready for each night watchman to mix himself a hot drink, carefully doling out the teaspoon ration of coffee, sugar and powdered milk. Also we stopped using our little paraffin lamp during the night watch, and used torches instead. The batteries for the torches were recharged from the wind generator and the solar panels, as was the radio battery. It occurred to me that *Hsu Fu* was becoming a microcosm of our own planet – we were using up our fossil fuel, the paraffin, but had an ample supply of renewable energy collected from the wind and sun. Long ago we had stopped throwing anything overboard, and carefully kept old tins, plastic bottles, coffee jars, or any item that might be reusable or turned to other functions. Above all, we never threw away any rope, even a strand of the shortest, most ragged, and knotted offcut.

Rope is the sinew of any sailing vessel. From Halong we had started out with poor-quality Vietnamese rope, supplemented it with extra coils of rope bought in Hong Kong, and then added yet more, best-quality manila rope in Japan. Still we did not have enough cordage. *Hsu Fu* consumed rope like no other vessel that I had ever sailed, and the reason was obvious: chafe. The constant flexing and twisting of the raft rubbed rope against rope, rope against bamboo, rope against timber. Rex was appointed the 'chafe inspector', and morning and afternoon he would make a complete tour of the raft, checking for signs of wear and tear. He, Trondur and Loi devised clever little bamboo tubes which they fitted as sleeves over ropes to protect them, and they arranged and rearranged the rigging to avoid chafing points. But still *Hsu Fu* devoured rope. Ropes broke under strain, or were worn through by prolonged use. We saved the broken pieces and spliced them together. We cut the ends off ropes that were too long for their job, and then joined the extra lengths together to make full lengths. But still *Hsu Fu* was not satisfied or took us by surprise. If a loose rope's end accidentally fell on the bamboo deck, it often slipped down into the gap between two bamboos as they rubbed and worked against one another, and was literally chewed to shreds as if being gnawed by a savage dog. Then we had to tease out the wreckage, comb the strands, twist them together, and laboriously try to repair the damage. All this would not have been too bad but for the fact that our rope was going rotten at an alarming pace. Trondur and I were puzzled. Best-quality manila rope which I had purchased in Shimoda, a fine, well-made honey-yellow rope that would last two years in the Atlantic off Europe, had gone rotten in five weeks. Sometimes it smelled bad. Sometimes it turned black. But always the rope fell apart, or became so weak that it could be snapped between one's hands. And on this rope our lives depended. The raft's bamboo hull was held together with rattan, but the cockpit and cabin baskets were lashed in place by rope, and only the rotting rope stopped us from being washed away.

On day forty-four since leaving Shimoda, five days after my accident, my ribs had knitted together enough for me to be able to leave the cabin for the first time, and gingerly make my way forward to the bows. The wind generator stood there on its bamboo pole, its six-bladed fan whirling away and driving a built-in generator which supplied twelve-volt power to the raft's battery. There was a faulty connection which had to be repaired, and after I had done the work, I paused and looked aft, down the length of the raft. I had been confined in the main cabin for long enough to see *Hsu Fu* with a totally new eye, and it was a shock. *My God!* I thought to myself, *How can we be at sea on this?* Everything about the raft looked on the point of collapse or of sinking. Waves were washing over half-submerged bamboos green with seaweed. There were ends of broken rattan poking up. Every length of rope had mends and splices. There was not one timber which did not have cracks and splints. The entire structure was creaking and groaning and moving. If the raft had been the skeleton of an old timber barn which I had unwisely entered, I would have run out into the open before the whole shed collapsed down on top of me in splinters and dust. Yet here we were going about our business every day on the open Pacific, calmly tying, knotting, mending, splinting, keeping the whole rickety structure together as a day-to-day routine, no more concerned than if we were on a small village pond and not 1,500 miles from land. People would think us totally mad, I thought, and remembered the comment of a Japanese fisherman at Shingu whom the local newspaper asked for his opinion as he was staring at the raft in

harbour and was told that the crew proposed to try to cross the Pacific. 'F . . . Hell' was his response.

Trondur reported that the rattan lashings seemed to be working loose in the centrebody of the raft, directly under the mainmast. He was not sure if any of the lashings had actually broken, because it was very difficult to see down into the spaces between the bamboos. But he detected a general loosening and slackening in the structure. On the other hand, he thought that the raft was not sinking, except very slowly. His confidence in *Hsu Fu*, as much as mine, was an important factor in encouraging the rest of the crew. Rex and Joe had great respect for his judgement and seagoing experience, and the two of them had consolidated their own roles. Joe was still the novice sailor, though he now had covered more sea miles than many amateur yachtsmen. He was perhaps more inclined to worry than anyone else, but he was also the person most likely to make jokes and raise a smile. He confessed to having the occasional despondent phase when the voyage seemed to drag on and on and we were getting nowhere, and then he felt tired and dispirited and turned in on himself. But these intervals of depression were brief, seldom more than two days long, and he would soon bounce back to his usual good humour, volunteering for jobs and, with his youth and energy, taking on the tasks that required muscular strength. Rex, similarly, was suffering from occasional bouts of withdrawal, but in his case it was to retreat behind his barrier of routine. He was always so unfailingly polite, so careful in following his set patterns, so methodical, that at times he appeared to be living separately from the rest of us. He even had a quirk which symbolised this: he had a habit of carrying in his pocket a small rag in a plastic bag to wipe his spectacles. When he sat down to use it, he would go through a slow ritual, taking off the heavy spectacles, methodically producing the plastic bag, unwrapping the rag, polishing the glasses lens by lens in strict sequence, and then replacing the glasses. During this ritual he looked both vulnerable and isolated – helpless without the glasses, his unfocused blue eyes surrounded by pale rings where the glasses had prevented tan, and lost in the routine of the act. By contrast, out of this measured withdrawal, would sometimes leap a bright unexpected flash of sardonic humour, which would spark off a round of banter and clowning between himself and Joe that had all the rest of us smiling.

Joe and Rex could interact with one another, so the real odd man out was Loi. He still had no more vocabulary than the few words he had learned on the way to Miyako. He still called the morning 'Good Morning' and evening was 'Good Evening'. He could count up to one hundred, and understood Up, Down, Lunch and Supper. But every command in running the ship was best reinforced by gestures. Like the others, his basic role had not changed. He was still the first to volunteer for any job, the cleanest in washing himself and his clothes, enthusiastic and cheerful. Yet I was a little uneasy. Loi came from a totally different culture to the rest of us, and without the ability to talk and discuss possible problems, misunderstandings could arise and then get blown out of proportion. All was well for the moment. Loi sensed that we all liked him very much indeed, and we were a genuine, close-knit team. Yet it would only take one outbreak of cultural confusion to damage the excellent atmosphere on board. If Loi, or indeed if any one of us on board, was unhappy, that feeling of unhappiness would disturb the others because we really did feel like a band of shipmates. The voyage had been notable so far, I reflected, for our maintaining such a smooth and good-humoured atmosphere on the raft. It was a credit to the self-control and the positive attitude of every member of the crew. Yet it was impossible to know exactly what each of them might be thinking. Take Trondur, for example. Anyone looking at him with his massive, workmanlike hands, all cuts and scrapes and scars, would have no idea that the same man who cut the throat of a thrashing shark would an hour later be reclining in the cabin, delicately sketching on a sheet of Japanese drawing paper. One day his drawing might be a fine representational picture of *Hsu Fu* sailing on the ocean; the next an abstract painting full of emotion and sensitive observation; or the third day it was a picture held in Trondur's imagination and transferred to paper showing the raft as seen by a fish swimming underneath it. With a broad sweep of blue watercolour washed across the page, the picture made you feel that you yourself were plunged three metres deep in the ocean and *Hsu Fu* was sailing right over you.

My own state of mind, as the voyage dragged out longer and longer and I began to see that it would extend far beyond the original plan, became more cautious and careful, even superstitious. I found myself writing in my journal for 20 September that I was:

'hoping quietly that perhaps we will enjoy an Indian summer. This is now my fifth maritime expedition, and if it succeeds, then I will have sailed right

around the world in vessels built in styles from no later than the eighth century and as old as the Bronze Age – skinboat, open rowed galley, Arab dhow, and now a bamboo raft. No boat has had an escort vessel or an engine, and all took risks with the sea, the weather, not to say financial risk and personal discomfort. Now I am aware that this present voyage is far longer, across more open water, in high and stormy latitudes, aboard a vessel half-sunk before it begins, and subjected day and night to flexing, twisting, and battering of thin-walled bamboo tubes – a grass not even a timber – ropes made of flimsy fibres, masts held up by jungle vines. So the risks are there, and they stretch far ahead, as we are only approaching a notional, not actual midpoint in this immense ocean. The season is advancing. Inevitably the winter gales will be upon us, with great waves and shrieking winds when our waterlogged and weary vessel, shaken and twisted until she is loose and slack in the rattan fastenings and the end-to-end joints, must hold together and not disintegrate. The rig must not snap so our masts and sails topple overboard. The weed-covered rudders, already loose and sloppy on their grooves, must hold and not part company with the raft or we will be left rudderless at the mercy of the waves. All this and we are barely halfway on the last, most demanding, and most dangerous sector. So superstition creeps in, good-luck charms to avert disaster – not to kill the albatross, never to mention that the journey is a foregone conclusion, not even to praise the recent fine weather for that presumption will be punished by change. If anything is going well, keep quiet about it and be thankful. If anything is going badly, the daylong battering and lashing of a gale, remind yourself that bad weather never lasts for ever and some time, however remote, the wind will abate and the waves calm down. If apparent catastrophe strikes – the mast or boom snaps, the drinking water is foul, the cooking paraffin found to be contaminated – then look for the alternative, repair or replace using whatever is available from other sources. And if that is not an option, accept the setback and place it in the perspective of the continuing voyage: that we are still afloat, still heading in the right direction, and that in however many days – fifty, sixty or ninety? – we may eventually make a landfall if in the meantime we learn to endure, make the best of circumstances, and do not tempt fate by taking any success or favourable situation for granted.'

The unvarying, perfect circle of the horizon all around, and *Hsu Fu*'s position judged each day by such small reductions in the number of miles yet to run, meant that we needed some markers to give us the feeling that we were actually making progress across that immense ocean.

We found those psychological milestones in the time zones which ran at right angles across our path. In those latitudes each time zone was about 720 miles wide, just the right amount to give a sensation that we were getting somewhere, and it was a distance which could be accomplished in a reasonable interval, usually fifteen to twenty days. Since leaving Hong Kong we had changed the shipboard clock three times already, and on 19 September we advanced the shipboard clock by one more hour, celebrating with a glass of hot sake – a gift from the Japanese fishermen who had sent it across on a fishing-line off Shingu two months before, though that seemed as if it had been in another age. To economise on paraffin we warmed up the sake in the hot water we had already used for cooking noodles, then divided it among the five of us. Now all of us, except Loi, were on the far side of the world from our homes, twelve hours different in time.

Four days later I wrote across the top of the page for my day's journal – 23 September *and* 22 September. That was the day when *Hsu Fu* sailed across the International Date Line in mid-ocean, and we gained a day on the calendar. Strictly speaking, the Date Line lay slightly closer to Japan than to California, but it was actually more than half way if we counted from our departure point in China. For us it was the major seamark of our entire Pacific crossing. It was the obvious halfway point, the dividing line where we began the long second half of our haul towards the American continent. Had we been a trans-Polar expedition walking across the ice-cap, this would have been our Pole and afterwards we would have felt we were on the downhill run. Ironically, we had been looking forward so much to crossing the Date Line that we almost missed the actual second. It was just after a late lunch of rice and bean curd that I switched on the little handheld position finder and saw that already the numbers on the little screen read 179.59.873 East. *Hsu Fu* must have caught a slant of wind and current for the numbers were mounting towards the magic 180 degrees as we watched. Moments later, we saw the East on the screen change to West and the numbers began to wind down backwards. We were across the Date line! It was an occasion to celebrate. I called for a toast in honour of the raft; Joe called a toast to the skipper from the crew; and Trondur just said briefly '*Skol!*' and then added quietly, 'This ship she give no trouble. We will get to America.' Silently I thanked him for his quiet confidence in the raft and an expedition which many had thought would never get afloat or, if it did, would barely sail a few miles offshore before the bundle of bamboos vanished beneath the waves. That was 4,000 miles ago. Trondur may be proved wrong about the crossing, I thought, but to have his unswerving confidence was a real boost to the crew's morale.

Now that we were poised in the middle of the ocean, with Asia and America the same distance on either side of us, I thought again about the theory that their ancient cultures had been in contact across the ocean. Needham had listed the cultural similarities by categories, beginning with systems of recording and writing, then discussing art, architecture and music, then religion and folklore, then natural philosophy, cosmology and astronomy, technology, and finally the evidence of plants and animals and diseases which seemed common to both China and ancient America. In every category he had found striking similarities: the writing of the Mayans of Central America resembled the Chinese in that they used square symbols, usually written in vertical columns, and which were sometimes read right to left. Or, again, in music the Aztecs used temple drums and wooden gongs similar to those found in Japanese and Chinese temples, and the panpipes played by Amerindians and Asians were graduated in the same way. Or, in the field of technology, both the Chinese and the Amerindians distilled alcohol using the same method which condenses the distillate on a convex still-head and gathers it in a central cup. This system is quite different from the method found in Europe and the Near East where the rising vapour is gathered in a concave still-head and then trickles down the sides to be collected in an outer gutter.

The list of clues went on and on, but even Needham had to admit that the evidence was always inconclusive, and that a final judgement kept slipping out of his grasp. The counter-questions were always the same – were the similarities genuine or imaginary? Could they be explained by simple coincidence? Was it possible that shared techniques were discovered twice, once on each side of the Pacific? There was always a good case to be made that Asians and native Americans were equally ingenious and imaginative, and could have discovered or developed most of the ideas, theories, and techniques all on their own.

Many apparent similarities became less convincing on closer examination. For example, both Chinese and the ancient Central American cultures seemed to have similar concepts about the world and heavens, and ascribed colours to certain directions. But the deeper the scholars dug, the more the differences rather than the similarities appeared. The colours were different for the different directions, and the cosmology grew more divergent not closer together. By contrast the likenesses of practical technology seemed more substantial the more the detail was examined. One archaeologist, Betty Meggers at the Smithsonian Institution, had shown a whole range of very detailed similarities between two types of early pottery, one type from Japan, and the other excavated in Ecuador in South America. Another American scholar, Stephen Jett, demonstrated how the humble-seeming blowgun, used in South-East Asia and South America, in fact involved a mixture of fifty-five technical elements, such as sights and arrow poison, of which thirty-two were common to both Asia and the Americas. A third group of researchers concluded that cloth made from the bark of plants, another seemingly obvious use of natural resources, actually involved specialised tools and techniques which were remarkably similar between Asia and America. Perhaps the most startling claim of all was made by the archaeologist David Kelley, who had worked at the University of Calgary. According to Kelley, the letters K,L, and M all occur in the same sequence in the Mayan, Greek, Hebrew and Hindu calendars, proving they were inter-related.

Attempts to substantiate the idea of trans-Pacific contact by employing the most recent scientific tools also gave unexpectedly ambiguous results. Genetic material taken from native American graves showed that the peoples of Asia and America came from the same stock, but could not define whether that link came from ancient migrations of peoples across the Bering Strait, or also across the ocean at a later date. Similarly it was thought that the physical characteristics of certain plants had provided firm proof of intercontinental contact. Cotton was the famous example. It was held that the New World was the only continent with native types of cotton which contained nothing but small chromosomes in their structure. The Old World, by contrast, had cottons which were unique for having only large chromosomes. When a hybrid cotton was discovered in the Americas which contained both large and small chromosomes in the proper ratio for an artificial hybrid, there was excited speculation that this proved that some agency – almost certainly humans – had brought Old-World cotton to the New World, and created the hybrid. But then it was discovered that there were, after all, some American native cottons which contained large chromosomes, so the hybrid could have been bred within the Americas by accident or design. The value of the evidence collapsed. Even the simple question as to why rice had not been cultivated in the Americas, if there had been trans-Pacific contact, produced confusing answers. Hsu Fu and his 3,000 colonists were said to have set out with the 'five grains' on board. If they, or other Asian sailors, had reached the Americas, how was it that they did not introduce rice cultivation? But then came the counter-question: how was it that the native Americans failed to cultivate their own native wild rice, just as – it seems – the Asians failed to cultivate maize which grew wild in the mountains between China and India. The Asians, for some reason, ignored the potential value of cultivating maize, just as the Americans ignored the idea of cultivating rice. The presence, or absence, of rice proved nothing.

A similar explanation had been put forward for the striking fact that the native Americans never exploited the use of the wheel. Indeed, it was thought for a long time that the wheel was never known in native America, and this was certain proof that there could never have been any contact with other cultures. But then small toys which ran on wheels were discovered in Mexican graves, showing that the idea of the wheel *was* known, but had simply been relegated to an amusing toy.

In short, for every argument there was a counter-argument, or a later discovery overturned the accepted wisdom. Peanuts, which all had considered to be a uniquely American plant, were found in four-thousand-year-old Chinese graves; a type of firefly once thought to be peculiar to South-East Asia had been found in South America. Coconuts, which some scholars claimed could only have been brought to the Americas by mariners, could have floated across the Pacific, and so forth. The discussion even brought in the humble body parasites found on corpses in native American tombs. These insects need warm temperatures to live and, it was pointed out, would never have survived the cold conditions when human migrations took place from Asia to America twenty thousand years ago. So the insects must have come across by sea, on rafts or ships carrying visitors from the Old World.

All this discussion would, of course, be settled once and for all if Asian artefacts had been discovered in the New World, and these artefacts could be shown beyond a shadow of doubt to have been brought to the Americas long before Columbus. There was no shortage of claimed discoveries. They ranged from 'ancient Chinese coins' which had turned up on the west coast of Canada, to alleged 'Chinese inscriptions' found in South America, to Japanese beads included in Mayan necklaces. But not one of these discoveries has been verified to the satisfaction of rigorous investigators. Eleventh-century Chinese coins found in British Columbia, for example, were shown by a Canadian archaeologist, Grant Keddie, probably to be recent imports by traders in the nineteenth century. And very often the exact location and circumstances of the discovery of an 'Asian artefact' in America were unknown or shrouded in mystery – usually a broad hint that the item came from an illegal excavation. In such cases no serious scholar was willing to risk his or her reputation by handling or studying stolen goods. It was essential to verify where the item came from, and to fix a precise date when it had been brought to the New World, because an early Asian artefact, like an old coin for example, may have been brought to the Americas long after the date of its initial manufacture. The 'Chinese inscriptions' could have been faked, and carved stone is notoriously difficult to date. So in the end there was no lack of enthusiasm to find evidence of trans-Pacific contact, but neither was there any lack of sceptics to deny that contact ever took place.

Convalescing on a bamboo raft of ancient design right on the notional dividing line between the two continents was very timely. I felt I had a foot in each camp. I could appreciate the doubts of the so-called isolationists who believed there had been no contact, and equally I was beginning to accept that trans-Pacific voyages were possible in the most ancient of vessels.

We did not have a blowgun on *Hsu Fu* but we soon had a bamboo bow and arrow. Trondur was frustrated by the increasing difficulty of taking fish on hook and line. The trouble was that as the water temperature

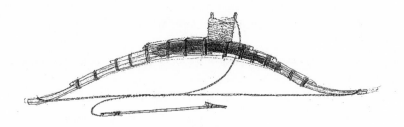

Bow and fish arrow

dropped, we were seeing fewer and fewer of our main prey, the dorados. These fish had been the hungriest and most aggressive, and had been our main catch using artificial flying fish as bait. As we travelled farther north and east, the flying fish had got fewer and fewer, and so, too, had the dorados. Now we saw them very rarely, and they were not hunting with their previous zeal. The other fish we caught were the yellowfins, which we had identified as a type of immature tuna. The yellowfins, too, were becoming wary and took the bait less often. But the main reason for the decline in fish-catch was the weather. It was very difficult to fish successfully when the sea was disturbed. The fish tended to move farther away from the raft in bad weather, and the bait was impossible to control in big waves. The solution, as far as Trondur was concerned, was to shoot the fish. He set about making a longbow with his customary crafts- manship. Selecting suitable lengths of spare bamboo, he split and shaped them into flat staves which he lashed together to achieve the correct lam- inated curve. Another piece of bamboo provided a handgrip, two projecting pegs served as points on which to coil the line attached to the arrow. The shaft of the arrow came from the handle of a bucket carried away by a wave long ago. Now Trondur straightened it, filed a flat, and working with fine fishing-wire tied on a barb painstakingly made from a discarded clip that once held together his artist's portfolio. The final result was a beautifully made bow, which required a twenty-pound pull, and drove an arrow clean through a yellowfin. Any fish that now came within five yards' range was a potential meal.

'Happy birthday and congratulations on your sense of timing,' said Rex as I emerged with excruciating slowness from the cabin on 25 September. Protecting my tender ribs, it still took me twenty minutes to get out of the sleeping bag and dress, and I felt as slow and deliberate as a South American tree sloth as I used my arms to haul myself cautiously out of the low cabin door, and lowered myself on the cockpit bench. A semi-inflated lifejacket served as a handy waistcoat to cushion the worst bumps and knocks.

'Thank you,' I replied, 'for remembering my birthday. But what do you mean by my sense of timing?'

Rex grinned. 'Well, you've arranged to be fifty-three on day fifty- three of the voyage since leaving Japan.' I had awakened to an odd smell of burning. Now I saw why. Joe and Rex shared the dawn watch, and Joe had spent the past hour preparing a birthday 'cake'. He had concocted it from porridge oats soaked in water, then fried with sugar and oil, and kneaded into two fist-sized lumps. The topping was a melted chocolate bar, sprinkled with a handful of soggy peanuts. The result looked like a misshapen, over-sized hamburger which we ate at teatime, and all agreed was absolutely delicious. Not a crumb was left.

That afternoon, too, the sea was calm enough for Rex to make another underwater hull survey, and check what changes had taken place to the fish and weed growth around *Hsu Fu*'s hull. Six weeks earlier he had been able to swim around the raft wearing shorts and a T-shirt. Now he had to put on a wet suit, and emerged after half an hour feeling very chilly. He reported that the effects of the drop in water temperature were very evident. Our escort of warm-water dorados had finally gone, and in their place two metres below the raft swam half a dozen tuna up to three feet in length. Also the cheerful little pilot fish in their yellow-and-black livery had been replaced by larger and more sombre cousins wearing strips of black and pale grey. There were still half a dozen of the slow-moving plankton feeders, but all the 'cellophane weed' had disappeared, and everywhere *Hsu Fu*'s underwater hull was growing a fine moss. Also a new seaweed had appeared, fine and stubby, and a startling purple. Rex dubbed it 'heather seaweed'. His report ended on a disquieting note. Across the forward third of the raft he had seen a large number of loose ends of rattan dangling down into the water. He could not tell whether they were broken ends, or perhaps the loose ends from underwater knots that had come undone. Only the forward third of the hull seemed to be affected. The rest of the hull was still neatly tied together. Nevertheless, his observation brought the first stirrings of unease. Was this the start of a serious deterioration of the hull?

Two days later came a hint that the close-knit unity of the crew was also suffering the effects of prolonged wear and tear. It happened just before the evening meal, and was completely unexpected. Loi had managed to catch three small yellowfins at precisely the right moment – just as Rex was preparing to take his turn in cooking supper. We had not eaten fresh fish for a couple of days, and the three yellowfins would make a splendid meal. Rex who admitted to being the worst cook on board, was determined to do them justice. He seized the yellowfins the moment they came aboard, filleted them, and had chunks of the yellowfins poised near the frying pan almost while they were still quivering. Turning to Joe, he asked him for the day's food supplies, and was issued with a single onion, half a packet of powdered soup and some rice.

'Can I have some garlic for the fish?' asked Rex.

'No, sorry,' answered Joe. 'The garlic ration for the day is used up, and the next clove will not be issued until tomorrow.'

Rex shrugged, and turned back to the frying pan, then checked under the bench for the cooking oil. He found the bottle of oil was empty. 'How about some oil?' he asked.

'No,' said Joe again firmly. 'If the oil has run out then we must wait until the next bottle is scheduled to be issued from stores.'

Rex, normally so well-controlled and polite, lost his temper. 'Then we can't fry anything,' he burst out. Picking up the precious onion, he hurled it overboard.

Joe seethed. 'If I put out a fresh bottle of oil now, it will all be used up well ahead of schedule,' he snapped. 'The only way to control consumption is to issue food in small quantities, and not make exceptions. What are you going to do next? Throw the soup packet into the ocean?'

There was a tense silence. Rex glared, and turned back to cooking. But his meal was a disaster – soggy rice and fish in a watery soup mix. There was a strained atmosphere in the cramped cockpit throughout the meal, and the tension only ebbed away at the time we were drinking our coffee. The mini-crisis had blown over, but I wondered if it was the prelude to a more profound breakdown in the remarkably even-tempered atmosphere we had maintained on *Hsu Fu* for the past twenty weeks.

Rattan rigging

13

THE GREAT
GARBAGE PATCH

[The voyage is] the longest and most dreadful of any in the world, as well because of the vast ocean to be crossed, being almost one half of the terraqueous Globe, with the wind always ahead; as for the terrible Tempests that happen there, one upon the back of another, and for the desperate Diseases that seize People, in 7 or 8 months, lying at sea sometimes near the Line, sometimes cold, sometimes temperate, sometimes hot, which is enough to destroy a man of steel, much more Flesh and Blood, which at Sea had but indifferent Food.

This is how an Italian traveller, Gemelli Careri, described his crossing of the North Pacific in the late seventeenth century. He was recalling a voyage he had made aboard the Manila Galleon, the treasure ship which sailed each year from the Philippines to Acapulco on the Mexican coast. The route of the Manila Galleon was nearly identical to the track being followed by *Hsu Fu*, and the story of the Manila Galleons had been central to my research in preparing the expedition. As no first hand accounts survived from Japanese or Chinese mariners on this route, something might be gleaned from the hard-won experience of the Spanish sailors who had tackled the same voyage under sail, bringing the silks, spices and porcelain of China to the New World. They had acquired an immense fund of information because the Manila Galleons plied regularly between the Philippines and Mexico, both belonging to the Spanish Empire, for a span of nearly 250 years. The Spanish ships, of course, were not to be compared to a bamboo raft. Even the early, smaller galleons were forty times the tonnage of *Hsu Fu*, but they, too, were slow-moving and often ramshackle. Above all, they faced the same weather and currents.

Crew and passengers of the Manila Galleon, 'the China ship' as it was often called, dreaded their experience. It was a long-drawn-out torment of overcrowding, poor food, disease, danger, and uncertainty. Sometimes two or even three ships set out from Manila, but usually it was a single large vessel crammed to bursting with returning colonists and government officials, and grossly overloaded with the finest haul of a year's commercial activity in Manila. Bales and packages were stuffed into the companionways, piled up on deck, so that in the first bad weather it was often necessary to throw priceless cargo overboard to lighten ship. The value of the cargo was so enormous that when the Manila Galleon was lost at sea it was a financial disaster for the colony. Usually the ships were victims of bad weather, but very occasionally they were captured by the enemy. In 1588, the year of the Spanish Armada, the annual Manila Galleon was seized by the marauding English captain, Thomas Cavendish. He sailed home with so much booty and gold aboard that when his ship *Desire* went on display on the Thames at Greenwich, the sails were made of blue damask, every sailor wore a gold chain around his neck, and the market price of bullion dropped throughout the kingdom.

But it was not the glamour of the Manila Galleons which concerned me. I was more interested in the sailing conditions and the track they followed.

In two and a half centuries the Spaniards still could not decide which was the best track. If they sailed too far south, they ran into head winds or calms. If they went too far north, they risked cold weather and gales. So they tried one route, then another, and switched between one course and the next. Their vessels were commanded by landsmen, usually grandees, but the choice of route and ship management was left to hardheaded professional pilots, master mariners who were very tough and competent. It was interesting to read their judgement. Outward bound, from Acapulco to Manila, they considered the voyage to be child's play. One master pilot was so confident of fair winds and easy seas that he left Acapulco aboard a ship's pinnace, not much bigger than *Hsu Fu* and made the passage to Manila with no difficulty. But going the other way, north past Taiwan and Japan, and then out into the Pacific was quite another matter. Then the vessels were full-sized galleons, carefully prepared for the trip which usually took six months. Obviously the captains worried about running out of drinking water, and so they rigged special rain-collectors of matting to channel the downpours, and carried extra water in bamboo tubes five feet long and as thick as a man's thigh. Another fear – not shared aboard *Hsu Fu* – was disease. Scurvy, or worse, often afflicted the crew and passengers, and in one macabre year the overdue Manila Galleon was found at sea, every member of its crew dead, while the vessel sailed on alone under untended sails. The Spanish colonial authorities alerted their settlements in California to be on standby to render assistance to the exhausted, half-starving crews, though usually they tried to make their landfall at Cape Mendocino, and then sailed along the American coast without stopping in order to get the nightmarish journey over as soon as possible. But it was not disease or starvation, which most alarmed the crews. They feared bad weather, and with good reason. Bad weather accounted for most of the losses – thirty galleons lost in 250 years. Their lament had a familiar ring: first they had to avoid typhoons off the Philippines and Taiwan, then they trudged across the long, tedious and increasingly chilly ocean passage, only to be faced with struggling through great gales off the coast of North America. One unlucky galleon reported encountering eighteen terrible storms during the crossing, and in 1600 the *Santa Margarita* beat about futilely for eight months without ever leaving the western Pacific when she went aground on the Ladrones, with only 50 of her 260 crew still alive.

Hunched in *Hsu Fu*'s bamboo cabin, reading the modern weather reports on the little laptop computer, it was easy to appreciate why the Manila Galleons took such hammering. Day after day the summary of North Pacific weather conditions listed gales and severe weather across a wide area. The main zone for bad weather was to the north of us, close to the Aleutian Islands, where the winds were regularly of gale force. But individual low-pressure systems would come swirling off the Japanese coast and head straight at us, bringing rain and strong winds. Occasionally such a huge storm system developed in the north that it swept up the little gales in its maw, and became one vast foul-weather system with a radius of a thousand miles, and we felt the winds on its outer edge. To appreciate the discomfort of life aboard the Manila

Galleon, I had only to look out of *Hsu Fu*'s cabin door and glimpse the grey, unfriendly ocean and sky that now surrounded us. The weather was unsettled and hostile. Half a day's fitful sunshine might be followed by a long night of rain and blustery winds. In a single evening, between sunset and midnight, we found ourselves lowering the sails in response to a sudden increase in wind speed, then hoisting them again when the wind dropped, then lowering them, then hauling them up again. A radio news report confirmed our suspicions. The summer had been the worst in those latitudes for forty years, and it seemed that early autumn was not much better.

Occasionally we were taken by surprise. Early one afternoon we were all tending to our normal chores, when Rex suddenly bawled out 'Squall!' at the top of his lungs. A nasty-looking wall of rain was rushing down on us about a mile away, the wind whipping up the white caps at its foot. We dropped the mainsail in time, but Joe and Rex were still wrestling down the foresail when the squall line hit. For a moment I thought the foremast would be wrenched out of the maststep, as the sail was flapped across like a slamming door. One rattan mast stay burst, so did the main sheet, and two of the bamboos stiffeners in the sail snapped in an instant. Luckily the mast itself survived, though for about five seconds as it thrashed and bent, I thought it and all the rigging would go crashing over the side.

The squall was a prelude to a fully-fledged gale, heralded well in advance by warnings from the meteorologists. The wind rose steadily, and we reefed down in matched response, first with four, then three, and finally only two panels in the fan-shaped mainsail. *Hsu Fu* rose and fell on big, though not yet dangerous, seas. Water burst regularly into the cockpit through a split in the stern quarter of the basketwork, and came squeezing up through myriad holes in the cockpit floor where the old tar was increasingly worn away. For company we had only storm petrels and tiny gadfly petrels flittering jauntily among the crests, together with our splendid, soaring, endlessly patrolling albatrosses. One or two albatrosses had been in sight since we left the coast of Japan, and now as many as a half a dozen of them were using the whorls and eddies of air current deflected by the jumble of waves beneath them. Often one was lost from view into the troughs so you would think the great bird must have crashlanded in the water, only for it to come sweeping jubilantly out of the trough fifty metres away from where you last saw it, dip one wing, and turn elegantly on that wing tip, skimming down into the valley of the next wave – a triumph of nature's aerobatics.

All day the gale lasted, with big seas building up and beginning to crash into the cockpit over the stern bar. One wave dumped several buckets of the Pacific all over our supper as Joe was straining Japanese soba noodles from the boiling water – the douche of cold salt water did nothing for their taste or temperature. Loi was now the unlucky one in the cockpit – twice he was caught by a big wave bursting over him when

Albatross

he was not wearing his foul-weather gear. Normally this would have been the cue for some sympathetic teasing and commiseration, but not now. Loi's lung infection, which Joe had diagnosed two weeks earlier, had responded to antibiotics only temporarily. After a few days the infection had flared up again, and with it came the same pain. Loi felt very unwell, and Joe was trying to treat the infection with a different type of antibiotic. But the pills had an unfortunate effect on Loi's digestion. Five or six times a day poor Loi suddenly pulled off his oilskins, scrambled out of his warm clothing and underwear, clipped on a safety harness, and perched on the submerged side bamboo suffering bouts of diarrhoea while the sea washed around his naked lower half.

Fortunately Loi's mutinous stomach did not stop him from working the raft. When a wave hit the rudder so hard that it snapped the tiller bar, Loi and Trondur rigged a replacement, using an oar handle and some twine, in less than ten minutes. The crew's morale was rock-solid even though we knew we were making little progress in the gale. Hove-to under just two panels of mainsail, the raft was being pushed a hundred miles sideways, to the south, while making just nine miles to the east, the direction we wanted. All tension between Joe and Rex had long since evaporated, and the two of them were on sparkling form. Joe was the expedition photographer, responsible for taking the stills photographs, while Rex had been learning to use our small video camera to gather material for a documentary film of the voyage. The two photography jobs overlapped, so Joe and Rex were working together, filming the more impressive waves sweeping down on the boat. Joe had clambered up to what was normally a dry spot on the cabin roof to film Rex at the helm as the waves came breaking into the cockpit. As luck would have it, the next big breaker hit at an awkward diagonal. It broke over Rex who gave a cry of satisfaction. But the wave crest then travelled on, higher than usual, to reach right up to Joe on the cabin roof, soaking him and the video camera. Rex's rejoicing stopped abruptly. A few moments later the two photographers came sheepishly to tell me that the video camera was out of action. In their enthusiasm they had failed to put the camera in its watertight case. It was impossible to be angry with them. Admonishing them would not repair the damaged camera, and we carried a spare. I much preferred to see Rex and Joe on such good terms than to chide them for their oversight and destroy their camaraderie. The previous day the two of them had borrowed Trondur's new bow and arrow, and were excitedly hanging off the stern of the raft, trying to shoot a yellowfin. Trondur had looked across the cockpit at me, with an approving twinkle in his eye, and said quietly 'Like two children!'

On watch that windswept night, my broken ribs well padded in the semi-inflated life-vest, I reflected that the morale of the crew would probably far outlast the raft itself. As a team we had barely begun to draw upon our reserves of mutual tolerance and respect. By contrast *Hsu Fu*'s material reserves were limited. Under a bright moon, the breaking crests surged almost luminous against the indigo and silver of the ocean, and in the moonlight the structure of the raft looked very thin and frail. I saw it as a never-ending drain on our meagre stock of rope and timber. Yesterday we had replaced yet another of the bamboo battens in the mainsail. It had broken during the first hours of the gale, and we had extracted the splintered pieces, selected its replacement from the small fence of bamboos that protected the sides of the cabins, cut the new batten to length and slid it into the sail pocket. The sail was repaired, the crew had shown its skill and competence, but the cabin side was now less well protected from the side-on breakers, and we had one less bamboo in reserve. Tomorrow I would ask Loi to replace another damaged tiller bar, cutting and shaping it from an oar handle. When he had done that, we would have just three oars left, not to row with as that would be useless in the ocean, but to provide a stock of long-grained timber. It seemed inevitable that well before we closed with the American coast we would be running out of material.

Dawn saw the north wind still blowing strongly, and a chaotic sea right to the horizon. The overnight damage was revealed as two rips in the mainsail, including one tear inside a panel which had been folded down, a bolt-rope seam around the edge of the sail splitting apart, another tear beginning in the leach of the sail where it stretched too tight and had begun to rip as it shrank in the rain, the broken tiller bar, all the port side bamboo posts knocked askew by the thumping of waves, and more vital, some of the ropes which tied down the cabins had worn through or snapped. Replacing these ropes was a priority. Should three of these ropes give way on the same side of a cabin – and it now seemed quite likely – the cabin would be washed off the surface of the raft and away into the ocean with fatal consequences for anyone asleep inside. Ironically, there was a general feeling of well-being. It felt good to have something important and challenging to keep one busy, even if it was damage control. This was a more positive way to look at what might otherwise have been seen as a setback with so many breakages in just thirty-six hours of high winds. Everybody was noticeably cheerful as they set to their jobs. Trondur stood in his big sea boots for hour after hour on the edge of the raft, stolidly working to replace the cabin lashings while the waves surged and churned around him. Loi repaired the tiller bar. Joe and Rex attended to the tattered sail, one on each side to stitch it through. By mid-afternoon all work was done except for the repairing of the sail rip, which Joe and Rex finished while Trondur volunteered to take Rex's turn to do the cooking.

Then we adjusted all four leeboards on the downwind side, so that *Hsu Fu* lay in her most comfortable position, at an angle of one hundred degrees to the wind. There she was as passive as possible to the weather, neither wracking nor bending unduly on the crests of the rollers. The newly mended sails were neatly tied down, the wind dropped, then picked up again, the watches changed through their regular four-hour cycle, life on board settled to its heavy-weather routine, two men in the cockpit, three men in the cabins. Outside there were black streaming clouds, and the sudden bright glare of a full moon, with moonbeams like white searchlights playing down through rents in the cloud cover. Inside was the boom of waves breaking on the flimsy palm thatch, the rush and trickle of water dripping through the lashing holes, and the sharper rattling splash of wave tops breaking into the cockpit basket. The off-watch crew waited patiently for the weather to change. Trondur made new fishing lures, glasses perched on the end of his nose like a Swiss watchmaker in a children's story; Joe studied his *Teach-Yourself-Spanish* book as he stretched out on the main cabin floor; I composed answers to the questions of the schoolchildren coming in over the radio link and took advantage of the rapidly spinning windmill to charge up every battery on board. Quite how Rex and Loi occupied their time in the forward cabin was a mystery. It was their private space, and I took care to intrude as little as possible. Loi probably snoozed and Rex wrote up his logbooks.

It was after he made his rounds next morning, day sixty since Shimoda, that Rex reported that a section of bamboo was coming loose from the main hull. I accompanied him to the spot. Peering over the side, I saw the end of a bamboo pole flapping free in the sea. One end was still fastened into the hull as it should be; but the other end was waving in the water. I looked more closely. I reached down and felt the loose bamboo, checking its size. The bamboo piece was about five metres long, and its large diameter meant that it could only be from the main hull structure. The loose end was not splintered and cracked, but neatly finished. Obviously the bamboo was the central section of a jointed fore-and-aft hull bamboo. I was fairly sure what had happened. Normally it would have been joined at each end into the other bamboos, like a section of a fishing-rod, and then lashed in place with rattan. For some reason one of the end joints had opened, the rattan lashing had come

238

adrift, and the bamboo had popped free. Rex told me that he had tried poking a bar down through the cracks between the hull bamboos, and found that the loose bamboo was barely attached at all. He could move it quite freely like a loose tooth about to fall out of the jaw. This was the first apparent casualty from the main body of the raft, and for the moment I was not too worried. The bamboo came from the exposed, vulnerable edge of the raft and would have been attached less firmly than the vast majority of the other hull bamboos, because the edge bamboos could only be tied inwards or upwards to their partners. By contrast, bamboos buried in the body of the raft were tied in four directions, to adjacent bamboos on all four sides, and would be more firmly held. Also this was just a single bamboo section. Its loss would barely effect the buoyancy of the raft, as there were at least another two hundred bamboos to go. Loi, when he came to inspect the damage, was confident. Perhaps he was thinking of the reputation of the raftmakers of Sam Son, but he indicated that the loss of the single bamboo meant nothing. With so many rattan lashings, he could not imagine that the raft would break up.

We went back to our chores. These were days to be philosophical and patient. A very welcome spell of fair winds ended in a brilliant sunset, made all the more spectacular by the single, unusually large, spout of a distant whale against the orange skyline. A false wind which began as a gentle breeze from the west, betrayed us by turning into the north and then, with no warning from the forecasters, increased to yet another gale which drove the raft even farther off our desired course. The rain became more and more frequent, not surprising with the change of season. The all-pervading dampness of rainy nights and days, reinforced by the occasional boarding wave and drenching spray, became a part of our lives. Nothing ever really dried out now that it was so thoroughly impregnated by salt sea air. When you rubbed your skin with a towel, the towelling was so soggy that it was difficult to say whether you were wetter or drier afterwards. At times the general dampness became so pervasive that you failed to notice. A wave came aboard when I was on watch with the hood of my oilskin unwisely left down. By then I was so used to being damp that I did not notice that the wave soaked my warm cap. It was not until I removed the cap an hour later in the cabin that I noticed dribbles oozing from it, and found I could wring out half a cupful of seawater.

The days began to blur into one another, as we deliberately ignored our slow rate of progress and paid no attention to exactly where we were on the map of the Pacific. We accepted that we were living within our own half-submerged world, and that our horizon could be twenty miles or a hundred metres depending on the weather, and it did not matter. *Hsu Fu* would advance at her own pace, depending on the wind speed and direction. Our task was to keep her seaworthy, and to make our own lives as comfortable as possible so that we were fit and alert to look after the raft. I took three position readings a day, and once a day reported our precise latitude and longitude by satellite radio to our friends in the Mariners' Museum in Virginia. Yet I did not bother to transfer the data to the small scale chart of the Pacific, except every ten days or whenever the sea was so calm that a little work with pencil and ruler helped to pass the time. Otherwise the chart itself stayed in its case, an artist's plastic portfolio, and I slept on it. The only concession we made to mark the passage of either time or space was to institute a weekly tea. It was Joe's idea. He had achieved such a success with my oatmeal 'birthday cake' that we decided to mark every Sunday similarly. Our stock of food was already so carefully calculated to last the next fifty or sixty days that we agreed to put aside a special allocation of sugar, keep back a few spoonfuls of oatmeal, and save an extra chocolate bar and some peanuts and raisins to make what amounted to a small and soggy currant bun which we would solemnly gather to eat every Sunday afternoon.

Our fishermen, Trondur and Loi, were again having a frustrating time. In heavy weather they could see their prey quite clearly, our escort of yellowfins swimming alongside the raft in the waves and swell. When the wave lifted high enough, the daylight shone through the water and back-lit the fish, so that we could watch them clearly, at eye-level to ourselves, finning briskly to keep on the leading edge of the wave. There were usually half a dozen fish, not large but certainly a mouthwatering size. But it was impossible to cast hook and line accurately enough into the disturbed sea to try to catch them. Finally, on the day when the waves and swell did diminish enough for profitable fishing, Loi and Trondur were on the same dawn watch at the ideal half-hour for a catch. I was woken by what sounded like a herd of buffalo stampeding across the cabin roof which sagged and bent alarmingly. There were shouts and cries, and I was about to scramble out to see what was the emergency, when a small yellowfin came bouncing in through the cabin door, thrashing and flipping its way around the cabin, in a shower of bright shiny fishscales and exuding a strong fishy smell. I seized the fish and promptly flung it back out into the cockpit where it was immediately joined by another yellowfin, seeming to fall from the sky. Then a third fish came dropping into the cockpit, and I peered out to find Loi and Trondur standing on the cabin roof throwing handlines into the sea and whisking out hungry yellowfins which were in a brief feeding frenzy. For the next two days we had yellowfin for every meal.

In the evening I called the crew together to remind them that good time-keeping was important when it came to changing over the watch. On board we ran a regime where each man spent the first two hours of his watch on standby, fully dressed and resting in the cockpit, while his partner steered the vessel. Then after two hours the standby watchman took the helm, his partner finished his turn of duty and went to his cabin space, and a new standby watchkeeper came on duty. I had noticed that Joe and Rex had been appearing as much as fifteen minutes late for their standby duty because when Trondur or Loi finished their turn, they would go forward to wake their replacement and then head for their own sleeping bags. Not until Rex or Joe had got dressed in wet-weather gear, a long process, did they arrive in the cockpit, and during this interval the helmsman was by himself. It was sloppy practice, I told the crew. The raft could not be handled in an emergency with just one man in the cockpit, and no one should go to his sleeping berth until his replacement had actually appeared fully dressed in the cockpit. That was the best time, too, when there were three men on hand, to reef sails, shift the raft from one tack to another, adjust lee-boards, or work the vessel. As usual I was reluctant to appear to be nagging an already excellent crew who must have been feeling tired and exasperated after nine weeks at sea in cramped, wet conditions. An incautious word, I felt, could spark off resentment. To my real satisfaction there was not a hint of resentment from anyone. Rather, everyone agreed that the sloppy watch-changes must stop, and Trondur jokingly announced that he would take care to wake Joe, notorious for his slow rising, half an hour early each watch-change to make sure he was ready on time.

Hsu Fu was now passing through the fringe of the 'Great Garbage Patch', an area of the Pacific notorious for its accumulation of floating man-made rubbish. We sailed slowly past scraps of broken fishing-net, white fragments of polystyrene bobbing high on the water, slimy grey-green plastic bags awash just below the surface. They were all held in a great mass of slowly circulating water to the north-east of the Hawaiian Islands, endlessly travelling on the ocean currents in an immense circle. Some of the debris would pass right through the circulation, and emerge on the other side to continue on towards the American coast. Marine scientists knew of the Great Garbage Patch, but wanted to have more information about how it worked and what effect it had. *Hsu Fu* had been asked to provide extra data. So ever since leaving Shimoda, Rex had been listing every item of floating rubbish which we saw, writing down the size, shape, type and colour, whether it was made of wood, plastic, metal or styrofoam. We had been pleasantly surprised to note how little pollution we had found in the sea close to Japan. Only once, for example, had we seen an oil slick, and that was barely the size of a tennis court. Later we had passed stray fishing-floats and quite a number of scraps of plastic sheets, usually the remains of heavy-duty plastic sacks. But on the whole we had found less pollution than we anticipated.

Now in the Great Garbage Patch the number of sightings soared. Sometimes we would be in sight of five or six pieces of rubbish at one time, and we reached out with a pole and managed to pull in a few items for a closer look. By far the most common were what we dubbed 'banana floats' – lozenge-shaped fishing floats, usually white or yellow, which had once been strung like necklace beads on the upper edges of fishing-nets. We saw hundreds of them, floating free, highly visible on the surface of the sea. There was an occasional bottle, always fun to pull aboard in case it contained a message or some worthwhile dregs. But they never did. The bottles were made of glass – oddly enough, only twice did we see a plastic bottle – and they were empty though we could sometimes read a label or guess what they contained, usually sake. Then there were the oddities, always plastic, which made us wonder how on earth they finished up in the ocean: a broken fly swat, a fan blade from a car engine, a child's doll. Shoes were another puzzle. Why were they always ladies slippers, never men's shoes and from the right foot, small size, well worn, and very gaudy? We had visions of small women dancing right-footed on the decks of liners until their shoes wore away and they kicked their right slippers overboard. By the time we picked them up on *Hsu Fu* the slippers, like everything else large enough to offer a gripping surface, were covered with revolting rubbery clusters of goose barnacles.

The Great Garbage Patch was popular with birdlife. Probably the seabirds found extra food among the small fish and marine animals which clustered near the larger items of rubbish. Above the tangled knots of old fishing-nets, still supported by their floats, always hovered seabirds, waiting for a meal. We identified two different types of albatross, four species of petrel, and a tern. Ironically the squalor of floating garbage was associated with an increase in sea life. The water temperature had risen slightly, and for a few days we even saw an occasional flying fish. There were very large predators, too, swimming beneath the scattered dandruff of flotsam. One morning the shark line that had been trailing behind the raft, off and on, for almost two months had gone slack. Trondur pulled it in and found the massive line had been bitten clean through by what must have been a very powerful set of jaws. It was our only really heavyweight line so he set a smaller version, and when I appeared on watch next morning, Trondur pointed silently to a splendid, shining silver-blue fish about four feet long, propped diagonally across stern. He had pulled it aboard an hour before, and the fish was so fat and muscular that he could stand it up almost vertically while sketching it. It was an albacore, a member of the mackerel family, and must have weighed twenty kilos. It had two long, thin forward fins, almost like wings, and was voted the best catch of the voyage, it made such good eating. We had fresh albacore steaks twice that day, and there was so much succulent meat on the animal that Trondur covered a wide plank with fillets of albacore which he painted with a mixture of sugar and salt

Albacore

to marinade them, and then carefully stored the plank up in the bows as a larder for the next few days.

The air now had a muggy, almost tropical, feel. The cabin roof was warm and wet to the touch, an unseasonal calm smoothed the sea, and there was a strange, slightly fetid atmosphere. To me it held overtones of rot and decomposition, perhaps imaginary because of my worries about the condition of the raft. There was now not the slightest doubt that *Hsu Fu* was decaying and losing her structural integrity. There was a general slackness about the vessel. Everything – rattan lashings, joints in the timber, knots in the ropes – moved and shifted loosely. Nothing was tight and snug any longer. As the raft moved up and down on the heave of the swell, *Hsu Fu* no longer flexed with the springy motion of a well-tuned fishing-rod or bow. She *rippled*, the bamboos moving against one another with a gentle rubbing motion. The worst situation was amidships, by the base of the mainmast. Here the bamboos of the top layer jostled up and down against one another as each wave rolled underneath them. They moved in sequence like the keys on an antique pianola when the pedals are operated. It was obvious that the rattan lashings in this area no longer held. This was not surprising as there had never been space to put in very many fastenings in this section of the raft when *Hsu Fu* was built. Now the surface was so slack that it was becoming dangerous. It was difficult to keep one's footing on the moving bamboos, and any rope which dropped on the deck here was immediately gobbled up in the shifting cracks. Loi and Trondur spent wet hour after wet hour crouched on their knees, trying to refasten the bamboos. It was dangerous work, attempting to push the last of our lengths of spare rattan down between the bamboos, then fish up the loose end, take a turn around the bamboo and make it fast with a decent knot. The risk of trapping one's hand between the moving bamboos was very real, and there was enough power in the twisting of the vessel to crush bones.

The two men came back with their hands fish-white with immersion in what was, fortunately, warm, almost soupy water. The ocean had so much plankton in it that the sea itself had changed colour. It was a rich, opaque green-blue, sometimes with a brown overtone, quite unlike the clear navy blue of the previous month. Rex scooped up a bucket of water and carefully poured some of it into a small white rice bowl. Against the pale background the plankton which swarmed on the surface were clearly visible. There was a whole galaxy of wonderful creatures –

Hsu Fu *'snaking'*

small elegant sea animals, living as individuals or in clusters. Some were no more than motionless translucent blobs. Others had hair-fine antennae waving like the fine legs of millipedes as they crept across the water, or they showed startling black and coloured centres in a globe of jelly and looked like frog's spawn or artificial beads which joined and unjoined in delicate chains to form sections of a necklace. Across this stew shot sea squirts, half an inch long and exactly like fountain-pen cartridges, propelling themselves forward in short jerks by shooting out water like tiny jet boats. Once, staring idly over the side, I saw a plankton cluster float past, which must have been eighteen inches across, a beautiful chain of violet-and-purple sacs, each as long as my thumb and glowing faintly. The chain was in the process of curling round as if to join and form a circle. It passed out of my view before the loop was formed, but it had already left the impression of an exquisite coronet of translucent floating gems.

The sun went down that evening on an amazing statement of the sea's richness. All day we had been gliding forward among thousand upon thousand of tiny Portuguese men-of-war, small jellyfish the size of a delicate porcelain coffee cup, bright blue in colour. The gentle lap of wavelets on the bow had thrown so many of them on the foredeck that a heap of them lay stranded by the base of the foremast, slowly changing from bright blue to indigo. As the sun sank even lower, almost on the horizon, the slanting rays glinted on the wind sails of their fellows. Each animal had spread a tiny membrane above the water as if to catch the slant of wind. There must have been millions of the small creatures, and the shimmering points of their sails resembled a whole rainstorm of water splashes frozen in still life.

Five days after Trondur caught the splendid albacore we faced our next crisis, and it appeared not from the ocean nor the weather, but from within the crew.

The evening had begun excellently. It was my turn to cook and I was about to fry up the last of the albacore, slightly rank after five days on the foredeck, when the colour and consistency of the meat reminded me of something. What was it? Then I remembered. The air-dried albacore flesh looked exactly like the finest Irish smoked salmon. So instead of cooking it, I sliced the meat and served it raw. It was even better than smoked salmon. As usual, after the first appreciative murmurs, we sat and ate our meal in silence. By now such silence was quite common.

Most of our conversation had been exhausted after eight weeks at sea, and each man simply kept himself to himself, and we appreciated the feeling of personal space that shared silence can bring. Nevertheless, we had all noticed that for the past week Loi had been unusually quiet. Indeed, he had seemed quite glum. We ascribed it to the fact that, like the rest of us, he was suffering from a temporary bout of boredom, enhanced by the continuing and constant pain of his lung infection compounded by the inconvenience of diarrhoea. Together they were enough to have made anybody miserable, and it was not surprising that Loi's shipwork had grown slack. He did not do his rattan work or carpentry with the same neatness. He left jobs half-done, or took short cuts which Trondur had to mend. I had tried hard to get Loi to communicate his feelings, and Loi had again spent hours preparing another dictionary conversation, listing the words he wanted to express. He had written them down and gone through the items first with me, then with Joe, and then again with Rex. It was a strange and sometimes incomprehensible catalogue, with words picked from the dictionary such as 'feeling of melancholy', 'difficulty', 'trust'. But the word he kept coming back to, again and again, was the Vietnamese '*quan ninh*'. It meant 'point of view'. It seemed that Loi was trying to tell us that he felt something was wrong, that he was feeling an outsider, that he looked at things very differently from the rest of us. Each of us, in his own way, had tried to cheer Loi up. But no one realised the extent of his depression.

That night, when Loi joined me on watch, he disintegrated. He and I had a small friendly ritual at the beginning of our shared watch. I would reach for two mugs and two packets of the instant drink mix which was our evening ration. The routine was unvarying, and I deliberately kept it as a technique of maintaining a personal link between us. I would hand Loi his packet drink, we would empty the packets into the mugs, add water, and stir the contents. Each politely offered the other the chopstick or spoon first for stirring. It was as formal and significant as a Japanese tea ceremony. Then as we began to sip our drinks I would offer Loi half of my single, carefully rationed, biscuit. He would accept, eat it, and then break his biscuit to give me half of his. At the end of our little snack he would gather up the mugs, wash them – he would never allow me to wash dishes – and then we would lapse into comradely silence. The ritual was always the same.

But this time it was totally different. Loi arrived with a slow shuffle, every move a deliberate signal that he wanted me to know that he was feeling unhappy. Instead of sitting down beside me as usual, he remained standing on the cockpit bench, gazing mournfully out to sea. I could see from his silhouette in the starlight that he was hanging his head. I reached for the mugs as usual, shone the torch on them, and coaxed 'Loi?' To my shock, he blurted out rudely, 'No!' I was startled because Loi was always so polite. I shrugged and made myself a drink, thinking it would be best to let him get control of himself. Ten minutes later I tried again to engage him in conversation with a friendly word. This time he turned away, and burst into tears. He did not sob loudly, he just cried steadily and quietly, occasionally pulling out his towel neck scarf to mop up the tears. Every now and again he mumbled indistinctly in Vietnamese, and I could distinguish the words: 'Hong Kong, Shimoda – *tot* (good) Shimoda – Rex, Joe, Trondur . . .' and then some more weeping. He was repeating what he had tried to explain to me three days earlier: that he had enjoyed the trip from Hong Kong to Shimoda, but had been unhappy ever since leaving Japan. This, of course, was not true. He had been in his element for the first fifty days, happy, hard-working, cheerful, briskly fishing, getting wildly excited when he hooked a fish, having the time of his life. Only in the last two weeks had the malaise set in, ever since his lung infection had taken hold. That sickness had begun to weaken his spirit as the treatment went on and on, seemingly without success. Yet his sadness had many causes: isolation, because he did not speak the language of his crewmates; boredom, as the boatwork grew more and more repetitive; loneliness, at being far from his family; a sense of inadequacy because he was ill and unable to do his full work; worry about his long-term health; constant diarrhoea brought on by his antibiotics; and probably a feeling of redundancy ever since Trondur came aboard, because Trondur could do all, and more, of the tasks normally done by Loi, whether fishing, splicing, carpentry, or metalwork.

But it was the linguistic barrier which overhung everything – Loi simply could not express his thoughts and feelings to us, and he felt left out. It was an almost unbridgeable gulf. I felt responsible and concerned, but also a twinge of frustration. It was not right to have a crew member so unhappy, and yet it was so difficult to do anything about it unless we could communicate. As he continued to cry, I reached out and laid a consoling hand on his shoulder, and kept it there as he went on crying.

'Loi, Loi,' I said soothingly, 'bamboo *tot* (the raft is good), Loi *tot* (Loi good), America forty or fifty days.' He cried some more. All I could do was keep my hand on his shoulder, and reassure him again and again – bamboo is good, raft OK, forty or fifty more days to America. After half an hour his crying ended, and he stood there quietly until the end of his watch. I went to my sleeping bag wondering how long his depression would last and if anything could be done.

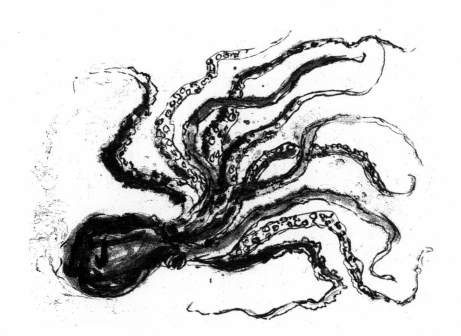

14

L OSING B AMBOOS

N ext morning Loi arrived late for breakfast and sat glumly in the cockpit, half-turned away from the rest of us, his face shielded inside the hood of his oilskin. He ate his tiny ration of cereal in mournful slow motion, to illustrate his unhappiness. He left his cup of coffee to grow cold, and then began weeping again. He brought out his home-made dictionary and word guide, and this time Joe and I both sat through the slow explanation, as Loi turned the pages and pointed out the words he wanted to express. The thoughts were much the same as before: 'point of view', 'attitude', but this time he added 'luggage'. Someone was stealing from his luggage. The crew was to investigate.

I was baffled. What did he think was being stolen? The answer was that he was missing a tube of toothpaste. By inference this meant he was accusing Rex of taking it because Rex shared the forecabin with him. Of course it was an absurd idea, and very sensibly Rex said nothing. He and Trondur were already climbing in and out of the cockpit and getting on with the normal morning routine of running and maintaining the raft. It was left to Joe and myself to try to untangle Loi's confused distress. It was a bizarre situation. We were cooped up aboard a soggy raft in the middle of the Pacific with a Vietnamese fisherman, who was suffering from loneliness, delusions and worry, largely rooted in his inability to communicate properly with the rest of us. Yet for nearly five months Loi had been a happy, hard-working and popular shipmate, and whatever his present problem we all knew that in the final analysis all five of us still formed an excellent team and were prepared to help one another to the very best of our abilities. It was a very comforting background to any plan to handle Loi's troubles, and I could see no better solution to Loi's worries than to make him understand how highly he was valued by the rest of us, that his anxieties were unfounded, and that we would reach America. Joe added the thought that perhaps Loi was also dispirited by his continuing lung infection and the fear that he would never get well.

Abruptly, another of Loi's worries surfaced: he feared we did not have enough food for the total voyage, now that *Hsu Fu* was travelling more slowly than planned. He had been making his own calculations of the amount of food held in reserve, and he had already looked up the words to harangue Joe who was in charge of the stores.

'We had food for one hundred days; it will be more than one hundred and twenty days before we get to America!'

Joe tried to reassure him that he had already cut back our daily rations to allow for the extra twenty days. But Loi was insistent — there was not enough food! As Loi stubbornly repeated his accusation, Joe began to get irritated.

'No! Loi. There is enough food. Please believe me.' But Loi kept repeating it over and over again — not enough food, not enough food. Then he fastened on the particular problem of coffee. He, Loi, had seen others — Rex and Trondur — helping themselves to extra cups of coffee on the night watch. They were not behaving correctly. He himself never had extra coffee on night watch. It was not fair. Their behaviour was wrong. It was a matter of 'point of view'.

At this stage it was obvious that Loi's worries and problems were not going to be solved quickly, and that the first priority was to make sure that his difficulties did not compromise either the proper running of the vessel or the morale of the rest of us, which amounted to much the same thing. Fortunately, Trondur, Joe, Rex and myself were not the sort of people who would be thrown off-balance by the situation, and I had no qualms about asking the others to treat Loi as normally as possible and to try to be as cheerful and positive with him as the situation would allow. I then spent half an hour updating *Hsu Fu*'s position on the main chart of the north Pacific Ocean. Calling Loi into the cabin, I showed him the raft's track since we left Japan, the line of little circles which indicated the daily distances we covered, our present position, and how there were about 2,000 miles left to go to the coast of California. Loi gazed at the chart and seemed to understand. He nodded, and was very

polite and respectful, his usual attitude to his skipper. But he was noticeably withdrawn, and for the rest of the day he stood moping in the
cockpit, huddled up in his oilskins, hands tucked in his pockets. Thinking
to give him some work to do and take his mind off his worries, I asked
him gently to make a wooden storage box for the hurricane-lamp. For
the first time during the entire voyage, he failed to respond instantly to
a request. He shook his head and mumbled, 'Tomorrow, tomorrow.'

The next watch that Loi and I shared was the graveyard watch from 4
to 6 a.m., and to my relief Loi arrived in the cockpit with a brief flicker
of a smile. Thank heavens, I thought to myself, maybe he has thought
over what Joe and I said, and has begun to see that his worries are
unfounded. Also, I hoped, Loi was such a fine seaman that he would
know that it was impractical if a crew member behaved in such a withdrawn and suspicious way. Throughout the two hours of our shared
watch he stood silently, gazing numbly out at the sea and again wept quietly for a few minutes. Once again I could do no more than put a hand
on his shoulder and murmur a few words to say that all would be well,
that he was important to all of us, and *Hsu Fu* was progressing satisfac-
torily. The first light of dawn was beginning to show by the time Trondur
arrived to take his turn at the watch, and Loi was more composed. The
three of us spent half an hour resetting the sails, and when we finished in
the cold chill of dawn, Loi asked Trondur if he wanted a cup of coffee.
Our ration was one cup of coffee per watch, so Trondur would have
been entitled to accept. But it just so happened that Trondur said no. I
saw Loi give a look of shocked delight. He interpreted Trondur's refusal
as a sign that Trondur had taken to heart his worries about the lack of
stores and also his complaints about excessive coffee-drinking. It was a
lucky fluke, and Loi was transformed. As soon as Rex and Joe appeared
for breakfast, he took them on one side and in sign language explained
that Trondur had refused coffee! Indeed, he himself had drunk a cup of
coffee when Trondur had not. The roles were reversed, and Loi was
convinced a new self-discipline regime had begun. The mood swing was
worrying, but at least it was an upbeat beginning to the day.

We needed some cheering up. The sky was obscured by gloomy,
slow-moving clouds, and *Hsu Fu* lay becalmed on a dismal, lead-coloured
sea. The calm meant that we could attend to the stray bamboo which had
begun to come loose nearly two weeks before. My broken ribs still
restricted my activity so Trondur volunteered to put on a wet suit and go

swimming to try to lash the bamboo back into position. We had already tried unsuccessfully to refasten the stray bamboo but it was too far to reach under the raft to make the repair properly. All we had accomplished was to stop the bamboo floating away after the last of its rattan lashings had snapped. We were happy to see that the bamboo pole looked to be in excellent condition. Its surface was still a healthy natural gold, mottled with light green patches of seaweed and with an occasional nut-brown band where the failed lashings had once gripped. Clearly the bamboo itself was not rotten. Even more hopeful was the fact that, after five months' immersion, the bamboo had not lost its buoyancy. It lay alongside the raft bobbing independently on the swell.

But when Trondur heaved himself back on board, water pouring from his saturated beard, he had sombre news. While he was tying the bamboo back in place, he had found that the bamboo lying adjacent to it, was also coming loose.

All of us could read the warning: the real threat to *Hsu Fu* was not that the raft would sink, but that she would fall apart.

As if to drive the point home, the next twenty-four hours produced the worst conditions possible for the survival of the structure of the raft. A gale swept down from the north, and heaped up rough seas to give *Hsu Fu* a battering that would have tested any traditional wooden vessel. Often the seascape was white to the horizon with line upon line of cresting breakers which smashed repeatedly into the side of the raft. The twisting and flexing was so continuous that both the hogging trusses, the tensioning ropes running down each side of the raft, burst. Their failure left the raft even more defenceless, and as the water poured across and through *Hsu Fu* we could feel the surge of waves shaking and vibrating the main hull. Life in the cockpit was miserable. The regular splatter of wave tops bursting in was interrupted by an occasional heavier crash as green water came aboard, and swirled around the basket floor. The extra weight of water was dangerous, so we jettisoned some of our spare cooking gear and water containers to make sure that there was free access to the sock valves, and that the valves themselves did not get blocked by loose items floating around the cockpit. By then there was so much water flying about that it was difficult to cook without salt water slopping into the pots and pans. At midday we heated up a kettle and poured the hot water on bowls of instant Japanese noodles, which we wolfed down before they too were drenched in ocean water. And in the evening we did not even attempt to cook, but ate a mess of cold spaghetti, before the off-watch crawled wearily into their sleeping bags. We were all damp, tired, and did not look forward to managing *Hsu Fu* through the long night watches. When I attempted to take advantage of the high wind speeds by coupling up the windmill generator, the windmill blades were already spinning so fast that a massive spark leapt fizzing and crackling across the electrical contacts, and I hastily unplugged the circuit before it burned out or dealt someone a dangerous shock.

Loi's behaviour added to the feeling of unease. Despite the atrocious weather conditions he insisted on standing all day on a cockpit bench, his upper body fully exposed to the gale, staring blankly at the ocean. The wind flailed him, and the breaking waves regularly dashed heavy spray over him so that his oilskins were running with water. But he just stood there, motionless, as if in a trance, refusing to sit down or to get behind the shelter of the canvas awnings we had rigged to protect us from the worst of the wind and waves. If any of us spoke to him, he ignored us. When night came on, he still remained standing in the gathering dark, refusing to go to his place in the shelter of the forecabin. The cockpit was so cramped that he was now in the way of the watchkeepers, and there was no space for the standby watchkeeper to stretch out and rest. This was unfair to the rest of the crew so I ordered Loi to go to his cabin, and when he seemed to ignore the order, I finally had to shout at him before he would obey. He moved forward reluctantly but instead of entering the forecabin, lay down on the cabin roof still dressed in his oilskins. It was a mad place to stay, possibly fatal if he rolled off the curved roof and into the sea, and certainly harmful to his sick lungs if he spent the night in the open, exposed to the spray and wind. Joe tried to get him to sleep in the forecabin, but he refused. Finally it was Trondur in the small hours of the morning who succeeded. He lost patience when he found Loi still stretched on the cabin roof, in the way of the sailhandlers, and by main force shoved him into the cabin.

Soon afterwards Trondur was waking me. He had been on the foredeck, and discovered that three more bamboos had broken free from the main hull and were hanging loose from the port side of the raft. I pulled on oilskins, clambered forward, and inspected the damage by the light of a hand torch. The three bamboos protruded at an ugly angle from the side of the vessel, half-awash in the waves. There was nothing to be done immediately. The crew was exhausted, the seas still heavy, and

without daylight we could not see what we were doing. I crawled back into my sleeping bag, and lay there listening to the sounds of the gale and *Hsu Fu*. Was that a new sound of thumping? Did it mean that more bamboos were breaking free? Had the ripple and upward heave of the cabin floor increased? Did it mean that the raft was breaking up? The remainder of the night passed drearily.

By dawn the gale had abated, and the daylight showed the full extent of the damage. Off the port side of the raft floated three sections of bamboo, separated from the main hull. Somehow, working in the darkness, Trondur had managed to attach short safety lines to all three bamboos to stop them floating off entirely and being lost. Two more sections, Trondur said, had broken free in the night and actually gone adrift. We would not see them again. Even as he spoke, a sixth and smaller length of bamboo came floating past the raft, just out of reach. Ten minutes later another short length bobbed past, and disappeared in *Hsu Fu*'s wake. As Joe and Rex looked on doubtfully, I began an inspection tour of the entire raft. Yard by yard I made a circuit of the main hull, checking the obvious weak point – the rattan lashings which held the entire structure together. The result was dismaying. I would reach underwater, leaning out over the side and plunging my arm as far as possible into the sea to grope under the hull and pull at a rattan lashing which seemed to be tight. More often than not, the lashing simply came apart in my hands. I stared at the broken strands of jungle fibre. They had not been eaten by fish or seaworm, but just seemed rotten. They were soft to the touch and easy to bend. Where once they had been whippy, they were now like straw. Occasionally a good stout lashing resisted my tugging, but by far the majority broke apart. On the deck it was the same story. Many lashings were loose and flapped around the bamboos they were supposed to grip. They were more like badly tied shoelaces. Right in the blunt bows of the raft, I could see gaps where entire bamboos were missing from the lowest of the three layers that formed the hull. Those that remained waggled up and down loosely, and it was obvious that several of them would be spat out forwards with the undulations of the hull. The middle layer of bamboos was more firmly fastened though they were still suspect. Only the top layer seemed secure. And even there, when I tugged at lashings which were easily accessible, they too snapped.

I called the entire crew to the cockpit, and told them my conclusion: the bamboos were fine. They floated, their internal air chambers were dry, and they retained their strength. The raft would not sink or snap. The menace was the lashing rattan. It was so badly degraded that I had serious doubts whether *Hsu Fu* would hold together all the way to America. But until I and Trondur had a chance to swim right under the raft and inspect the full width of the underside of the hull it was difficult to make a judgement. Meanwhile I proposed a step-by-step plan: first, I would send a signal to the Mariners' Museum explaining our predicament, and asking them to contact the United States Coastguard as we were now much closer to America than to Japan. I would ask the Mariners' Museum to tell the Coastguard that I was worried about the structural integrity of the raft, and that I would like to discuss a possible procedure in case we had to abandon *Hsu Fu*. But for the moment the museum was to tell the Coastguard that we were in no danger, and would have a much better idea once we had a chance to swim under the raft and assess its condition. Our contact with the Coastguard was simply precautionary. Secondly, I told the crew that we would bind around the raft three broad yellow straps which I had brought along for just such an emergency. The straps would not be capable of supporting the structure of the hull, but they should hold together the loose bamboos and stop them floating off if more rattan lashings gave way. Thirdly, we would keep sailing forward normally, repairing, running and maintaining the raft in the usual way until the underwater survey had been done. At that point we could decide whether or not we should abandon *Hsu Fu*.

My little speech was greeted with nods of approval. No one had any amendments to the plan, and Joe spoke for all of them when he said quietly, 'It would be a pity to have to leave the raft after we had got so far.' After breakfast, the sea having moderated, we installed the girding straps. It was tricky work, which Trondur directed, to loop the belts around the raft and then pull them tight. An unexpected bonus was that the emergency work galvanised Loi out of his melancholy. With manic energy he threw himself into the task of securing the belts. He stripped off his clothes and jumped overboard to free the straps when they got stuck under the raft. He hurled himself into each chore, tying and pulling with frantic energy. It was the catharsis he needed, and he finished up wet, shivering and exhausted, but feeling once again a partner in the team, and clearly much higher in his own estimation.

It took most of the day to fit the girding straps, and then we turned our attention to the cockpit. It looked like a battle had been fought across it. There were bits and pieces of equipment washing back and forth in a couple of inches of water; the side awnings had split their seams where waves had burst them; and every pot, pan and jar was half-full of seawater where the waves had flooded in. It was dark by the time that we had cleared up the mess, and my message to the Coastguard had been acknowledged by our friends at the Mariners' Museum. Then it was a question of trying to recuperate our strength and energy while we waited for the next development in the saga of *Hsu Fu*.

Fortunately the next twenty four-hours, day seventy-eight, allowed some respite. The wind was steady from the south-west so the raft made encouraging progress. We were so drained by our recent efforts that we relied on habit and routine to see us through the tasks of the day. There was a listless and tired feeling on board. Everyone was noticeably quieter, each man thinking about the chances of whether we would be forced to leave the raft. Loi, too, was affected by the subdued atmosphere. Joe and I spent an hour in the afternoon trying to get him to explain his concerns more precisely, and through the familiar thicket of phrases about 'point of view' and 'troubles' we managed to get one or two smiles from him. For his part he succeeded in making us understand how difficult it was for him to feel so alone, and that he was surprised and puzzled why he still failed to learn to speak much English. Joe and I detected that he was sliding back into depression after his energetic peak of the previous day, and it was no surprise when he said that he wanted to leave the raft and go home. It was a symbolic gesture. He knew very well that it was impossible to get off *Hsu Fu* in the middle of the Pacific, and find his way back to a village on the coast of Vietnam. To take his mind off his worries, I suggested that he wrote out a message for his family. I would try to send this message to Truc in Hanoi and have it relayed to Sam Son. Loi brightened, and hurried to the forecabin to find pencil and paper.

Late that afternoon a message came in from the Mariners' Museum to say that they had been in touch with the US Coastguard who, by lucky chance, might have a patrol ship passing through our area in the next few days. I went to sleep feeling more optimistic, and awoke to the cheerful news that during the night the wind had held good and *Hsu Fu* had advanced another thirty miles towards California.

My spirits were dampened very quickly. At breakfast a short length of bamboo was seen floating away behind the raft. Obviously it had come away from the hull, and that meant the yellow girding straps were not holding the bamboos together as we had hoped. A quick visit to the fore-deck revealed the truth. The flexing motion of the raft was spewing short lengths of bamboo out of the blunt bows like a boxer spitting out broken teeth. We could slow down the rate of loss by draping lengths of fishing-net, salvaged from the sea, over the blunt bow but it was only a temporary measure. Eventually we would lose all the short lengths of bamboo from the bow, and though they were not essential to the buoyancy or strength of the main hull, their loss would expose the larger, longer hull bamboos to the action of the waves. In short, *Hsu Fu* was unravelling. The consolation, as Trondur pointed out, was that the process was still very gradual. A single-hulled vessel would already have ruptured and sunk with such weak fastenings, but our bamboo *Hsu Fu* was falling to pieces only slowly. There was no risk of sudden failure. The key question, of course, was just how long would that disintegration take? How soon would the raft become unsafe?

Loi was well on his way down into the depths of a mood swing. Removing his boots, he climbed the mizzen-mast to replace a rope which was so rotten that it felt soft and slithery like suet. When he came down, he put his boots on the wrong feet and left them there like an angry and frustrated child. It took an hour and a half to talk him gently into a better mood, and learn that when he talked about 'state of mind" he was not referring to the rest of the crew, as I had thought, but to his own feelings. He could not understand, he managed to tell me, why he was overwhelmed by such a feeling of unease and melancholy. He did not find the voyage itself so difficult or uncomfortable, so why was it that he felt so depressed? He had written out the message for me to send to his family, but it was in Vietnamese and his writing was so difficult to read that I had to ask him to make a fair copy.

About four in the afternoon we were sitting quietly in the cockpit when, astonishingly, there came the sound of a big multi-engined plane, flying low overhead. We could see nothing. The sky was totally obscured by thick, grey cloud, its base no more than 200 feet above the sombre ocean. There was so little daylight it felt like a late winter evening. Five minutes later the sound came again, and this time we could identify the direction. There to the south of us was an unforgettable sight. Tucked down between the cloud base and the sea, heading straight at us, was a large four-engined aircraft, all its lights blazing through the murk. It was a magnificent spectacle, an impressive exercise of modern technology set against a hostile and stormy backdrop of nature. The air shook as the big aircraft passed low overhead, one engine feathered to save fuel, and we could read the insignia of the US Coastguard painted on its fuselage. Then it climbed, condensation trails streaming back from its wing tips, and was lost from view back into the cloud base. We heard it turn, and again it made a low-level pass just to the side of us. Out tumbled a flare which hit the water and began to give off grey smoke, a signal that they had seen us. By then I had dug out the little VHF walky-talky handset and was speaking to the pilot.

The plane was an Orion P-3, a long-range search aircraft of Patrol Squadron 4 of the US Coastguard based in Hawaii, 1,100 miles to the south-south-west. Their squadron command had received a signal from the Coastguard Communication Centre in Alameda, California, asking for a plane to locate *Hsu Fu* and they had flown for almost four hours to reach our last reported position. *Hsu Fu* had barely moved since the time I had last contacted the Mariners' Museum, and the Orion had picked us up on radar on their first pass. I marvelled at the precision of the raft's little handheld satellite location system which had enabled us to tell the museum such an exact location. The pilot of the Orion asked if we needed help, and sounded disappointed when I told him that all was well on board. He had been given no information why we came to be on a bamboo raft in the middle of the ocean, and for an hour he flew in slow circles while he listened to the unlikely story of how *Hsu Fu* had sailed from Hong Kong to Japan and then out into the Pacific. He had news for us: the long-range US Coastguard cutter *Jarvis* was in the vicinity. Under normal circumstances *Hsu Fu* was far outside the patrol area of the Coastguard, but by an extraordinary coincidence when our message had been passed by the Mariners' Museum to the Coastguard Communications Centre, *Jarvis* was *en route* to her home base in Hawaii after finishing a patrol off Alaska, and passing very close to the raft. In fact, said the pilot of the Orion, *Jarvis* had been only seventy miles away from us when she received the message, asking her to find us and offer any assistance. It was a very generous and wholly unexpected offer from the US Coastguard. Soon afterwards, as the last of the dull light faded, we saw the superstructure and radio masts of a big cutter steaming towards us, navigation lights bright in the gathering dusk.

The cutter's first boarding party arrived in the dark, skimming their way towards us in a large inflatable support boat. It comprised a lieutenant, a junior lieutenant and a petty officer dressed up in bright red overalls with US COASTGUARD in huge letters on their backs, and delivered by a worried-looking young coxswain and crewman operating the support boat which bounced and hovered uncertainly around our strange-looking vessel. I had to smile to myself at the seriousness of our visitors. They were methodical, polite, and patient. They brought a gift of oranges and Danish pastries for our breakfast, and a huge list of questions which had to be answered and written out on forms held on clipboards. There were enquiries about nationality, names and addresses, passports, ship's documents, details of our life-raft, safety equipment, radio beacons, flares and so forth. As the lieutenant wrote down the replies, I could see him mentally reassessing *Hsu Fu*. This was no madcap venture as his inventory lengthened to include the latest high-technology locating devices, ocean-standard self-inflating life-raft, special design survival suits if we had to abandon ship, and so forth. Indeed *Hsu Fu*'s survival equipment was probably of a higher standard than that carried by the Coastguard. Nor could our crew have looked in need of much help – a Faeroese Islander who was a Neptune lookalike, a Vietnamese raft sailor who had made his living on the sea, Rex with 80,000 miles under sail to his experience, myself on my fifth long-distance sea expedition. And in Joe we even had our own ship's doctor, a luxury that *Jarvis* with her 180 crew members could not boast.

'Is there anything you need really urgently,' asked the lieutenant.

'Yes.' I replied firmly. 'Rope and paraffin for the cooker!'

'Anything else?'

'Well, we have to take a really good look under the hull of the raft as soon as the sea is calm enough. Would it be possible to borrow or buy a pair of spare flipper feet?'

At last the lieutenant, Gary Lakin, visibly relaxed. 'I think so. I have got a couple of sets of flipper feet in my cabin, and I would be happy to make you a present of one of them.'

The Orion aircraft had departed, heading back to Hawaii, and after an hour's visit the boarding party returned to Jarvis. The cutter would stand by overnight, and in the morning would deliver the rope and other items we had asked for. I was very grateful. I realised that the crew of *Jarvis* must be eager to get home for their shore leave after several weeks on the Alaska patrol, and their meeting with *Hsu Fu* would delay them for twenty hours.

Gary Lakin and his team reappeared promptly in their inflatable dinghy at 7 a.m. bringing a huge coil of extra rope, flipper feet and goggles, and a gift of more food. Trondur put on the goggles to make his first dive under the raft, while I climbed aboard the inflatable to be shuttled back to *Jarvis* to meet and thank her commanding officer.

Captain Scott Merrill was a tall, greying man, with a kindly face and a quiet manner. His chief concern, he said, was for the safety of *Hsu Fu's* crew. From what he had heard from the boarding party, we were experienced, prudent, and our safety equipment was of a very high standard. I explained – after thanking him profusely for bringing his ship to see us – that the appearance of *Jarvis* was a wonderful surprise. No one had told us that a Coastguard ship was in the area, or that an aircraft would be flown to look for us, and that when I contacted the Coastguard in California all I had intended was to try to set up a smooth procedure if it proved necessary to abandon the raft. Captain Merrill confirmed that it was remarkably lucky that his ship was so close to *Hsu Fu*. There were only two Coastguard cutters in the Pacific area which had the long-range capability of *Jarvis* and his vessel was in transit, not only patrol. Normally it would take four or five days of steaming for a Coastguard vessel to have reached our position, and except in a real emergency that intervention would never be authorised.

After five months of living on the raft it felt very strange to be sitting on a normal chair, facing across a varnished wooden table in *Jarvis*'s wardroom as I talked with the cutter's captain. I had become so accustomed to life aboard a bamboo raft that I felt light-headed in the air-conditioned, scrubbed and painted surroundings. Climbing up the series of metal ladders to reach the officers' quarters, I was clumsy and awkward in the sea boots and thick clothing we normally wore aboard the raft. Entering the centrally-heated wardroom was like stepping into the tropics, and I had been obliged to strip off layers of clothing and finally sat down wearing only my underwear. The strangest sensation of all was the motion of the room. The wardroom was high in the ship, so as Jarvis rolled gently on the swell, the room swayed from side to side. Even sitting down I found myself grabbing the edge of the table to stop falling off the chair. It was very odd that tiny *Hsu Fu* was so much steadier than the big long-range cutter.

Captain Merrill could not have been more helpful. He warned that if we wished to leave *Hsu Fu* this was our only chance to do so. No other Coastguard ship would be in the area again for weeks, or even months. I replied that I would have to consult with my crew, but I was fairly sure that they would want to go on with the raft voyage. In that case, said the captain, we must be sure to report our position daily to the Coastguard in California. When he got to Hawaii he would supply the Coastguard Communications Centre with a complete update on our status. If another ship did try to make a rendezvous, it would not be easy. *Hsu Fu* was so small and so low in the water that the cutter using her most sophisticated search radar had not spotted us on the radar until we were within eight miles. Without the help of the Orion patrol aircraft *Jarvis* might never have found us at all.

Finally Captain Merrill sent for the weather charts for the area, and showed me that *Hsu Fu*'s best chance of avoiding bad weather was to stay just south of the forty-degree parallel until we were 500 miles off the American coast and then turn north-east. But, he cautioned, the seasonal weather was deteriorating. The autumn and winter gales had already begun.

As I left the wardroom to return to *Hsu Fu*, I paused for a moment outside on the cutter's companionway. I was high above the surface of the sea. It was the first time I had ever had the chance to look down at the bamboo raft from such a vantage point. *Hsu Fu* was about half a mile distant, sails up and heading slowly eastward over a low, grey-blue swell. The raft seemed minuscule set in the middle of the huge ocean. Clear-cut against the sea horizon rose the distinct, unmistakable silhouette of her three junk sails. They were black and sharp and elegant as if trimmed with a razor from black paper. The raft looked tiny, vulnerable, but in an odd way, very seaworthy.

Delivered back to the raft by *Jarvis*'s support boat, I stepped aboard with one question on my lips: 'Well, Trondur, what do you think about the rattan fastenings under the hull?'

Trondur looked wet and tired. He had only just peeled off the wet suit used during his inspection. He paused, as deliberate as ever, before he replied. 'By the bow it is very bad. Nearly all the rattan is rotten. And along the sides the same – just like on top – all the fastenings broken or weak. But in the middle and stern of the raft, everything looks fine.'

'Do you think the raft will hold together?'

Another pause. 'It's not dangerous now, and we can try to fix the forward bamboos in some places.'

I glanced at Joe and Rex. Their faces told me everything I needed to know. They wanted to go ahead with the China Voyage, not abandon the

raft. Lieutenant Gary Lakin was watching me closely. Unknown to me, he had taken each crew member aside during my absence, and asked them if they wanted to leave the raft. None of them had.

'Well, I accept Trondur's assessment,' I said. 'If you are also happy with it, then we proceed with the voyage.'

Both Joe and Rex nodded promptly. Clearly they had discussed the decision already. Loi, I knew, was my responsibility as captain. He must have understood what was being discussed, but he gave no sign that he really wanted to leave the raft. If he did go with *Jarvis*, it would be an administrative nightmare to get him, as a Vietnamese citizen, from Hawaii to Hanoi. I was sure that the raft and the team meant more to him than any idea of abandoning the project. I would have to discuss the matter with him later. For the moment, my decision was clear.

'The China Voyage goes forward,' I confirmed.

I had guessed Loi's attitude correctly. The following day I sent his message for his family to Truc in Hanoi, asking him to relay it to Sam Son. Later Truc sent back a translation from the Vietnamese original. It read simply, 'Loi asked Tim to send message home. On 10 October due to strong wind, four bamboos dropped off lowest layer of raft. Tim and crew have consolidated raft so voyage can continue successfully.'

Jarvis resumed course for Hawaii, and our special semi-aquatic world closed around us again. It was the world we knew and preferred for as long as *Hsu Fu* stayed reasonably safe. *Jarvis* had been a contact with another, strange society which we were not yet ready to rejoin. While I was aboard the cutter Captain Merrill had asked me if my crew would like to visit his ship, take a hot meal and have a hot shower. When I checked with the others, all of them had politely declined. They felt more comfortable and at home on the raft.

Loi's mental state was our chief concern. When *Jarvis* had been on hand, he had watched the big modern vessel with interest, but given no sign of wanting to leave the raft. Now in an attempt to break down the language barrier, I tried again to start regular language lessons, sitting beside Loi in the cockpit and rehearsing sentences and vocabulary. Loi seemed to enjoy himself for the first lesson but then, abruptly, halfway through the second lesson he baulked and began a diatribe. He was Vietnamese, he announced roughly, he wanted only to speak Vietnamese. The rest of us should speak English and talk among our-selves. That was normal. He was prepared to stand watch and steer the ship for forty or fifty days or however long was necessary. That was his wish and his duty. He would always be at his post. He did not need to sleep or take turns at watchkeeping. He would be on watch all the time. By now he was almost incoherent, turning the pages of his Vietnamese-English dictionary with shaking hands and reading out words at random. Then he stood up again on the cockpit bench, stared out to sea, and began mumbling to himself in Vietnamese. The rest of us let him mutter. We preferred that he should at least talk to someone, even if it was to himself.

Joe was coming to the view that Loi's mental state was unlikely to improve, and that he would either continue with his mood swings or become increasingly withdrawn and then inactive, or – in the worst case – turn violent. I could not accept this last possibility. Loi was essentially a very gentle person, though it pained me to see him rambling on, repeating the same words, unable to communicate, and that we were so fumbling at understanding his thoughts. I told Joe and Rex not to become obsessed by Loi's predicament, and that as long as Loi remained a working member of the team, we should carry on as normal.

Jarvis's gift of extra rope provided a distraction. The Coastguard cutter had left us with several lengths of spare towline, and these we now cut up and rigged as extra mast stays in case the disintegrating rattan shrouds should snap and we lost *Hsu Fu*'s masts overboard. It was tiring and tedious work, lowering and pulling up sails, hoisting Trondur, our key worker, to the masthead to slip new loops of cable over the mast top, tightening down the new shrouds to the correct tension, but it kept Loi active, and the crew worked well as a team. The brief interval of calm weather had been replaced by an unsettled sequence of heavy rain showers and variable winds which might rise to near-gale strength in the night, and by dawn the next day have dropped to a gentle breeze. We ignored the weather changes and concentrated on our daily chores, fortified by large helpings of bacon, fresh bread, eggs and vegetables which *Jarvis* had left us. We were not just hungry for the fresh food; we knew we should eat it up before it went bad, and by 24 October, day eighty-two, we were back to our regular diet of dried and tinned fish, rice and noodles. Now, however, we could cook our meals without fear of running out of fuel. The cutter had not carried any paraffin aboard, but it turned out that the wicks of our simple Hanoi cookers would burn the same fuel that ran *Jarvis*'s engines and we had been given forty litres, enough to last us for the forseeable future.

In two or three days *Jarvis*'s visit had faded until it seemed like distant history. We were reabsorbed so completely into our shipboard life that all that concerned us was the ocean life around us and the little details of our daily existence. Thus we celebrated the brief return of the silver-and-gold dorados which provided a couple of wonderful meals, then they disappeared. We took up again the twice-daily routine of the chafe patrol. Joe began to suffer from mouth ulcers. Our hand torches for the night watch began to break down. Months at sea had rusted their connections so they flickered irritatingly. The terminals of their batteries, recharged daily, developed a coating of rust in only twelve hours. Trondur, usually a tower of strength, began to suffer from back pains and occasionally had to take a midday rest on the cockpit bench.

The truth was that the crew, as well as *Hsu Fu*, was wearing out. It was a gradual process, and I was so close to it and part of it, that I would never have noticed but for the little video camera we carried aboard to make a documentary film of the voyage. Peering into the tiny eyepiece of the camera to review the video tapes had the effect of making me an outside observer, seeing life on the raft as if from a distance. I suddenly noticed how exhausted the crew looked. I saw drawn faces, sunken eyes, deeply etched lines in skin, and heard a slower, nearly slurred speech pattern. They were symptoms of an all-pervading tiredness. Rex was the most difficult to judge because his features were usually hidden by glasses, his red beard and the hood on his red suit. But his eyes, when he took off his glasses, looked tired. Trondur was very pale, his eyes red-rimmed, his cheeks sunken even behind his massive beard, and his hands where he had been tying in loose bamboos were slashed and battered by barnacles. Loi had a withdrawn expression, a slightly glazed look and, on the video tapes, I could detect a slower comprehension of what was going on around him. His former sparkle and quick response were missing. Joe was the most changed of all. He had begun the voyage looking very young, barely in his early twenties. Now he seemed a full ten years older. His boyish, eager manner had been eroded, and was replaced by a steadier, more self-confident but exhausted appearance.

A series of gale warnings added an edge of tension to the creeping advance of fatigue. We were sufficiently tired for all of us to wish to avoid, though not yet dread, the advent of a gale, and for most of 25 and

26 October the raft lay under thundery skies, the wind shifting and erratic. That night the thunder rumbled and sheet lightning flashed ominously among towering clouds, sinister and black in the moonlight on the southern horizon. A sudden confused swell indicated a not-too-distant storm, with the swells coming short and fast from different directions and making the raft lurch and sway as if she were sailing, although we had lowered all three sails and made them fast to prevent chafe on rigging, and the irritating clatter of battens on the mainsail. As the swells subsided and the morning sun came out, I knew that I had to take the chance to make an underwater survey of the hull for myself. My ribs had healed enough to let me manoeuvre gently underwater, and I could no longer expect Trondur to take the responsibility of monitoring the state of the raft's hull. It was a chore I did not relish, but I pulled on the clammy wet suit, Gary Lakin's flippers, and with Rex holding the end of a safety line attached to a chest harness I gingerly slipped overboard.

I fell into a bright, hard, blue world. The water was quite warm and so clear that it was like dropping into an aquarium. There beside me was the raft's escort, almost within touching distance. There were no yellowfins nor dorados, but eight or ten of the bland, plump, grey fish, up to sixteen inches in length, which pottered along in the shadow of the raft, swallowing fragments of plankton which came slowly swirling past in the current. The fish were momentarily startled at my sudden appearance, but after a while they ignored me. There was a distinct shiver and quiver of alarm among the two dozen or so black-and white pilot fish which darted about, close under the raft and sometimes hid among the bamboos. But soon they came peeking out again, and resumed their flickering little rushes as they investigated small grains of food matter. I looked downward and the water was so clear that directly beneath my feet, maybe thirty feet down, I could see the pale outline of a shark lazily keeping pace. It was only a small shark – about three feet long – so I ignored it and began the survey.

My first impression of the hull above my head was how elegant and how travel-worn it looked. Line upon line of bamboos were arranged in their neat rows, and the raft's flat bottom still turned up at the edges just as designed. Down the length of the raft I could see the tips of the eight leeboards sticking downward from the hull like stiff fins. The ends of the boards were crusted with barnacles. The colours were the intense blue

of the surrounding sea, the grey coating of barnacles, and here and there a patch of the honey golden-brown of natural bamboo. Rex on deck moved along the edge of the boat, holding the end of the safety line like leading a dog on a lead, as I worked my way down one side of the raft, and then up the other, diving down every yard to swim briefly under the hull, check the bamboos, and tug at the rattan lashings.

Across the forward part of the hull, for a third of the raft's total length, spread a short dark beard. It was rattan, dozens of broken ends of it, dangling down like stubble. When I could reach between the bamboos and tugged on a rattan lashing, it usually felt soft and weak and broke in my hand. Then as I worked my way aft, the conditions improved. There were fewer broken lashings hanging down, and when I tested a binding it seemed adequate, though I refrained from pulling too hard.

I worked my way right round the stern of the raft where Trondur and Loi had recently relashed the rudders, then up the port side. It was the same story: the centre and aft sections of the raft were in quite good condition but the forward third of the hull was severely degraded. Between the second and third leeboards I found two bamboos which had broken all their lashings. They were held in place only by their buoyancy. I could wobble and rattle them with ease. I could see no method of lashing them back in place, and so swam on towards the bow. There I could count the gaps — five in all — where entire sections of bamboo had worked themselves free and floated off. Reaching up into one of the gaps I fingered the lashings of the middle layer. Once again some of the lashings snapped like rotten thread at the slightest tug; others seemed to retain about half their original strength. Again I dared not pull too hard for fear of unravelling the raft.

I clambered back on board. Rex and Joe were looking at me anxiously. Trondur had used a face mask several times along the side but had never gone right under the raft, and he looked less worried.

'It's not as bad as I feared,' I said. 'I think there is enough strength left in the hull structure to carry on for at least a couple of weeks.'

'Will she survive four or five more gales?' asked Joe.

'Yes, I think so,' I replied. 'I certainly don't think we need to evacuate the raft quite yet.'

Now my hands, like Trondur's, were running blood from barnacle gashes. As I stripped off the wet suit, I thought over our situation. Had

I made a mistake months earlier in Vietnam when building the raft? Under it I had noticed that the fastenings made from round unsplit rattan were surviving better than the fastenings of half-round split rattan. Should I have specified round rattan throughout the raft? If so, would *Hsu Fu* be in better shape now? It was impossible to tell. There was nothing left to do but to keep travelling forward, monitor the hull whenever the sea was calm enough for me to swim under the raft, and hope for favourable winds. One thing was certain: I must not allow the voyage to become an obsession and blind me to the risks involved. We were aboard *Hsu Fu* as an experiment, not as a do-or-die mission. To stay on *Hsu Fu* or to leave the raft should be a decision reviewed on a daily basis. The survival of the crew was my prime concern.

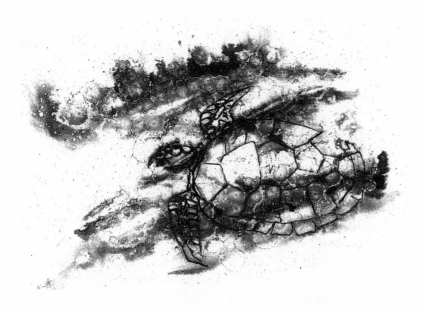

A THOUSAND MILES TO GO

The bull killer whale gave no notice of his arrival. Rex and I were standing on the bow of the raft, completely absorbed in a discussion about the leeboards, when the animal surfaced beside us. No film technician arranging the special effects for an adventure film could have created a more spectacular debut. One moment Rex and I were relaxing at the edge of the raft, quietly talking, the sea empty and calm beside us; the next moment out of the water two or three metres away from us slid a great, black, sabre-shaped fin as smoothly and silently as if it had been pushed up by a hydraulic ram. The fin was as tall as we were, and its glistening rise in total silence made the moment all the more breathtaking. For a moment Rex and I gaped, and then Rex dived into the cabin to fetch his camera. But it was too late. The killer whale was in motion, swimming slowly around the raft to take a closer look. The water swirled over its huge back in deep ripples, and a whirlpool spun off the trailing edge of the big fin as the massive body forged deliberately ahead. The whale was about thirty feet long, half the length of *Hsu Fu,* and would have weighed about seven tons. If he had wished, the animal could have used its weight to tip up the raft as killer whales do when feeding on seals in the ice fields. There the whales deliberately tilt the floes so that seals slide off into the water and into the jaws of their attackers. There was no doubt that the whale was curious. We were still on the fringe of the Great Pacific Garbage Patch, and the whale was one of the larger predators which feed on the fish and dolphins in that rich area. The animal had come directly and deliberately to the raft, and spent a minute or two investigating us closely. What the whale saw did not whet its appetite, for the great beast made a shallow dive under the stern of *Hsu Fu*, swam under us, and then accelerated away, heading north-west and staying close to the surface, dipping and rising so that the black-and-white patterns on its body were clearly visible. Standing quite so close to the big animal, our feet in the water beside it and virtually part of the same aquatic world, had made the encounter seem extremely immediate.

Trondur, Joe and Loi had joined us to watch the killer whale's close-quarters patrol.

'Very big. Has to be a male,' commented Trondur.

'Doing at least fifteen knots by now,' added Rex, as the big animal sped away in the distance.

They took a cool professional interest which matched the matter-of-fact way they were dealing with the crisis of our disintegrating home. The previous noon we had been eating lunch in the cockpit when I spotted another short length of bamboo, about three metres long, floating away in the wake. It was perhaps the tenth bamboo I had seen adrift since the raft began to come apart.

'Bamboo!' I called, and pointed aft. The others merely raised their heads to take a look, noted the size and diameter of the lost bamboo, then calmly went back to their food.

'Probably came from the lowest layer, somewhere between the second and third leeboards,' was the only comment, from Rex. It was as though they had lived all their lives on a bamboo raft that was beginning to fall to pieces 1,000 miles from land, with the ocean 4,000 metres deep beneath them.

We were quietly confident that whatever might happen to *Hsu Fu* we would be able to give the raft the best chance. Despite our tiredness we knew we could still help the raft, and as captain I did not doubt the abilities of the crew. Their ingenuity was in the tradition of long-distance sailors faced with a lack of materials. Even after five and a half months on board they were still devising ways of improving, as well as repairing the raft. Their materials were now salvaged bits of timber, old tins and plastic sauce bottles, even scraps of lost fishing-net hooked out of the sea. Despite his worries Loi spent hours working with mallet and chisel to shape new locking pins for the leeboards, or constructing an elegant new shelter with a curved pagoda roof to protect the helmsman's position, using lathes split from a loose hull bamboo that we had been unable to lash back into position. Trondur was now designing a second fish-bow. His original longbow was losing its springiness, so he was cutting out the pieces for a crossbow.

October ended with a blazing reminder that we were closing on our destination. Half-past nine that evening I was on watch, the only man awake while Loi, the standby man, was dozing beside me on the cockpit bench. The night was clear and cool, the stars bright, when a brilliant spot of light appeared in the sky to the south of us. It was too low and luminous to be an orbiting man-made satellite, much too fast to be a high-flying aircraft, yet too slow and too flat in its trajectory to be a meteor. As the bright spot moved onward, it began to leave a glowing trail across the night sky. I realised what it was: a space shuttle entering the atmosphere on its final run-in to earth. I had a grandstand view, with no city lights to dim the spectacle, no air pollution or clouds to obscure the thrilling arc of the falling craft. I could trace its exact path as the spacecraft streaked onward, lower and lower, finally disappearing over the horizon leaving behind it a fiery trail which stayed etched in the black night sky for at least two minutes. The shuttle, I told myself, was probably in its approach to touchdown in the United States. In just a few seconds it had crossed a gap which would take *Hsu Fu* at least thirty days to cover, if all went well, and even then there was no guarantee that our 2,000-year-old design of vessel would make the distance. Where would I rather be? Cooped up inside a space capsule at the mercy of technology, unable to affect the course of events, or here with my colleagues on a slow-moving raft where our efforts might control our destiny. My choice was clear: I would prefer the raft. Fifteen minutes later I switched on the radio to listen to a newscast and heard the report that the space shuttle *Columbia* had touched down safely with a crew of seven astronauts aboard after completing a medical test programme.

November opened with grim warnings of a 'developing storm' and we took what precautions we could. Trondur and Rex spent all day double-checking and splicing the sodden and rotting ropes which held the cabin baskets on to the hull, and Loi tried his best to secure the half-dozen loose bamboos which had begun to sidle sideways out from under the edge of the hull. Often knee-deep in water on the outside edge of *Hsu Fu* as the waves lapped up and across the raft, Trondur tackled the main cabin, while Rex and I worked on the forecabin.

'Can I use some new rope for this job?' asked Rex, looking at the mangled remains of a manila rope that twenty-four hours earlier had anchored the forecabin in position. He asked my permission to use new rope because we were desperately short of traditional rope. Only a few metres were left in the spares barrel, and for weeks we had been knotting, splicing, and salvaging every strand of old rope to hoard our supplies.

'That's OK, Rex,' I answered, and he took what he needed, and I thought no more about it. Twenty-four hours later my journal read:

'Driven thirty miles north last night by continuing strong southerly winds. Joe remarked that I've been very pensive and quiet these past few days. I must be

tired, like we all are. If Chinese mariners made this voyage in ancient times, they came ashore in pre-Columbian America so exhausted they would have been on their knees.

'Our "developing storm" developed! By dusk the wind increased to forty knots from the south-east, and seas to thirty feet, very confused and cross-matched. They were racing here and there, and when wave tops collided, throwing up great spouts of water. In other parts the squalls built up great walls of water, rolling down towards us, the entire top of the wave breaking in a foaming crest. At first we kept up two panels of sail, but at 11.30 p.m. the wind changed forty-five degrees for ten minutes, rising to forty-five knots, then eased and switched back in direction. During that crucial ten minutes I feared the wind pressure would rip the mainmast out. Loi and I were on watch, so I yelled at him "Down! Down!", pointing at the mainsail. He clambered forward, loosed the ropes, and threw his weight on the sail to bring it down. The ends of the halyards flew out horizontally to the wind, there was no time to secure them. My cries of "Down! Down!" alerted Joe and Trondur, both off-watch and unable to sleep in the cabin where the roar of waves, the whoosh of wash-through water, and the moan of the wind were too disturbing. They tumbled out of the canvas flap door and helped Loi lash down the mainsail. Then we lay ahull, under a three-quarter moon while all around us the storm raged, tearing the sea to shreds. Hsu Fu rose and fell on the waves, which were now racing past her. Occasionally she lurched and tipped at an angle on a wave face, giving rise to thought of "Will she capsize?" But most shocking of all were the impacts of waves which happened to peak and crest just as they swept up to the raft. Then the top of the wave broke free and smashed into the side of the raft, while the body of the wave washed under. The impact was shattering: shaking the entire raft, and felt especially clearly inside the flimsy bamboo cabin which shook and bent under the blows. "Like a missile landing," was Joe's description, as tons of water thundered right over the cabins, obscuring them completely. At the worst time the frame of the cabin, small timbers lashed together, creaked and groaned, and sometimes split with a terrifying crack. The cabins bent and buckled under the weight of water, twisting and squashing out of shape. The same thought was in everyone's minds: will the bamboo-and-leaf-mat cabins survive or will they be washed away as their bindings snap, or will they simply fold inwards trapping the occupants?'

These were exactly the foul weather conditions I had feared when we strengthened the cabin tie-downs in Japan. All night I anticipated the

awful moment when the cabins and the cockpit basket would break adrift. Next morning the wind was still so strong that a three- or four-inch-thick layer of fog seemed to cover the ocean. It was, in fact, a fine mist of spray still being ripped from the sea by the gale. We saw that the cockpit had been shifted bodily sideways by the force of the water, and the forecabin had been knocked askew. The forecabin now lay at a definite slant across the deck of the raft. I asked Trondur if he would again check the tie-down lashings. To my consternation Trondur exploded in rage. He was an awe-inspiring sight, his beard jutting out fiercely and his brow knotted in anger.

He roared, 'Yesterday I work all day with rotten rope, breaking in my hand, all day in the water. You won't let me have good rope. But when you tie down forecabin you use maybe three metre good rope. How can I work if you don't give me good rope.'

I was totally taken aback, and then remembered allowing Rex to use a short length of new rope the previous evening.

I had rarely seen the normally placid Trondur so enraged, and the last thing I wanted was our most skilled sailor and one of my oldest friends to turn uncooperative.

'Trondur I trust your judgement,' I said. 'Where you need good rope, take the best rope.'

'Rope! Rope! Always this story of rope,' thundered Trondur. He, too, I realised, was showing the strain, and when Trondur Patursson lost his temper, then conditions were getting really near the margin.

Trondur soon simmered down, and with Rex he went to refasten the cabins, using the last of the good rope. Loi, revitalised by the need to do emergency repairs, sat on the forecabin roof, replacing rattan lashings which had snapped. Joe and I tried to find a method of untwisting the heavy nylon tow rope which *Jarvis* had given us in order to make it into smaller cords. We failed. The thin strands of white nylon were so slick and soft that they slipped and slithered and failed to grip.

'Mermaids' hair' was Joe's name for it. During a break in our labours I switched on the little handheld position finder to check where we were. *Hsu Fu* was 999 miles from Cape Mendocino in California. Without noticing, we had passed the final waymark that we had set ourselves.

I had climbed on the roof of the forecabin to help Loi, and the two of us were replacing a broken lashing when the sound of breaking water warned me to look to windward. A larger-than-normal wave was racing down on the raft. It roared under and through Hsu Fu's hull, and the heavy crest was brought to an abrupt halt as it smacked broadside into the superstructure. The weight of water slammed Joe, who was at the helm, from one side of the cockpit to the other, and knocked the wind out of him. Fortunately, Trondur was working on the lee side of the main cabin, so he was sheltered from the onslaught. I had no idea where Rex was, for the water was sluicing right over the forecabin roof and threatening to wash Loi and me into the ocean. Loi grabbed with both hands for a crossbar and clung on. I had time to leap like a lemur on to the boom of the foresail, and wrap arms and legs around it while the water poured past.

Joe, recovering from his knockdown, poked his head up to make sure that we were all right. 'I was sure,' he said, 'that both you and Loi had been washed overboard.'

Five hours later the weather bulletin confirmed that we had indeed passed through an official 'storm' with winds of fifty miles an hour. By then we were too busy to care: we were rebuilding the front end of the raft in an operation which, five months earlier, I would have believed impossible.

Loi had called me to look at something in the forecabin. He rolled back the bamboo-slat matting to expose the basketwork weave of the cabin base. It looked awful. A great bloated bulge was swelling up from below, like some huge boil about to burst. If it did split, it would rupture the floor of the cabin and let in the ocean. Something, and it was impossible to guess what it was, was driving upward into the cabin base so powerfully that the pressure had snapped the three-inch-thick floor beams. Their jagged ends were poking upward in raw splinters.

We had to see what was causing the damage under the cabin and put it right in a hurry. But the base of the cabin was tied down to the raft's hull, with water surging up through the bamboos and washing against it. The only way to gain access was to lift the cabin right off the deck and hoist it up in the air in mid-ocean to see what was underneath. It seemed a crazy thing to attempt but we had no choice. In mid-Pacific we began to take our home to pieces.

First we untied the ropes and rattans which fastened the forecabin to the deck. Several of the ropes were badly frayed, and all the original rat-tan lashings which were supposed to hold the cabin to the raft, were rotten and useless. I could pull them out by hand with a gentle tug, though they had been wrapped four times around the bamboos. I threw the decayed rattan overboard. When all the cabin tie-downs had been removed, we slid a rope under one side of the basket base, and while Joe and I at one end, and Loi and Rex at the other pulled upward, Trondur heaved on a large bamboo he had stuck as a lever under the side of the cabin. Using the flex and movement of the raft to help us, we shifted the cabin from its foundations. We literally prised it off the deck, the sticky tar which had been applied back in Sam Son pulling away in shreds and streamers. Inch by inch we tilted the cabin on its side until it leaned at an angle. Our battered forecabin now looked like the canopy of some decrepit truck jacked up for repairs in some Third World country. But we were not in the African bush or the mountains of Tibet – we were tumbling the cabin on its side in the middle of the ocean.

When the cabin was high enough for us to crawl underneath we slid a leeboard under it to stop it from falling and crouched down to take a look at the trouble. The cause of the damage was immediately obvious: the end of one of the curved 'dragons', the heavy fore-and-aft timbers, had broken its fastenings, and was driving upward into the base of the cabin. Trondur and I looked at the damage thoughtfully. It was serious.

'We could cut out the dragon entirely,' I said, 'and dump it overboard.'

'I have a better idea,' said Trondur. 'Why don't we cut the dragon free, slide it aft under the cabin, and lash it down in that position to help strengthen the raft. It will no longer act as a spring but at least it will give the cabin a more solid base. And we must do the same for the other dragon on the opposite side. It also will soon break.'

For six hours Trondur and Loi crouched under the sticky uptilted base of the forecabin, doubled up in the narrow space, the waves splashing up into their faces and around their knees as they lashed the two dragons into their new positions. I was astonished how they could manage to do the work under such difficult conditions, literally tying the raft back together, half underwater. It was a skill at which they were now getting a lot of practice.

Taking advantage of the uplifted cabin to give access, I asked Joe and Rex to sew canvas patches over the worst of the holes on the basketwork floor. In two places the holes were so big you could put your fist through them. It was the first time Joe had seen just how flimsy the basketwork cabins really were, no sturdier than a good-quality woven basket sold in a garden supply shop.

'My God,' he observed, 'and to think I have been sleeping and living all this time on the ocean in such a thin and weak shell.'

Damp, grey, and blustery, the weather continued to gnaw away at the raft and her crew. For the next five days we had no respite. At times it was so clammy and miserable that there was little to do but retreat into the leaky cabins and get on with our individual tasks: Trondur produced pencils and watercolours to do his drawings and paintings; Rex wrote up his nature log; Joe kept records of his stills photography and checked through the medical supplies. The damp air aggravated Loi's lingering lung infection, and he complained that the chest pains had returned. But there was little that Joe could do to help. He had tried every combination of the antibiotics we had on board, and was running out of tablets. Loi's spirits, luckily, were noticeably on the rise. He was quiet, but not gloomy and his bouts of crying had ended. Occasionally he would start talking to us in Vietnamese, and we did not mind as it was obvious that talking was a help to him, even if his hearers did not fully understand. We could grasp that he was usually talking about the first sector of the voyage from Hong Kong to Japan, and his visit in Tokyo, and remembering it with happiness. Having work to do was the best medicine for his troubles, and he carried out his allotted tasks much more competently and efficiently than when he was in the trough of his depression. The turning point in his recovery had been a message from his family in Sam Son. Truc had relayed the message to say that Loi's family were all in good health, and they were proud of him. The message arrived in English, and I had trouble in translating it into Vietnamese for Loi to understand. He did not know the word for 'proud' given in the English-Vietnamese dictionary. I consulted Joe.

'Why don't you say that Loi's family "applaud" him,' he suggested. I tried the new version, and Loi beamed with pleasure.

Loi had been keeping his own notes of the voyage, writing down details of the raft and its condition in a notebook I had given him in Hong Kong. When he got home to Sam Son he would be able to tell the other raftbuilders how their handiwork had held up to a major ocean voyage. By 8 November, day eighty-seven, he had used up all the pages in the notebook, and came to ask me if I could give him some extra paper. He showed me the final entries of his diary, ticking off on his fingers the days in which he had seen bamboos drifting out from the side of the raft, 2 November, 4 November, 6 November, 7 November – 'Bamboo bye-bye, bamboo bye-bye,' he repeated, really quite jauntily.

That was the first part of our dilemma: the heavy weather was shaking *Hsu Fu* to pieces. Day after day of heavy seas meant that the raft was being thrashed and rattled, and the hull was slowly and steadily shedding bamboos as the weakened rattan fastenings snapped. We could even anticipate the moment when loose bamboos rolled up from under the hull: it always happened when we changed tack after a bout of strong wind. As long as *Hsu Fu* lay steadily at the same angle to the wind and waves, any loose bamboos stayed trapped in their places beneath the hull. But when we changed the direction of sailing, and the raft tilted gently to a different angle, this released the trapped bamboos and they floated to the surface on the windward side of the hull, bobbing up accusingly. If the weather had been kinder, the wind more consistent, or the sea calmer, our raft would have been holding together better. But it was unreasonable to expect fair weather so late in the season; we were experiencing normal late-autumn conditions. So we battled on, trying to calculate just how fast the raft was breaking up, and doing our best to rescue any loose bamboos before they floated off, and fasten them back into position.

There was a second, equally serious, part to our predicament: the wind was against us. This was bad luck. In late autumn we could normally have expected either a mix of winds from different directions or, better, a high proportion of westerly winds in our favour. On the contrary, we had days of head winds, or gales so strong that we were forced to drift defensively without making much headway. The result was that *Hsu Fu* was slowly being driven in a circle. On day ninety-two we had crossed the imaginary line of 1,000 miles between us and California. Two days later we had only 925 miles left to go. But then the wind turned, rose to gale force, and by day ninety-six we were once again back to the 1,000 mile mark, and on the wrong side.

It was this backward drift which I, as skipper and navigator, had to think about as I lay at night in the bamboo shelter and listened to the chorus of creaks and groans and cracks of bamboo and timber all around me. When we crossed the 1,000-mile mark, I had fallen into the elementary trap of beginning to look forward to a fixed point as the end of the voyage – say 27 or 29 November – instead of concentrating, as I had repeatedly advised all the others to do, on the closer targets and forgetting the long-range destination. Now I had to readjust my thinking, and it was not easy in surroundings which were becoming increasingly uncomfortable.

By now everything in the cabin was very damp – clothes, sleeping bags, even the writing paper for my journal was so saturated that it was more like blotting paper. Ordinary ink ran into a blur, and the sharpened end of a pencil or a ballpoint pen ploughed into the softened surface. I changed to using a special waterproof paper – and gave Loi the same – and sat writing up my notes amidst the smell of wet socks and damp sweaters. Beneath me the basketwork of the cabin floor was now so full of pinholes that the sea could be heard squeezing through in thin fountains whenever a big wave rolled under the raft and pushed against the cabin base. Occasionally, after a larger than usual wave had passed under us, I would switch on my torch and crawl around trying not to disturb the others, and shine the beam down through bamboo-slat floor to see the glisten of water swirling back and forth in the bottom of the basket. If the wave had broken aboard, I would shine the torch upward, running the beam along the wooden uprights of the cabin to check if they had developed new cracks, or probing with the light to locate the source of drips. I was worried that the so-called 'dry area' in the very centre of the cabin under the tent canopy was getting smaller and smaller as water splashes and drips gradually invaded this last dry zone. The 'dry area' was not a question of comfort, but of safety. Here I had to operate the electrical equipment – charge batteries for the torches or the radio, and operate the laptop computer which sent our messages to the outside world. I was very conscious that if the radio or the computer failed, then we would be on the first step to possibly fatal isolation. In an emergency I could switch on the satellite distress beacon, but if I did so, there would be no way of knowing whether its signal had been heard or whether help was possible or on its way. As long as the radio was working, we could continue to send in daily position reports, receive weather forecasts, and in the event of having to abandon the raft, exercise some planning over the evacuation.

So it felt comforting, as well as slightly strange, that all through our ordeal with the heavy weather we maintained our daily radio contact with the schoolchildren far away in Virginia who were following our progress. As the raft wallowed in the ocean, the spray rattled over us, and we laboured to keep our vessel in one piece, I wrote out each day a brief report of our activities, sent the words up to the hovering satellite, received and answered questions, all as if we were safely on dry land. The children were thrilled to hear about the killer whale, asked if we were tired of eating so much fish, and wanted to know what we did with our spare time. To that question I answered that we now had less and less spare time because *Hsu Fu* was demanding more and more care and maintenance as the voyage lengthened and the vessel began to disintegrate faster. When we were free to relax, Joe studied Spanish, Loi dozed or fished, Trondur fished and read the only Danish language book he had brought with him, Rex dozed and read, and I listened to the news broadcasts on a pocket-sized shortwave radio. Where would we like to be if we could be on land? asked one student. At our own homes in the various countries, I replied, Trondur in the Faeroe Islands, Rex and Joe in London and South-East England, Loi at his village in Vietnam where his wife was running a shopping stall with some money I had lent her husband, and myself in the small village on the coast of County Cork in South-West Ireland, where I could look out at the herons stalking along on the shore of the estuary outside my study window. The schoolchildren must have been recording our daily position reports on the map, for on day ninety-eight came the question: is it frustrating to have the raft go so slowly?

That question followed the worst night of the voyage. The sky was so covered with storm cloud that it was already dark by five in the evening. The black ocean around us was lit only by white wave flashes like manic grins, and in my tiredness I had the impression of a mindless destructive force out there in the heaving abyss, waiting to destroy the raft, waiting with limitless power and biding its time. To shake off the sense of threat I had to concentrate on the physics, think of pressure gradient, wind speed and relative wave height, to make some sense of such a constantly hostile environment. I suspected that I was almost alone in being so concerned by our situation. Rex, as usual, seemed unflustered by danger and discomfort; Loi and Trondur appeared entirely at home on the ocean even when it was turbulent. Only Joe, as far as I knew, was prone to letting his imagination run free. For the last five days, ever since the weather had deteriorated, he had been, he confessed to me, in a down-beat mood.

I had finished my watch and was curled up in my sleeping bag in the cabin when there was a terrific crash, and water came sluicing on to my head as if several bucketfuls had been hurled through the cabin door. This was the first time that a wave had actually broken into the cabin, cascading in through the roll-up canvas flap. My first thought was – the cockpit has flooded! Second – the electrics! Water trickled down on me as I fumbled for a torch. When I got it to work, I could see dripping mayhem everywhere at the aft end of the cabin – our clothes, the plastic sandwich boxes which contained all the vital electrical equipment, all were glistening and running with water. It was obvious that *Hsu Fu* had been struck by the biggest boarding wave of the voyage so far. I crawled on hands and knees to the cabin door and raised the soaking flap.

'Are you all right?' I called anxiously to the cockpit watch. Water was swirling outside too. I could see the black sheen of Trondur's long sea boots and the gleam of his heavy yellow cape. Rex was looking dazed. He had been sitting under Loi's newly woven helmsman's shelter when the big wave dumped itself over the cockpit. The entire shelter had bent, pressing down on Rex's head and forcing him to crouch double. Then, miraculously, the shelter had sprung back into its former arch, and he could come upright. The matting roof of the main cabin, on the side where the wave had hit, had been peeled upward by the force of water. Splints of bamboo stuck up at odd angles. More worrying, the entire cockpit basket appeared to have been knocked sideways. Trondur, calm as always, was on the point of climbing out of the cockpit to stand out on the side of the raft, thigh-deep in waves, and fit extra lashing ropes in case the cockpit threatened to wash away entirely. My head and shoulders soaked, I returned to my wet sleeping bag and wondered how long the raft could take such a battering.

Daylight revealed that in some ways the damage was not as bad as feared – the cockpit had merely been smashed out of shape, not shifted from the foundations by the force of wave. The cockpit dodger – the strip of canvas hung up to keep out the wind and spray – had been split open by the wave, and could be sewn up. The cabin roof could be repaired, though we would have to cobble it with odd bits of rattan salvaged from rotting mast shrouds, because Loi had used up all his stock of spare rattan lengths. But when Trondur and I met on the foredeck as we did our inspection tour of the damage, we had both reached the same conclusion: the raft could not take much more punishment of that ferocity. Her structure was failing. She could survive one, two, perhaps even three more gales provided they were brief. But a prolonged gale of three or four days would probably finish off the raft. The danger was not the piecemeal loss of hull bamboos – *Hsu Fu* could continue to lose individual bamboos for many more days without foundering. The real worry was that the last rattan bindings which held the main raft crossbeams to the bamboos would give way. If the crossbeams and bamboos separated, then the raft had no more shape or form. It would become nothing but a bundle of bamboos jumbled together and loosely held. That would be the end. Soon afterwards the individual bamboos would float away on their own. The hull would be so distorted that it might simply roll over upside-down. Because the cabins and cockpit baskets covered two-thirds of the deck, it was impossible to check on the condition of all the vital crossbeam lashings. But nearly half of the lashings we could inspect had already snapped.

I judged that if we were to make land, we had to have better weather. But it was now past the first week in November, and more gales were expected. Privately I rated *Hsu Fu*'s chances as no better than 50/50, but did not say so to the crew. Our best course was to press forward as soon as the wind changed in our favour, hope for good weather to get us to land, and reduce the rescue distance if we had to evacuate the raft.

We spent a quiet afternoon and evening as the wind slowly moderated. Everyone was aware that our situation was growing increasingly difficult. There was no despondency, just a matter-of-fact acceptance that we were not making progress towards America, and that the raft was slowly expiring beneath us. Our contemplative mood was reflected in our reaction to the appearance of another large sunfish which came swimming up alongside the raft. Its disc-shaped body was clearly visible, four or five feet across, and the greeny-grey upper fin wavered close beside us for ten minutes, within harpoon range. Previously we might have thought about catching the sunfish for its liver, but the memory of the last sunfish and how little we had managed to eat, together with the thought that we might not need much more food, restrained us. We just sat on the cabin roof, silently watching the animal swim beside us until the sunfish turned aside and vanished below the waves.

As usual it was Trondur who proved to be the most resourceful under these trying circumstances. He gathered some scraps of spare timber and spent the rest of the afternoon with mallet, chisel and knife, making an old-fashioned spindle whorl. He explained that on his family farm in the Faeroes, it was customary to spin a special soft rope from sheep's wool. These woollen ropes were used to tie together the legs of the sheep when they were being transported in small boats out to the small islands for their summer pasture. Only rope made from raw wool was soft yet strong enough to bind the legs of the sheep without scarring or injuring them. In the Faeroes, apparently, the spinning of wool was men's, not women's, work and, of course, Trondur knew how to spin by hand and also how to make the correct size whorl. With the home-made whorl he now proposed to respin the 'mermaids' hair' strands from the nylon tow rope and make it into short lengths of cord.

Characteristically for him, too, Rex noted a coincidence in the diary of our voyage. 'Nine hundred and ninety-nine miles to go on day ninety-nine,' he commented at breakfast, tactfully omitting to say that this was the second time that we had passed the 1,000 miles-to-go mark. By the following evening the weather seemed perfect: there was a fine sailing breeze all night long, and the next morning was bright and clear, though chilly. The problem was that the breeze was still from the wrong direction, and although *Hsu Fu* was moving well through the water, we were going sideways and not decreasing the distance between us and California. We were marking time, and this was something we could not afford to do. It was not just a question of waiting until the wind changed: the delay had used up one more week of the raft's limited lifespan, and not much of that life remained. After the usual frugal breakfast of a handful of oatmeal and dried fruit I made my daily patrol of the vessel. I was aware that the previous twenty-four hours had not been unduly severe on the raft. The sea was still too rough to dive under the hull for a proper inspection, but the waves were moderate, and we had changed tack only once or twice. So it was all the more worrying that even after these comparatively gentle conditions I found that another large bamboo had worked loose on the starboard side, and that several more bamboos were spewing out from the bow, including one which was large and long enough to be a major bamboo from within the main hull. There was also a serious problem with the heavy bamboo which ran like a toe rail all the way along the full length of the raft on the starboard side. This was a key bamboo. To it were fastened all the ropes holding up the three masts. The bamboo was made of two handpicked sections joined end to end. Now the two sections had snapped apart, and the rail was kinked. It was a sign that *Hsu Fu* was breaking her spine. As soon as possible I had to swim under the raft again, and examine the true condition of the hull. In the meantime I had the uncomfortable but distinct impression that *Hsu Fu* was much more limp and floppy.

16

FAREWELL TO HSU FU

One hundred days at sea since leaving Japan, and *Hsu Fu* was looking like a makeshift rope factory. That afternoon Trondur showed Joe and Rex how to use the spindle, and they were busily spinning lengths of three-strand nylon cord out of the 'mermaids' hair'. The cockpit was criss-crossed by white nylon strands, and as fast as the spinning team prepared the cords, they were carried off by Loi and Trondur and used to lash down the vital toe-rail bamboo. The atmosphere on the boat was charged with a sense of purpose and the satisfaction of meeting a challenge. It felt good to be doing something positive and useful. The last, maverick, gale had headed off southward and we knew that we had been luckier than another vessel caught in its path. The radio reported a distress signal put out by an unidentified vessel in difficulties some 500 miles to the south of us. So although the wind was still blowing steadily and strongly from the east and *Hsu Fu* was still being driven farther and farther away from California, we had found a new rhythm to our day-to-day existence. We concentrated on our spinning speed and technique, until it took just twenty minutes to prepare a two- or three-metre-long lanyard, five minutes more to burn and seal the ends so it did not untwist, and hand it on to the lashing team.

The immediate priority was to secure the broken toe-rail bamboo, but it was not the major problem. We still had to find out how to stop the hull bamboos from coming loose and floating off. Essentially, we had to think up a way of sewing up *Hsu Fu* at sea. And there was very little time for invention. By the dawn of day 101, two more main hull bamboos had rolled up from under the raft, and were hanging there, loosely flapping off one side of the hull.

Joe stripped off his oilskin top and shirt, leaned outboard, and looped a rope's end around one of the loose bamboos. The bamboo had broken all but one of its lashings, so we hauled it dripping on the deck to check its condition. We found that it was one of the thickest bamboo lengths, obviously a central hull piece. Section by section we examined it for cracks and flaws. Most of the individual compartments of the giant bamboo, divided by the internal walls, were intact. We tapped them with Loi's machete and they gave off a satisfying tight sound. Only one section responded with a soggy flat clunk. Breaking it open we found that the section had split, and let in seawater which had gone fetid and now gave off a foul smell of rotten eggs. But overall there was very little wrong with the bamboo, and it was still strong and buoyant enough to do its job as part of the hull. When we reached to the end of the bamboo, the last three sections, we found something we had not encountered before: shipworm.

This was the plague that many experienced sailors had warned us about. They had been sure that teredo, or shipworm, would fasten on the bamboos of Hsu Fu's hull and chew it to pieces in the first few weeks of our venture. Yet it was only now, almost six months later, that we had come across the first clear evidence that teredo were attacking the bamboo. There were the unmistakable pinholes which showed where the seaborne larvae of teredo had attached themselves to the bamboo stalk and drilled their entry to the wall. Joe took the machete and cracked open the infected section of bamboo. Inside the outer wall of the bamboo ran the hollow galleries which were the trails of the feeding grubs, where they had eaten out the fibre which was their food. Each gallery ended in the shipworm which had done the damage. The slug-like pink-and-white grubs were in some ways revolting to look at, yet it was impossible not to admire how brilliantly nature had designed them. Each fat little worm was a perfect drilling machine, its head a series of cutting plates which chewed on the fibre and fed the material back into the animal's digestive tract. As a species the teredo formed one of the most destructive elements in the ocean, and these tiny animals had sunk more wooden ships than all the gunfire in naval history. Ironically, they were only a secondary threat to Hsu Fu. A severe case of teredo infestation would have sent a closed hull vessel to the bottom of the ocean, but our raft was still buoyed up by nearly 200 bamboos, and the majority of them would have to be severely chewed before the raft would sink. Compared to the problem of the rotten fastenings, the dreaded ship-worm was of minor interest.

Trondur and I had each been pondering the same vital question: we had found a way to make more rope by spinning it for ourselves, but how could we use it to stitch together the bamboos of the raft? Almost a year earlier in Sam Son the raftbuilders had tied together the raft on land, working in pairs from both sides, passing the fastenings from top to bottom or from side to side, one man on each side while the raft was held up in the air on a building frame. Out in the middle of the Pacific we had access to only one side of the raft, the top surface. The rest of the raft was submerged in the water. Somehow we had to devise a system which meant we could pass each new cord down through the body of the raft, loop the cord around a group of bamboos, retrieve the free end of the cord back through another, different, gap between the bamboos, and tie the two ends together on deck. All this had to be done while the raft was moving through the water, and the waves were surging through the wash-through structure.

The loose bamboos at the very edge of the raft were easily dealt with. Here the work was very wet and uncomfortable, but at least it was straightforward. Someone – usually Trondur or myself – leaned right over the edge of the raft, took a deep breath, and plunged his head and shoulders underwater. Reaching as far as possible under the raft, he groped for the end of a stiff wire which his work partner had already pushed down through the narrow gaps between the bamboos. The wire had a loop in the end, and the underwater worker fumbled around until he could feed the end of a lashing lanyard through the wire loop. Coming back out of the water, a nod to the second man, and he hauled in on the wire, hopefully pulling up the nylon line between the bamboos. The cord was then knotted down tight, and the outer bamboos were held in place.

This system was effective only as far as the underwater worker could reach, say, the width of three or four bamboos. That left the main body of the raft, some twenty-nine or thirty bamboos across, still to tackle. It was impossible for a diver to go under the raft, and stay there long enough to help out. He would not be able to hold his breath long enough, and the sea was very rarely sufficiently calm to allow any underhull dive. Also the bottom of the hull was covered with sharp-edged barnacles which would have cut his hands to ribbons.

At first we experimented with using the flow of water under the hull to carry the loose end of the lashing to where we wanted. We fed the lanyard down through one gap between the bamboos in the middle of the hull, opened up an adjacent crack with wedges, waited for the current to carry the end of the cord sideways, and then fished up the loose end – if we could see it – with our stiff wire. This method allowed us to tie together a few more bamboos, but it was not enough. We needed to work out a way of threading the lanyards around the bamboos in the spots where they would do the most good. Eventually we hit upon a solution: Trondur straightened out two bucket handles, joined them end to end, and bent one end into a hook. It looked like a giant crochet hook. One man then thrust this implement down through a gap between the hull bamboos, so the hook projected into the ocean below the raft. Meanwhile, two other crew members had taken the lanyard and tied it between the ends of two six-foot-long poles. Starting in the bow of the raft, one on each side, the two men pulled the lanyard taut between the two poles, which they plunged overboard, stretching the line under-water like an upside-down clothes line. Holding the line taut between them, they walked back along the raft until the line, moving down the hull, hit the projecting metal hook. The man with the crochet hook

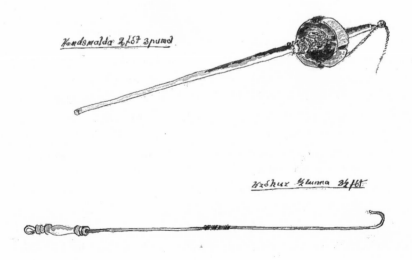

Spindle whorl and giant 'crochet hook'

could feel the slight tug as the lanyard touched the hook, and he pulled upward. With luck he gathered up the lanyard between the bamboos, and could fasten it in a loop. Then, with the line still held tight by his two colleagues, he could reach down with the crochet hook into the adjacent gap between the bamboos and pull up the lanyard a second time, and complete the knot. A stranger seeing this process in action would have thought the two men with the bamboo poles had lost their senses. They would have looked like a couple of lunatics engaged in some mad version of survey work, or trying to touch the bottom of the Pacific Ocean with sounding rods.

We laboured in this strange fashion all day on 13 November and then again on 14 November. It was a minor triumph each time we succeeded in catching up the lanyard on the hook, and fastening together a batch of bamboos, usually in bundles of three or nine at a time. We concentrated on the foredeck of the raft because it was here that we had the best access to the surface of the hull, and it was here, too, that the underwater rattan lashings were most rotten.

But the work was very tiring. We were exhausted by trying to balance on the slippery, seaweed-covered edge of the raft and manipulating the bamboo poles at the same time, or kneeling on the foredeck to grope with the hook between the bamboos. Even Trondur, at the end of the day, was grey with fatigue and troubled by back pains. Yet we refused to give up. We needed to learn whether we had the materials and skills to repair the raft because this would give us a choice. If there was nothing we could do to mend *Hsu Fu* then we would simply be forced to evacuate the disintegrating structure, and admit defeat. If, however, we found we had the means to keep the raft together, then it would be our decision whether we would evacuate *Hsu Fu* or stay aboard, and we were reluctant to feel that we had run out of options.

Keeping our options open also meant that we had to plan exactly as if we were going to continue with the voyage for as long as it might take, maybe another twenty or thirty days, to get to land. So at lunch on 14 November Joe introduced us to the new diet. He called it the 'weight loss' special, and it comprised three cups of coffee per man every twenty-four hours; half an onion per day between the five of us; and two basic meals of our well-tried combination of rice or noodles with dried bonito or tinned tuna. With that ration Joe calculated we had enough food to sustain us to an American landfall, if the raft kept afloat.

But would *Hsu Fu* hold together long enough to cover that final 1,000 miles? Were we able to nurse the bamboo raft across the last gap?

It was the all-pervading, all-important question, and the only way to develop an answer was to monitor the raft's rate of collapse as closely as possible, and calculate the efficiency of our response.

So on the afternoon of 14 November, day 103, I took advantage of a moderately calm sea to dress up in the wet suit, and dive under the raft once again. My intention was to compare *Hsu Fu*'s hull condition with what I had seen two weeks earlier after the visit of *Jarvis*. At that time I had judged that the raft was deteriorating, but still safe enough for us to continue aboard her.

Now I found something new. My first impression was purely subjective and emotional: the escorting fish had gone! I could see just five or six of the sleepy, plump grey fish, and only two or three little grey-and-white-striped pilot fish instead of the previous cloud of twenty or thirty. There were no dorados, yellowfins, or sharks swimming about in our company. The sea was nearly empty, and *Hsu Fu*'s hull looked strangely naked and lonely. *Our fish escort know something*, I thought to myself irrationally. *They are abandoning us.* I looked down the length of the hull, and felt better. From underwater the broad, slightly curved hull platform looked unchanged. It still kept its shape, and the stiff fins of the dagger boards still projected downward in workmanlike fashion. I came back to the surface, took a deep breath of air, and plunged back under the raft, pulling myself across the undersurface of the forward section. I could see the white cords of Trondur's new lashings wrapped around several bamboos in the correct places. The crochet-hook system certainly seemed effective. But there was something missing. Then I realised what it was. Two weeks earlier when I had swum under the raft, the entire forward section of the hull had bristled with the short lengths of broken rattan, dangling down in the water. Now they were gone. The ranks of bamboo extended in bare, plain sequence, sprinkled with small acorn barnacles and shrouded in a light film of fine sea moss. It was obvious that the ends of broken rattan were so rotten that they had been washed away. On the starboard side I could see at least six gaps in the row of bamboos where individual bamboo poles had broken free and floated away.

When I moved towards the stern of the raft, I had an unpleasant shock. Two weeks earlier, the centre and stern sections of the hull had been neatly and smoothly bound together. Now, the centre and stern were hung with exactly the same beard of broken rattan ends which had heralded the impending disintegration of the forward section. The entire integrity of the hull was gone.

There was a slight sea surge which made it difficult to manoeuvre safely under the raft, and I was beginning to feel chilled. So I clambered back on board, and described my findings to the rest of the crew gathered in the cockpit. I pointed out that we were now about 1,200 miles from land and that it would require at least twenty-five days to reach the nearest point of the American continent. I asked for everyone's comments and their ideas on what they would like to do next, stressing that this was only a preliminary discussion because conditions under the raft had not allowed me to make a thorough survey, and I wanted each person to have ample time to think over his own response to our situation. As skipper, I was very conscious that we were such a well-integrated and supportive crew that each man not only deserved to make his views known, but knew that we would all respect what he said.

As the most experienced sailor, Trondur spoke up first, and as usual he was succinct. He would be very sad to have to leave the raft, he said, because it was such a beautiful and unique vessel, and had served us so well, bringing us through such extraordinary experiences on the sea. He could not answer whether we should abandon or stay with the raft. All he could say for the moment was that once the bamboos in the centre and stern section began to break free, they would go at an accelerating pace, and that because the cabins and cockpit baskets blocked any access from the deck, it would be impossible to stitch back the bamboos in those areas using our crochet technique. Also he doubted that we had enough heavy nylon rope to spin the number of lanyards we would need.

Joe spoke up to say that it would be a shame to leave the raft after having come so far, and that he would like to stay on board for one more bout of heavy weather to see how the structure held up. Rex agreed with him. He felt that we should keep sailing forward as long as *Hsu Fu*'s sailing performance was not impaired. Loi had been looking on, clearly understanding what we were discussing. I unfolded the chart of the North Pacific and showed him how *Hsu Fu* had been driven in a circle by head winds and gales during the past ten days, and that it would take at least another three weeks, perhaps a month, to reach land. He understood, nodding vigorously, but made no comment.

There was no need to reach any final decision that day, I said. Each person should think over what he had heard. As the organiser of the voyage I was more than satisfied with what we had already achieved. As far as I was aware, we had made one of the longest raft journeys in modern times. It was probably the record for any modern raft journey in northern waters. As an experiment in maritime archaeology and long-distance voyaging in ancient craft we had completed our programme by taking *Hsu Fu* as far as we could using the traditional materials we had to hand. We had no more natural fibre rope and no more rattan. If we chose to keep going forward, repairing the raft with lanyards of modern nylon rope, then that was for a different reason to the original motive for the China Voyage. We would not be testing the bamboo sailing raft as it might have existed 2,000 years earlier, we would be setting ourselves a test of seamanship and our own stamina.

That night, during the watches, the crew would have the chance to discuss among themselves what we had talked about in the late afternoon, and refine their ideas. During the long quiet hours of darkness I, too, would have a chance to gauge their opinions.

Trondur took the first turn at the helm, and I was touched by what he told me that evening. Trondur revealed how his love of the sea interacted with his sensitivity as an artist. Reaching an American landfall, he said to me simply, was of no interest to him at all. It was completely unimportant. What mattered to him was having had a good time on the voyage, and enjoying the sea. Our voyage had been a very good one. He was content. In addition to the sketches and paintings he had already made, he had acquired images and ideas which he would work up into finished drawings, lithographs, painted glass, and watercolours when he got home. His only sorrow would be to leave the raft. But then, as he put it, leaving a boat after a long voyage was a sad moment even if you left it in harbour at journey's end. To abandon it in the ocean, still afloat, was even sadder. He gave me something else to think about. On the day, eleven weeks earlier, when we had harpooned the sunfish he had scratched two marks on the crosspieces in the bow, using the point of a machete to mark the water level at that time. Now the water level was two inches higher. It would not have been significant for an ordinary boat, but for a raft with barely any freeboard, it was an important loss of flotation. *Hsu Fu* was definitely sinking into the waves.

Joe, who shared the first half of my watch with me, had also refined his ideas about staying on the raft for one more bout of bad weather. He was still prepared to remain with the raft, he said, but admitted that he had the least sea experience in reaching such a decision. If the more experienced crew members judged that abandoning the raft was inevitable, then it was better to get the evacuation over as quickly as possible. He could see no point in prolonging the time we stayed aboard.

Rex had been talking matters over with Loi in the forecabin. Loi was hopeful that the raft could hold together for another month while he, Rex, was entirely prepared to go on with the voyage provided that the sailing performance of the raft was sufficient, and that the living conditions and safety measures were still adequate. I had to smile to myself at Rex's remarks about living conditions being adequate. Of all of us, Rex had the highest tolerance of wet, cold and discomfort. As Trondur had once remarked to me, Rex seemed positively to enjoy being wet. So if Rex ever felt that living conditions had really become intolerable, then *Hsu Fu* would be well underwater.

The night was calm, with a light fog shrouding the raft and hiding the stars as the first hint of grey dawn light began to seep through the darkness. I heard a series of heavy splashes in the still water around us. The noise lasted for about ten minutes. It was a school of dolphins surfacing and diving, moving around the raft and examining it. We had not seen dolphins since October, and again I thought to myself, irrationally, *They are coming to say goodbye.*

As the light strengthened Joe and Rex pumped up the little inflatable dinghy, and paddled off as far as the safety line would reach. They wanted to photograph and film *Hsu Fu* from a distance while there was still time. Already there was an unstated feeling that our evacuation was very likely, and there seemed to be so many last-minute details to attend to. There were all the unfinished items on our work list — the photographs to take, the sketches to draw, the notes and measurements to be made — so now it seemed almost as if we were facing an imminent deadline.

After breakfast I went under the raft again, this time wearing gloves to protect my hands. Now the sea was almost flat, and I could take a more thorough look at the condition of the hull. What I saw confirmed my impressions of the previous day. None of the fastenings of the hull could be trusted any longer. I swam down the starboard side of the raft, diving every yard and counting the gaps left by missing bamboos. Each time I surfaced for breath, I called out the length and position of the gap to Rex who made a tally of the losses. Then I worked my way up the port side. In total I counted that one quarter of all the bamboos on the lowest tier were gone. That in itself was not too disastrous. It represented less than ten per cent of all the hull bamboos, and most of them came from the forward section of the raft, or the sides. But each time I dived down and found a gap, I had hauled myself across to the gap, so I could reach in with my gloved hand. Groping around, I had hooked my fingers over the rattan lashings which held the middle layer of bamboos in places. The rattan felt brittle yet grainy, like the thick stalks of dead reeds in winter. When I gave a tug, the lashing disintegrated easily. It happened every time. Looking upward, I saw a small cloud of sediment and broken fibre drift away in the current.

After forty-five minutes I clambered back on *Hsu Fu* and found that Trondur was now in the rubber dinghy, floating off the stern, sketching. When he had finished, it was my turn to take the little craft and paddle round the raft, making a slow, deliberate circuit of inspection. From a distance *Hsu Fu* looked just as elegant and eye-catching as when I had viewed her from the height of the visiting Coastguard cutter. The raft with her three masts was still one of the most unusual vessels afloat, an astonishing profile of three junk sails seeming to rise directly from the surface of the sea, scarcely any portion of her hull visible. But seen from up close, there was a very different, almost mournful impression. Everything was very worn and shabby. The sails were faded and ripped. There were emergency lashings and knotted ropes everywhere. The timbers were bleached and out of true. The bow no longer swept up jauntily, but hung down on the waves. The whole profile of the vessel had changed. Once it had been a purposeful, tense curve. Now it was out of shape, hog-backed, and slack. When each low swell rolled under the hull, *Hsu Fu* no longer flexed and sprang back into shape with the passing of the wave. She gave a long, loose, limp ripple which sagged down the length of the hull. *Hsu Fu* looked utterly spent.

Back on board I made a drawing of a fish's-eye-view of the hull, marking the bamboos which were missing from the bottom layer. When I showed this drawing to the crew after lunch, Trondur quietly produced his own sketch of the top surface of the raft. As practical as ever, he had gone around the raft, noting the spots where he would be able to tie in extra lashings, and he had calculated how much rope he would need. Our two sets of drawings coincided, and so did our calculations. We estimated that only forty per cent of the hull of the raft was accessible with our crochet hook, and could be repaired. The remainder of the raft would have to be left as it was, because the cabins or cockpit made it impossible to reach down between the bamboos. Trondur had calculated that to stitch new fastenings into the accessible areas would take at least two weeks of continuous work, two men spinning cords, three men lashing the bamboos in place. We had just enough 'mermaids' hair' to make the lanyards, but we would also need day after day of good, calm weather for the repairs.

I looked around the faces of the crew, as they sat thoughtfully. Trondur's information, and my own description of the condition of the hull, was the sum total of the evidence available to reach a decision whether to stay on *Hsu Fu* or, evacuate the raft as unsafe. The new findings were much the same as those of the discussion we had the previous day.

'Joe,' I asked, 'what is your feeling?'

'We will all have to help Trondur,' he replied. 'He cannot be expected to shoulder the main burden of repair.'

'That's understood,' I replied. 'We can all learn the techniques, tie the knots and help. What I would like to hear is whether you think we should leave *Hsu Fu* now in an orderly evacuation, or carry on for a few more days and see what happens in the next spell of bad weather, or press on in complete determination to reach land.'

Joe looked perplexed. 'I really don't know,' he said. 'I will go along with whatever you all decide.' Then he paused, and said, 'Tim, I think that in the end it is your decision. This is your project and we are here to support you. We all have our own points of view, but I think we would accept your judgement.'

'I agree with that,' added Rex. 'I believe we can go on as long as the raft is still sailing, and living conditions are not too uncomfortable. But it is your decision, Tim.'

'Trondur?' I asked.

He nodded. 'You decide.'

'Give me half an hour to think it over,' I said.

While the others carried on with their various chores, I made a final tour of the raft, clambering all the way around the outside rail, and trying to see the vessel dispassionately. I noted the snapped toe rail, the edge of the hull platform, now only an inch above the water. I noted the mends in every length of rope, the bundles of string and knots. A low wave washed across the foredeck. I saw the splints and cracks and repairs in the timbers and the bamboo poles of the superstructure. Another wave, slightly larger, washed across the foredeck and this time I saw how it flowed halfway up the canvas-flap door to the forecabin where Rex and Loi slept, exposed to the full force of the Pacific surging the foredeck. Then I noticed how their cabin no longer sat straight on the raft. Colin Mudie's words came back to me. 'Rafts are notorious for their initial stability, but then their sudden angle of capsize.' The lower that *Hsu Fu* sank in the water, the less stable she became. Loi and Rex slept in that cabin, what chance would they have in a gale if the vessel capsized or a wave washed over, snapping the ropes which tied it down. The ropes were fastened to the crossbeams, but the crossbeams were no longer fixed reliably to the bamboos below them. Their rattan fastenings had rotted away. We could go on, I knew, struggling forward, keeping the raft afloat. But for what? To reach America in a vessel tied together with strands of modern nylon rope. That would destroy the point of the experiment.

I returned to the cockpit. 'When you decided to join the expedition with me as leader, you did so knowing that I am a careful and cautious person who does not take unjustified risks. You knew that I had always brought back my crew alive from my previous expeditions, or you would not have volunteered to travel with me. When I began the China Voyage project, it was not to get to America on a bamboo raft with the same approach that a mountain climber sets himself to reach the summit. The purpose of the China Voyage was the doing – the research, building, and sailing of a bamboo raft, the experience at first hand of the conditions that early raft sailors would have known, the intimate life of the ocean, and to record all these things as well as possible. That is why we have an artist, a photographer, and now, after Rex learned the trade, a video cameraman on board. With the exception of the closing scenes, you have all done your work well, and that work is complete. I know Trondur's drawings will be good; Rex's video will make a fine documentary; Joe, your photos will be fine. To me the arrival on the American shore would be a great moment, but it would add little to what we have already shown by bringing a sailing raft to this point. We have investigated the physical possibility of cultural contact between ancient Asia and America by this type of vessel. The data we have gathered about long-distance raft sailing is what is important, and I would leave those people who read our account or see our film to judge whether trans-Pacific journeys were possible in such vessels. I do not believe that the risks attached to pressing on are justified. As skipper I am responsible for all our safety. And while each one of you is prepared to go on individually, it is my judgement that we should evacuate the raft taking our notes, drawings and tapes with us. I would like to see us carry out the evacuation in as professional a manner as possible.'

My voice had grown unsteady. I was trying to remain objective and to present a clear summary, but my eyes were prickling with tears. Leaving *Hsu Fu* was the right decision, so I was surprised to find that the idea of leaving the raft had such a powerful effect on my emotions. From the very first day I had decided to undertake the project I had always accepted, indeed prepared for, the eventuality of evacuating the raft, so why I should be so moved by that decision was beyond my immediate understanding. Perhaps it was because the project had been such a phenomenal experience, whether searching for bamboos in the mountains of Vietnam, building the raft on the beach of Sam Son, living on the ocean, or any of a countless number of experiences. In the end the China Voyage had dominated my life utterly so I was inevitably affected by its conclusion. Also the total support of the crew had an impact. I was deeply touched that they had placed their lives and their work unhesitatingly on my judgement.

Trondur, as the senior crew member, responded. After a long pause he said, 'I am sure you are right, Tim. It is always very sad to leave a boat in the sea but it has been a good voyage. I have enjoyed being on the ocean.'

I began to explain my decision to Loi. But there was no need. He had seen from our faces what was going on. He was heartbroken. '*Bon!* Sad! Sad!' he said. 'No America.' For him perhaps the decision was the hardest result. He would have to return to Sam Son to explain to the men who built *Hsu Fu* that their raft had not reached America, that their laborious work had been done for nothing. 'Bon, bon,' he repeated.

The poignant moment was soon relieved by a touch of farce. On the laptop computer I typed out a message to the US Coastguard Communications Centre in Alameda, California, giving our exact position and explaining that I judged the raft no longer safe, and that I had decided to evacuate *Hsu Fu*. Could the Coastguard advise the most sensible method for a controlled evacuation? I sent the message off twice, once to our friends in the Mariners' Museum asking them to forward it to the Coastguard, and once to the Coastguard direct. Some time afterwards I received a reply from the Museum to say that both messages had been received, but the Coastguard Communications Centre was finding it technically difficult to establish direct contact with the raft. They did not have the right equipment in operation. The only way they could

communicate with me was via the museum. So the comical situation arose whereby the Communications Centre in California with its immense resources was reduced to telephoning the museum staff in Virginia, and asking them to relay their messages to me. Meanwhile the briefcase-sized computer on a bamboo raft was successfully sending messages direct to the Coastguard.

Bureaucracy added to the burlesque. The first question that came back from the Coastguard was, was I declaring an emergency? To which I replied, no, I was not declaring any emergency, and there was no immediate risk to life; *Hsu Fu* would stay afloat for days or even weeks, and that I only wished to arrange an evacuation with the least inconvenience possible to anyone who might be involved. Promptly came back the bureaucratic response that unless I declared an emergency, the Coastguard could not intervene. I sent the obvious reply: 'There was no emergency now, but unless some arrangement was made, there would be an emergency later.' It produced the desired effect. The museum relayed a message to say that the Coastguard would check to see if a merchant ship in our area could divert to pick us up.

Four hours later we were advised that a Japanese-owned container ship, *California Galaxy*, had agreed to help. We could expect a rendezvous in eight or nine hours.

This interchange of messages had taken us well into 16 November, day 105, and kept the atmosphere on the raft remarkably cheerful. I insisted that all three sails were kept hoisted, and that *Hsu Fu* should still be underway when help reached us. As keeper of the food stores, Joe sanctioned the opening of our hoarded tin of cocoa so the night watch had hot chocolate to drink, the ultimate luxury. Then it was a matter of preparing to save the important items on board *Hsu Fu*, double-sealing the packages of video tapes, book notes and drawings, deciding what few personal items to keep. We knew that we could take only the minimum. We had been told that the *California Galaxy* carried a motor lifeboat which would be lowered to pick us up. Space would be very limited. The question was: would the rescue ship reach us in daylight while there was still light to conduct an orderly evacuation?

Even while we were still packing the last items, Rex called out 'Ship in sight!' And there, not two miles away, lights blazing in the evening sun, was the container ship heading directly for us. The second officer came on the VHF to say that no pick-up by lifeboat was possible. They would try to manoeuvre their ship alongside, and lift us off directly. Trondur shook his head and gave me a meaningful glance. 'Like climbing a mountain,' he said. The situation had changed entirely. From being a straightforward pick-up, the evacuation itself would be the most hazardous moment of the entire voyage. Every moment that our small raft stayed alongside a large ship in mid-ocean increased the risk of being thrown into the sea, or crushed. The slightest swell would toss our fragile raft against a steel ship and smash it to smithereens. Luckily the swell was as low as we had seen it for weeks. Consummate seaman to the last,

Trondur began lashing barrels to the side of *Hsu Fu* to act as fenders. But it was a puny gesture.

Within moments, or so it seemed, the huge black side of the container ship was looming over us. Tiny figures gazed down from the rail. 'Please prepare ropes so we can hoist baggage,' I had asked on the VHF. But no ropes came down. Instead, from a point halfway along the *California Galaxy* someone threw a heaving line. I had asked on the radio for a heavy line to be lowered from the container ship so that we could attach *Hsu Fu* and swing in alongside the larger vessel. But *California Galaxy* had thrown a line from amidships. It was not the right place. The towline was too far aft, and *Hsu Fu* was dragged under the towering stern of the huge ship. It was a terrifying situation. The swell was heaving the stern of the big ship up and down beside us, and just beside the propeller. If the stern came down on top of *Hsu Fu* we would be crunched to toothpicks. As it was, each time the great black stern slapped down, a great gush of water shot sideways across the raft. 'Ropes! Ropes!' we screamed up at the crew gazing down at us. No one seemed to understand. 'Rope! Rope!' I was roaring with frustration. Then I picked up a rope on Hsu Fu and pointed at it. Someone understood, and at last a rope-end was flung down. Loi and Joe frantically lashed four kit-bags to it – cameras, film, video tapes, artist's drawings – it didn't matter in what order or how, but those records were the China Voyage. They had to be saved. 'Hoist! hoist!' we were yelling and I gave the international dockers hand sign to pull upward. The men above understood and heaved away. The cluster of bags whisked off *Hsu Fu*'s deck, hit the stern of the *California Galaxy* like a bunch of grapes, and were whisked upward. 'Rope! rope!' we yelled again. Another rope came down and another consignment was hauled up out of sight.

Hsu Fu was rubbing against the great black steel cliff, there were heartrending groans and cracks from her bamboos. 'Rope! rope!' Now the mainmast had swung against the *California Galaxy* caught under a rail, and as the swell lifted *Hsu Fu* some of the rattan stays snapped with alarming sounds, the mast swayed and groaned. 'Look out!' Loi, Rex, Joe and I dived for the cockpit, glancing up at the mast. It creaked, swayed, but held. 'Rope! rope!' The immense stern of the container ship slapped down on the sea beside us with a huge hollow boom, and the water sprayed out, soaking the raft. This was distinctly too close. Now the mainsail had caught in the superstructure, and was being twisted and turned like some deliberate torture. I glanced forward. A rope-ladder dangled down near Trondur who was handling the bowline. It was his escape route.

Boom! the great stern thundered down again.

'All bags gone!' said Joe. He was white with shock but coping splendidly.

'Loi! Rex! Go! Go!' A second rope-ladder now had been thrown over the stern and Loi and Rex went up it, cumbersome in their yellow survival suits. Boom! down again came that black crushing stern.

'Joe! On your way!' and he ran up the cabin roof, and seized hold of a rung of the ladder. But for some reason, he found the climb very difficult. Awkwardly, slowly, he hauled himself up. I watched, dreading an injury. The ladder hung right next to *Hsu Fu*'s mast which scraped the steel stern of the big ship, and the spar threatened to maim any climber or knock him off into the sea. If anyone fell between the container ship and the raft, he would not stand a chance. I took another look forward. Trondur was halfway up his rope-ladder, dangling over the sea. It was time to go. I grabbed the machete from its sheath in the cockpit, and began to haul myself upward, blade in hand. There was one last service I could do for *Hsu Fu*, piniponed to the destructive side of our rescuer. Hands helped me over the rail.

'All safe?' I asked Rex.

'Yes, there are five of us on the stern deck.'

'Cut her off!' I wanted *Hsu Fu* to be free, to sail on. That was why I had insisted we hoist all sail before we left her. The stern line was cast off. Now just the forward line remained. A seaman took the machete from my hand and I stood beside him as he swung it and chopped the heavy cable through. Now nothing held *Hsu Fu* to the great ship.

I returned to the aft rail and looked down forty feet. It was a bird's-eye view to our home for the past six months. It was all laid out. The cockpit, the two bamboo cabins, I could see my binoculars on top of the main cabin lying where I had left them in the scramble to evacuate. I could see the loose bamboos sticking out underwater on the starboard side. A sailor had brought a hand-held floodlight and shone it downward. The light glittered on the water slopping between the bamboos of *Hsu Fu*'s wash-through hull. In the swell I could see the tired, weary hull flex limply. But the three masts still stood, and despite the terrible battering, *Hsu Fu* was intact as no normal vessel would have been. Flexible and resilient as ever she accepted the punishment and survived.

I expected *California Galaxy* to move off now we were aboard. But no! The man with the floodlights was talking on his walky-talky to the bridge. He was waiting for the raft to drift or be blown clear before starting the great propeller turning. *Hsu Fu*'s sails were filling and she nuzzled the dangerous stern of the container ship. 'Let her go! Let her go!' I said to myself as another handful of bamboos were crunched by the container ship. We were all safe, and it was time for our raft to be on her way. Finally there was a shudder beneath my feet as the propeller began to revolve; a boiling whiteness of water in the spotlight and the upsurge washed *Hsu Fu* away. *California Galaxy* began to edge forward and slowly *Hsu Fu* reached the edge of the floodlit zone and passed on into the darkness beyond. By then all three sails had filled and began to move her gently through the water. She was on the port tack, her tillers central, and she was still heading for America. With all five of us safe and uninjured on the container ship, I knew it was the right decision to leave the raft, but it was a desperately sad moment. She had served us so well for 5,500 miles. Now she would sail on without us. Her silhouette faded into the blackness, the weary shabbiness was invisible, only the elegant shape of her three roach-fin sails could be seen faintly against the black sky. How long would she sail on by herself? To circle forever in the great whirlpool that the ancient Chinese believed to exist in the Eastern Ocean? To join the other debris in the great Pacific Garbage Patch? To break up in pieces or be eaten by shipworm? Or perhaps to be carried by the current and washed up one day on the American shore.

EPILOGUE

The container ship took nine days to complete her crossing to Tokyo, the same distance that our raft had needed 105 days to accomplish. It was a curious sensation to be retracing our track at such speed. Looking down on the ocean waves from the bridge, forty feet up in the air, I felt both relieved and yet deprived that we had been so totally separated from the element which we had come to understand and appreciate. The ship, churning through the water at what seemed like a heedless pace, was well run. Vigilant lookouts manned the bridge, instrument dials monitored wind speed, engine thrust, and minute changes of direction. But the realities of the sea were far away. There was no human hand on the helm. *California Galaxy* was steered by computers reading satellite positions; the bridge team worked in shirtsleeves, bending over glass-topped chart tables. This was a different world, isolated safely behind armoured glass. Even when you pushed open the heavy, watertight steel door leading to the open wing bridge and stepped outside, there was still no real sensation of being on the ocean itself as we had known it on *Hsu Fu*. The container ship created such a wind speed of her own that the natural surface winds whose nuances and flickers had ruled our lives for half a year were barely felt. It required an effort to imagine what it would be like to be down there again on the surface of the sea, semi-submerged as part of the ocean itself. From the bridge of the container ship our raft would have seemed no more than a scrap of waterlogged flotsam. Yet Captain Nagata of the *California Galaxy* was very respectful of the North Pacific. His vessel shuttled back and forth across the Pacific on a regular two-weekly run as orderly as a train schedule. But the vessel's winter and summer tracks were changed according to the frequency of bad weather, and even a 30,000-ton vessel like his own fled the risk of typhoons.

For the crew of *Hsu Fu* the container ship was like a decompression chamber, an invaluable halfway stage between our strange ocean-soaked life and the normal world to which we would soon be returning. We had been allocated spare cabins in the crew quarters, and there each man kept himself remarkably busy. Trondur's cabin soon looked like an artist's studio as he taped working drawings to the walls and began to prepare his raft pictures for publication as lithographs or to show them at art exhibitions in Scandinavia. Joe and Rex spent hours logging their stills photographs and the video film from the trip. I shut myself up in the cabin provided for me, and started on the long chore of transcribing the handwritten notes of the voyage. Loi slept like a dead man. For him the transfer to the *California Galaxy* was a curiously numbing release. It was as though his entire system had switched off the moment he came aboard the large vessel. He shared his cabin with Rex, and most times that Rex came back there, even at midday, he would find Loi sound asleep, and difficult to wake, like a damaged animal recuperating. Loi slept for hour after hour, getting up for meals and for a few hours in the evening. When he was awake, he was quiet, dead-eyed and listless until, luckily, he made friends among the crew of the container ship. From deck-hands to middle- rank officers the crew of the *California Galaxy* were Filipinos. Only the four senior officers were Japanese. The Filipinos were vivacious, warm-hearted and hospitable, and two of them in particular made Loi feel very at home in the little recreation room set aside for the crew to spend their free evenings. There Loi as usual established contact through smiles and sign language, and found himself among people with whom he could communicate in his uncomplicated way. By the time *California Galaxy* docked in Tokyo, most of Loi's former sparkle had returned, and he was more like his old self, though quieter, graver, and more self-confident.

In Tokyo we held a farewell party, not at some restaurant or bar, but in the little house Nina rented. There we all sat down crosslegged around the low Japanese table, crammed together in a small upstairs room which was as crowded as if we were back in the cockpit of *Hsu Fu*. Only Geoffrey, running his business in Hong Kong, and Mark, who had returned with his Japanese girlfriend to Hong Kong by then, were absent. The rest of us took turns to cook dinner, each to prepare one dish, rather than one meal as had been the custom on the raft. It was a quiet, deeply felt farewell, because we knew that some of us would probably never meet again. Loi would be returning to his village, the others to Europe, all of us sent home by air by the generosity of our sponsors at DHL, who pronounced themselves well satisfied with the achievement of our voyage. Their Hong Kong office had followed our daily reports with fascination, and all were relieved that we were safe and well after our adventures. They sent us the map on which they had plotted daily the raft's position, crawling across the graph paper until it ended in an eccentric little loop where the winds had driven *Hsu Fu* in a circle before we abandoned the raft.

The next day the team broke up. Joe took Loi to Tokyo Airport to make sure he got on the correct flight, and reported that in the airport Loi, the villager from Sam Son who previously had never even been as far as Hanoi, sauntered off as if he had been travelling on intercontinental flights all his life. Joe sent him off with a medical report and a written request to any doctor in Vietnam: please would a doctor give Loi a thorough medical examination in a hospital and check his lungs for fear of a deep-seated infection. Weeks later Truc would send me a note to say that Loi had been passed fit and well, and was back in his village, a hero.

Once the others were safely on their way back to their homes, I too took the plane home. As the aircraft climbed out of Tokyo's airport, and turned its nose away from the Pacific, I asked myself if, given the opportunity, I would undertake the China Voyage project again. The answer was no: the voyage had been such a good one, so enjoyable, and so memorable, that anything else would seem an anticlimax. By covering eighty per cent of the distance across the ocean from the mainland of Asia to the mainland of America we had served the principal research purpose of our project. We had learned a great deal about bamboo rafting in the North Pacific, and shown that it was possible to regard the bamboo sailing raft as a trans-oceanic vessel. Going the last 1,000 miles would not materially change the results of our expedition. Of course, this did not stop me from speculating about the changes that I would make to the raft if I were to try again, changes that might give a vessel a better chance of crossing the entire ocean. Perhaps, I thought to myself, *Hsu Fu* would have lasted longer if I had decided to use round rattan, not split rattan, to hold the structure together. Maybe the raft would have held together better if we had painted tar on the lashings and given them a protective coating. And, naturally, I wondered if the raft would have got to the American shore if I had decided that we should stay aboard at all costs, steering her eastward even while the structure was failing.

The answer was that *Hsu Fu* would probably have made the shore, if we had been lucky enough to avoid very heavy weather. But I was still sure in my own mind that the risk to life would not have been justified. And what if we had decided to stay the winter in Japan after the first season's sailing from Hong Kong? We could have refurbished the raft in Shimoda, dried out and checked the lashings, then set out on the main Pacific leg at the start of the next summer, taking advantage of a better sailing season. Such a scenario would have been possible for the first explorers like *Hsu Fu* and his colonists if they had decided to continue eastward. And what, too, would have been the effect if we had started our own voyage, not from Hong Kong but from farther north in China? That would have reduced the voyage in length, so that the 5,500 miles we covered would actually have brought our raft all the way to America. The combination of a shorter distance, a layover in Japan, and tarred fastenings would probably have brought us to the American mainland. But that was all speculation, and after six months on the raft I felt something more important had to be taken into account. If I embarked on the same voyage a second time, it would be impossible for me to see the ocean again with such a fresh, receptive eye. And where would I ever find such a first-class, happy crew again, such a magnificent team? Let others make the final 1,000 miles in their own replica craft if they wanted to, my crew and I were well satisfied with what we had done, and would always value the experience.

Where did that leave the theory of trans-Pacific contacts, the idea that had originally sparked the concept of the China Voyage? The short

answer was that we had demonstrated the feasibility of raft sail
that given a decent vessel and average weather luck a raft could n
crossing. We had also shown how sea survival in those latitu
humanly possible, and that a raft crew could survive even if th
unintentional voyagers driven out to sea by gales or carried aw
hostile ocean current. But equally we had shown how diffic
exhausting the voyage was, and that if such trans-Pacific voyage
made 2,000 years ago, then the survivors would have come ashc
pitiable state. Would their arrival have influenced the high cult
native America? Perhaps so, but only in certain limited areas. Nc
the China Voyage was over, I could understand how materials b
from Asia might not survive the very harsh conditions of an ocear
ney – for example, the grains of the 'five seeds' taken aboard H.
original colonising fleet might all have been destroyed. Barely a h
of rafts would have got through, and on them perhaps the majority
sailors would have died, leaving scarcely any artisans or skilled far
too few to accomplish a settlement or act as tutors to native Amer
Much more likely, I thought to myself, the Asian mariners wh
come ashore in the Americas were those who travelled there by mis
the accidental voyagers who were swept away by gales or strong
rents. Such visitors, even if they did step ashore alive, would have
more to offer than what they had brought in their heads, their kn
edge and the skills associated with the sea. So perhaps the ingen
principle of leeboards – known on both sides of the Pacific in anc
times – was a genuine foreign import into the Americas, or some ol
ideas connected with navigation had been brought from across the se
star knowledge, calendars and the rest. But these contributions wc
have added just the lightest, superficial gloss to native American ci\
sations already well developed. So, in the final analysis any trans-Pac
voyages would have been of marginal significance.

Where was *Hsu Fu* herself? That was a question that I would be ask
again and again during the next months. On the final afternoon
California Galaxy came in sight, I had found time to take several sheets
the special, virtually indestructible notepaper on which I had made n
sea journal. Using indelible ink I had written out several copies of tl
same message which Rex had then fixed to various parts of the ra
structure before we left *Hsu Fu* for the last time. The message read:

THIS IS THE BAMBOO SAILING RAFT
HSU FU
ABANDONED AT SEA ON 16 NOVEMBER 1993
AT 31.41N 148.27W, 1000 MILES
FROM THE COAST OF AMERICA AFTER A
VOYAGE OF 5,500 MILES FROM HONG KONG.
HER CREW ARE SAFE.
ANYONE FINDING THE RAFT PLEASE
CONTACT THE MARINERS' MUSEUM, NEWPORT NEWS,
VIRGINIA, USA, STATING PLACE AND DATE OF FIND.
NOTES OR PHOTOGRAPHS OF THE CONDITION OF
THE RAFT WOULD BE APPRECIATED.

THANK YOU FOR YOUR HELP.

TIM SEVERIN, LEADER, THE CHINA VOYAGE EXPEDITION.

Since then, nothing more has been heard.

A CKNOWLEDGEMENTS

The China Voyage was generously assisted by friends and supporters in so many countries that the only sensible way to organise my thanks to them is geographically. To these friends, wherever they are, I want to say how much my crew and I appreciate their kindness and assistance. Their intervention made a tremendous difference, and this is my happy chance to cite them for their contribution to the expedition.

In Ireland: Susie Pope, Tom Kitt T.D., Tony O'Connor and Bill Harpur (RTE), Sean McCarthy and Michael Hegarty (Hyperion), John Kenny and Laura Donnelly (Portable Software Solutions).

In the United Kingdom: Sarah Waters, Julian Grant and Helen Knight (Trimble Navigation), Cecilia Lawrence (DHL), Cecil Coleman (Arthur Beale Ltd), the Strzelecki family (Henri Lloyd), Dr Stephen Bell and Kenneth Parker (Firdell), George Durrant (Lumic/Ampair), Gordon Head (Zodiac), Paul Alder (Portable Software Solutions), Paul Moxham and Nigel Owens (Husky Computers), Henry Hopkins and Brian Kane (Sony Broadcast), David Monkhouse (Vinten Broadcast), Philippa Scott, Max Malavasi (Aquaman/Pelican Cases), Amanda Hill (Jordans), Clare Stephens (Lyons Waddell).

In Vietnam: Mr Tran Hoan Minister of Culture, Information and Sports, Mr Vuong Thinh Director of International Relations Department, Duong Duc Hong Director of the International Press Communication Centre, Do Thi Hoang of the Foreign Affairs Office, Qang Ninh Province, William Ong (DHL), Judy Rapp (British Embassy).

In Hong Kong: W.T. Lee, Georges Beau, Herman Fung, Daisy Poon, Allen Yau, Ho Si Man, Peter Yau, Jane Leung (all DHL), Raymond Fong, Pollyanna Li, Judy Lau, Martha Lo Ho Yin (all Hong Kong Telecom), Phil Weaver (SARC), Mark Houghton (Leadgate Industries), Royal Hong Kong Yacht Club, Arne Dimblad, Trish Harwood and Laura Weston (Rowland Company), Jill Kluge and Julie Amman (Mandarin Hotels), Aberdeen Boat Club especially David Watts, Nanette McClintock, Laurie Gilbert, Wayne Moran.

In Taiwan: Dr Chin-Ming Lu and Dr Chi-Chuag Cheng of the Taiwan Forestry Research Institute; Taiwan Yachting Association.

In Japan: Akira Yagiu, Roy Igareshi, Keiko Atsumi, Keiko Akatani, Teiko Homma (all Mediahouse Inc.), Allan Morrison, Masamichi Kashiwabara (DHL), Mike Lee (Cable & Wireless), Dave O'Gorman (Barclays Bank), Hidetoshi Ito (Shimoda Boat Service), Mr Shimoji, Mr Yamamoto, Mr Sumi, Mrs Motoko Slevin, Clint George (all Shingu City), Liam English, American Computer Services on Okinawa.

In the United States: William Wilkinson, Linda Kelsey and Mary Dykas (all Mariners' Museum), Brian Sullivan and Lisa Burt (Watermaker), Bill Graves and Mike Davis (National Geographic Society), Betty Meggers (Smithsonian), Wayne Brandt (Trimble).

In Singapore: Ian Lloyd.

In Germany: Eike Schmitz and Lars-Peter Barthel (Atlantis Film).

In Canada: Grant Keddie (Royal British Columbia Museum).

In Australia: Tom Vosmer, Bill McGrath.

Naturally there are certain key individuals who were of vital significance, and to whom a very special debt of gratitude is due: David Allen OBE, Chairman of DHL Worldwide Express, was one of the first people with whom I discussed the idea of the expedition, and he gave his unswerving support right from the start. In Hong Kong Peter Tilby, again of DHL, mixed calm competence with good humour as his office ran our communications link with the outside world, while the DHL staff supplied invaluable practical back-up. Also in Hong Kong, I would like to thank Chris and Karen Jaques for providing such a welcome oasis of family life. In Taiwan Michael Garvey gave practical help, and introduced me to the magic circle of the Irish business community spread around the Pacific rim. My chief mentor in Japan was Hiroshi Iwai whose advice and thoughtfulness have left a deep impression. Finally, no one on dry land could have done more on our behalf as we sailed the

North Pacific than Ray Foster. With the participation of the staff at the Mariners' Museum at Newport News he operated the satellite radio link which, after successfully telling the schoolchildren of the educational network about our day-to-day experiences, brought a safe conclusion to our adventure.

To all of them, I would like to say . . . many, many thanks for all you did so unstintingly on behalf of the bamboo sailing raft *Hsu Fu* and her crew.

Tim Severin
Ireland